PERGAMON INTERNATIONAL LIBRARY
of Science, Technology, Engineering and Social Studies
The 1000-volume original paperback library in aid of education,
industrial training and the enjoyment of leisure
Publisher: Robert Maxwell, M.C.

Behavioral Treatment of Alcoholism

PGPS– 60

THE PERGAMON TEXTBOOK
INSPECTION COPY SERVICE

An inspection copy of any book published in the Pergamon International Library
will gladly be sent to academic staff without obligation for their consideration for
course adoption or recommendation. Copies may be retained for a period of 60 days
from receipt and returned if not suitable. When a particular title is adopted or
recommended for adoption for class use and the recommendation results in a sale
of 12 or more copies, the inspection copy may be retained with our compliments.
If after examination the lecturer decides that the book is not suitable for adoption
but would like to retain it for his personal library, then a discount of 10% is
allowed on the invoiced price. The Publishers will be pleased to receive suggestions
for revised editions and new titles to be published in this important International
Library.

PERGAMON GENERAL PSYCHOLOGY SERIES

Editors: Arnold P. Goldstein . Syracuse University
Leonard Krasner . SUNY, Stonybrook

TITLES IN THE PERGAMON GENERAL PSYCHOLOGY SERIES

Vol. 1.   J. WOLPE – *The Practice of Behavior Therapy* (2nd Edition)

Vol. 2.   T. MAGOON *et al.* – *Mental Health Counselors at Work*

Vol. 3.   J. McDANIEL – *Physical Disability and Human Behavior* (2nd Edition)

Vol. 4.   M. L. KAPLAN *et al.* – *The Structural Approach in Psychological Testing*

Vol. 5.   H. M. LaFAUCI & P. E. RICHTER – *Team Teaching at the College Level*

Vol. 6.   H. B. PEPINSKY *et al.* – *People and Information*

Vol. 7.   A. W. SIEGMAN & B. POPE – *Studies in Dyadic Communication*

Vol. 8.   R. E. JOHNSON – *Existential Man: The Challenge of Psychotherapy*

Vol. 9.   C. W. TAYLOR – *Climate for Creativity*

Vol. 10.   H. C. RICKARD *et al.* – *Behavioral Intervention in Human Problems*

Vol. 11.   P. EKMAN, W. V. FRIESEN & P. ELLSWORTH – *Emotion in the Human Face: Guidelines for Research and an Integration of Findings*

Vol. 12.   B. MAUSNER & E. S. PLATT – *Smoking: A Behavioral Analysis*

Vol. 14.   A. GOLDSTEIN – *Psychotherapeutic Attraction*

Vol. 15.   F. HALPERN – *Survival: Black/White*

Vol. 16.   K. SALZINGER & R. S. FELDMAN – *Studies in Verbal Behavior: An Empirical Approach*

Vol. 17.   H. E. ADAMS & W. K. BOARDMAN – *Advances in Experimental Clinical Psychology*

Vol. 18.   R. C. ZILLER – *The Social Self*

Vol. 19.   R. P. LIBERMAN – *A Guide to Behavioral Analysis & Therapy*

Vol. 22.   H. B. PEPINSKY & M. J. PATTON – *The Psychological Experiment: A Practical Accomplishment*

Vol. 23.   T. R. YOUNG – *New Sources of Self*

Vol. 24.   L. S. WATSON, Jr. – *Child Behavior Modification: A Manual for Teachers, Nurses, and Parents*

Vol. 25.   H. L. NEWBOLD – *The Psychiatric Programming of People: Neo-Behavioral Orthomolecular Psychiatry*

Vol. 26.   E. L. ROSSI – *Dreams and the Growth of Personality: Expanding Awareness in Psychotherapy*

Vol. 27.   K. D. O'LEARY & S. G. O'LEARY – *Classroom Management: The Successful Use of Behavior Modification*

Vol. 28.   K. A. FELDMAN – *College and Student: Selected Readings in the Social Psychology of Higher Education*

Vol. 29.   B. A. ASHEM & E. G. POSER – *Adaptive Learning: Behavior Modification with Children*

Vol. 30.   H. D. BURCK *et al.* – *Counseling and Accountability: Methods and Critique*

Vol. 31.   N. FREDERIKSEN *et al.* – *Prediction of Organizational Behavior*

Vol. 32.   R. B. CATTELL – *A New Morality from Science: Beyondism*

Vol. 33.   M. L. WEINER – *Personality: The Human Potential*

(Continued at back of book)

The terms of our inspection copy service apply to all the above books. Full details of all books listed will gladly be sent upon request.

Behavioral Treatment of Alcoholism

Peter M. Miller, Ph.D.
University of Mississippi Medical Center
Jackson, Mississippi

PERGAMON PRESS

OXFORD · NEW YORK · TORONTO
SYDNEY · PARIS · FRANKFURT

U.K.	Pergamon Press Ltd., Headington Hill Hall, Oxford OX3 0BW, England
U.S.A.	Pergamon Press Inc., Maxwell House, Fairview Park, Elmsford, New York 10523, U.S.A.
CANADA	Pergamon of Canada Ltd., P.O. Box 9600, Don Mills M3C 2T9, Ontario, Canada
AUSTRALIA	Pergamon Press (Aust.) Pty. Ltd., 19a Boundary Street, Rushcutters Bay, N.S.W. 2011, Australia
FRANCE	Pergamon Press SARL, 24 rue des Ecoles, 75240 Paris, Cedex 05, France
WEST GERMANY	Pergamon Press GmbH, 6242 Kronberg/Taunus, Pferdstrasse 1, Frankfurt-am-Main, West Germany

First edition 1976

Library of Congress Catalog Card No. 75-22415

0 08 019518 0 (FC)
0 08 019519 9 (HC)

Typeset by Santype International Ltd., Salisbury
Printed in Great Britain by A. Wheaton & Co., Exeter

To Gabrielle, Michael, and Melanie

Contents

Preface   ix

1. A Behavioral Formulation of Alcohol Abuse   1

    Introduction   1
    Use Versus Abuse   2
    Traditional Models of Alcohol Abuse   3
    Behavioral—Empirical Model   9
    Factors Influencing Alcohol Consumption   10
    Behavioral Treatment Procedures   17

2. Behavioral Assessment   23

    Drinking Behavior   23
    Social—Emotional Behavior Patterns   35
    Analysis of Social—Emotional Functioning   36

3. Aversion Therapy   46

    Introduction   46
    Chemical Aversion   49
    Electrical Aversion   55
    Covert Sensitization   62
    Methodological Issues   66
    Conclusions   71

4. Teaching Alternative Behaviors: Assertiveness, Relaxation, Self-Control   77

    Introduction   77
    Assertive Training   78
    Relaxation Training and Systematic Desensitization   85
    Self-Management Behaviors   87
    Miscellaneous Alternative Behaviors   95

5. Operant Approaches   99

    Positive Reinforcers   99
    Negative Reinforcers   100
    Consequences Which Decrease Behavior   101
    Schedules of Reinforcement   103
    Setting Events   103
    Therapeutic Intervention   104

viii   Contents

6. *Marital Interaction*   116

    Wives of Alcoholics   116
    Husbands of Alcoholics   117
    Alcoholic Couples   118
    Social-Learning Formulation   119
    Altering Marital Interactions   122
    Obstacles to Behavior Change   130

7. *Controlled Social Drinking*   135

    Introduction   135
    Social Drinkers Versus Alcoholics   136
    Treatment Approaches   139
    Social Drinking Versus Abstinence   150
    Conclusions and Future Trends   151

8. *Comprehensive Behavioral Approaches*   156

    Introduction   156
    Examples   157
    Specialized Populations   163
    Conclusion   171

9. *Conclusions and Future Trends*   174

    Clinical   174
    Experimental   177
    Societal   178

Author Index   181

Subject Index   187

Preface

The last several years have witnessed a tremendous increase in public attention and concern over the social and health implications of alcoholism. As the nation's most abused drug, alcohol affects the lives of approximately nine million individuals in the United States alone. If the extent of alcohol abuse is to be significantly decreased, consistently effective treatment methods requiring a minimum of time, effort, and monetary expense must be developed.

Behavior modification, as a clinical approach emanating from the principles of learning developed in experimental psychology laboratories, has potential for accomplishing this goal. This approach offers the field of alcoholism two distinct advantages. First, it brings with it a number of empirically based treatment strategies whose effectiveness has been demonstrated with similar behavior problems. Second, and most important, behaviorists have insisted on a scientific–evaluative approach to treatment. Thus, objectivity of measurement is combined with the application of experimental methods to evaluate treatment effects. Such an orientation should be a welcome asset to a field that for so long has relied upon limited appraisals of therapeutic outcome.

The application of behavioral therapies to alcoholism is not entirely of recent origin. Indeed, references to the use of electrical aversion conditioning for modification of drinking patterns date back to 1928. However, along with the current national interest, behaviorists are applying their technologies to alcohol problems on a far greater scale than has previously been attempted. This has led to a proliferation of more sophisticated and more comprehensive therapeutic programs.

This book represents the first major attempt to organize, within a single volume, the diverse methodologies of behavior modification as applied to the treatment of alcoholism. The material presented here should be useful to both professionals and nonprofessionals working in the field of alcoholism and those interested in the more general field of behavior modification. These include psychologists, psychiatrists, social workers, physicians, nurses, alcoholism counselors, mental health workers, sociologists, law enforcement officers, personnel managers in industry and a variety of others who have contact with alcoholics and their families. The text will have research as well as applied clinical implications and, therefore, will interest academic professionals and students. The book would also be useful as a primary or adjunct text for the rapidly growing number of alcoholism courses currently being taught through undergraduate and graduate programs.

I am indebted to my colleagues, Michel Hersen, Richard Eisler, and Leonard H. Epstein, for their critical analyses of early drafts of chapters together with their assistance in providing more clarity to ideas expressed in the text. In addition I gratefully acknowledge the efficient efforts of Laura Wooten and Pat Schaeffer in typing the manuscript and of Mary Plunkett in preparing the indexes.

About the Author

Peter M. Miller, Ph.D. is currently Associate Professor of Psychiatry (Psychology) at the University of Mississippi Medical Center. He is the author of over 40 research articles in the field of alcohol abuse and related problems. Dr. Miller is also Editor-in-Chief of *Addictive Behaviors*, a major professional journal encompassing alcoholism, drug abuse, obesity, and smoking.

CHAPTER 1

A Behavioral Formulation of Alcohol Abuse

Introduction

While the excessive use of alcohol has been an individual clinical problem for generations, widespread social concern over alcohol abuse is relatively new. Historically, apathy regarding abusive drinking as a social problem appears related to a number of misconceptions in relation to the extent and nature of this disorder. One common misconception is the notion that alcohol abuse is predominantly a problem of older, unmotivated, Skid Row males living in the deteriorated areas of the city. In fact, approximately 95% of alcohol abusers are *not* in this category but rather, are young to middle-aged men and women most of whom are functioning in employment and in families. On the basis of a recent national survey, Cahalan, Cisin, and Crossley (1969) concluded that the highest proportion of heavy drinkers in the United States is found among men aged 30 to 34 and 45 to 49 and among women at ages 21 to 24 and 45 to 49. In addition, the highest rates of alcohol-related problems occur in men under the age of 25 years! Alcohol abusers often do not become visible to society until the long-term aversive consequences of their heavy drinking become evident. Thus, at age 60 an alcohol abuser may be repeatedly hospitalized due to medical, employment, and/or financial reasons and finally be recognized and labeled as an alcoholic.

Another myth regarding alcohol abuse relates to its relationship to other drug substances. A popular belief is that the abuse of drugs (e.g., heroin, barbiturates, amphetamines, marijuana) is (a) more widespread than abuse of alcohol and (b) more personally devastating than alcohol abuse. This myth is easily dispelled when we examine the incidence of alcohol versus drug abuse. Approximately 10% or 9 million individuals out of the 90 million drinkers in the United States are alcoholics. Compared to approximately 200,000 heroin addicts, possibly 750,000 marijuana abusers, and 300,000 to 500,000 abusers of sedative drugs, alcohol abuse represents a significantly more widespread social phenomenon. As with many of these drug substances, alcohol has physically addicting properties such that termination of use after extended periods of excessive consumption leads to physiological withdrawal symptoms. The acute and chronic physical and psychological concomitants of excessive drinking have been well documented (NIAAA, 1970).

1

A third myth relates to the treatment of alcoholism. While the notion that alcohol abuse is a treatable disorder as opposed to an immoral or sinful act seems to be currently accepted, a marked pessimism regarding the likelihood of therapeutic success is apparent among professionals and laymen alike. Certainly, treatment success varies widely depending on chronicity and the stability of the alcoholic's life as he or she enters treatment. A recent critical review by Emrick (1974), however, indicates that approximately two-thirds of alcoholics involved in psychological treatment programs demonstrate significant clinical improvement.

Use Versus Abuse

The differentiation between alcohol *use* and *abuse* is a complex one. While our society has certain general prescribed situations in which drinking is appropriate (e.g., cocktail party, before a meal, wine with a meal) and at times even when drunkenness may be considered appropriate (e.g., New Year's Eve), the general attitude is one of ambivalence. That is, the norms fluctuate not only between socio-cultural groups but also within these groups. Since society has no established norms, definition of abuse must come from elsewhere.

One approach is to base the definition of abuse on the *amount* consumed. Due to individual differences in tolerance and the circumstances under which alcohol is consumed (e.g., prior or subsequent to eating a large meal) such a definition is not a very useful one.

Another system involves the diagnostic classifications of the American Psychiatric Association (1968). Alcoholism, defined as drinking which chronically interferes with physical, personal, or social functioning, is divided into three types. The first two are based on the number of times an individual becomes intoxicated in a year's time. *Episodic Excessive Drinking* constitutes intoxication as frequently as four times per year while *Habitual Excessive Drinking* refers to twelve intoxications per year or under the influence more than once a week. The third classification, *Alcohol Addiction*, is based on either (a) presence of withdrawal symptoms, (b) daily drinking, or (c) heavy drinking for a period of 3 months.

Jellinek (1968) devised a classification system based upon various physical and psychological concomitants of drinking. He classifies various levels of alcoholism as (1) *Alpha* (no loss of control; alcohol used to cope with life), (2) Beta (no dependency but obvious physical concomitants of excessive drinking are apparent), (3) *Gamma* (physical dependence together with loss of control), and (4) *Delta* (completely unable to abstain from alcohol even for short periods of time). A similar but more comprehensive system is that devised by the Criteria Committee of the National Council on Alcoholism (1972).

Alcoholics are categorized into three diagnostic levels based upon the presence or absence of various physiological, clinical, behavioral, psychological, and attitudinal indices. Indicators include such factors as physiological dependency, alcoholic "blackouts", drinking despite negative social-environmental consequences, and alcoholic hepatitis.

The major drawback of these definitions is their reliance on static categorical systems which add little to the treatment of the individual alcoholic. It would appear to be more useful to identify alcohol consumption along a continuum ranging from complete abstinence to moderate drinking to excessive drinking. In this sense alcoholism is seen not as a separate entity but rather as a behavioral excess to be modified in a downward direction. In addition, social, emotional, cognitive, marital, employment, and medical problems correlated with the excessive use of alcohol must be identified and altered. Within a behavioral framework objective assessment of functioning in each of these areas in lieu of diagnostic categorization serves as a basis for establishing a list of specific treatment goals.

Traditional Models of Alcohol Abuse

The recent interest in alcoholism has also intensified efforts to develop more effective treatment strategies. Traditional treatment approaches include individual and group psychodynamic therapy (Brunner-Orne, 1958; Silber, 1959), psychodrama (Weiner, 1967), milieu therapy (Kendall, 1967), medications such as tranquilizers, antidepressants, and LSD (Abramson, 1960; Kissin and Charnoff, 1967), disulfiram (Gerrein, Rosenberg, and Manokar, 1973; Lundwall and Baekeland, 1971), transactional analysis (Steiner, 1969), and community abstinence groups (Alcoholics Anonymous, 1955). Unfortunately, the question of which techniques are more effective than others remains unanswered due to a general disregard for objective evaluations of therapeutic outcome using these procedures.

Implementation of treatment strategies is also complicated by the fact that etiological factors involved in chronic abusive drinking appear to be extremely complex ones. Although speculation and theorizing abound in the alcoholism field, these factors have not as yet been clearly delineated. This lack of knowledge seems directly related to the paucity of direct factual information on the causes of abusive drinking. In spite of the scant data on etiology, numerous theoretical models have been proposed to explain the alcohol abuse phenomenon. In turn, treatment approaches based upon these theories have been devised and are being implemented despite the lack of evidence for their efficacy.

The behavior modification model of alcoholism, while far from being completely structured or evaluated, offers a more systematic approach to the development of viable treatment strategies. The rationale and specific research findings upon which behavioral treatments are based will be discussed in this chapter. Subsequent chapters will include descriptions and evaluations of various behavioral alcoholism treatment techniques.

For comparative purposes, the status of other current theoretical models will be briefly described. These explanatory systems include the disease model, sociological model, physiological model, and the psychological model. The ultimate goal of research would not necessarily be to discredit these models in favor of a new one, but rather to glean from each empirical data relevant to the understanding of alcohol abuse. Presently alcoholism appears to be a complex phenomenon related to various sociological, physiological, and psychological factors.

Disease Model

The disease model views alcohol abuse as a progressive, irreversible disorder. As initially proposed by Jellinek (1960) the concept applies to those individuals who demonstrate a "loss of control" over their drinking. The traditional interpretation of this model, as far as treatment is concerned, is that "once an alcoholic, always an alcoholic". This is why members of Alcoholics Anonymous who are currently sober are referred to as *"recovering alcoholics"* though they may have been sober for as long as 10 or 20 years. This "loss of control", evidenced by irresistible cravings or urges, leads to continued drinking to the point of intoxication after one drink is consumed. Colloquially, this is often stated as "First Drink, Then Drunk" (Sobell, Sobell and Christelman, 1972).

This model was originally proposed and fostered in an attempt to change the status of alcoholism from an immoral, sinful act to be ignored or punished to a disorder of behavior in need of treatment. It appears that this goal has been at least partially accomplished. It may be that alcoholics themselves have been indoctrinated with this disease concept even more successfully than the general public. Sobell, Sobell, and Christelman (1972) surveyed 30 inpatient alcoholics regarding their attitudes concerning "loss of control". Fully 67% felt that if they had one drink they would inevitably continue drinking until they were drunk. In addition 77% felt that once they had drunk 16 ounces of liquor they could not voluntarily terminate their drinking.

Currently, a number of investigators are questioning the continued usefulness of this model. Part of the problem results from the exact meaning of the term "disease" since there have as yet been no specific etiological factors conclusively demonstrated to be pathognomonic for alcohol abuse. In this respect the term "disease" can often be misleading and often therapeutically counterproductive.

Many writers infer that "alcoholism" represents a phenomenon which is etiologically and descriptively different from excessive drinking, problem drinking, or abusive drinking. Thus, a drinking *continuum* exists until a point is reached when the individual *has alcoholism*. This mistaken notion often leads to circular reasoning regarding etiology. Thus, one might determine that someone is an "alcoholic" because he has lost control of his drinking (that is, he never drinks in moderation) and perhaps because he evidences dependent and irresponsible behaviors. When asked why this individual has lost control and why he exhibits dependency and irresponsibility the answer is often, "because he is an alcoholic!"

Therapeutically, the usefulness of the "loss of control" or disease concept is highly controversial. Alcoholics Anonymous considers this notion to be central to the maintenance of sobriety in their members. There are, however, several countertherapeutic elements in this conception which have been delineated by several authors (Robinson, 1972; Sobell and Sobell, 1974). Clinically, the disease concept tends to take the burden of responsibility for change away for the alcoholic. Thus, the oft quoted phrase, "How can I do anything about my drinking? I've got a disease." Alcoholics often assume that either detoxification and/or medical treatments will "cure" their alcoholism. In fact the disease concept places the responsibility for treatment of alcohol abuse with the physician. As Robinson (1972) has pointed out, the medical profession is often ill prepared to deal with this problem even to the point of being unwilling or unable to even recognize its existence.

The loss of control myth also frequently provides the alcoholic with a rationalization to continue drinking to the point of intoxication after one or two drinks. Thus, he or she is told that resistance to continued drinking after one drink is impossible. The reasoning is that even one drink is as bad as twenty drinks. Reactions of friends and relatives perpetuate this reasoning. That is, many spouses respond as negatively to the alcoholic's consumption of one drink as they do to ten drinks. Thus, he may as well drink the ten since he is being "punished" equally for both mild and excessive drinking.

In this regard, the "recovering" alcoholic is often not given credit for "relapses" during which he consumes one or two drinks, terminates drinking, and then remains sober once again. The author is reminded of a story regarding an AA member who had been completely abstinent from alcohol for 20 years. This lengthy period of sobriety was accompanied by recognition and status within the AA group. Prior to receiving a special commendation for his efforts, however, the individual reinstituted his past drinking behavior for a brief 2-day period. His drinking during this time was rather moderate and he returned to complete abstinence after the drinking episode. Unfortunately, the social consequences of this "relapse" were profound. Not only did the individual lose considerable recognition within his AA group, but the special commendation award he was to receive was cancelled. In addition, at AA meetings he could no longer say "I'm Joe Smith and I've been sober for 20 years!" but rather "I'm Joe Smith, and I've been sober for *two weeks*." Both his efforts at abstinence for 20 years and his ability to terminate his drinking after 2 days were unrecognized.

Arguments regarding the pros and cons of the "loss of control" hypothesis could continue *ad infinitum* with no resolution. The most productive effect of this controversy has been the recent proliferation of research efforts to test its validity.

Consistently, the available research does *not* support the notion of "loss of control". A number of investigators (Merry, 1966; Williams, 1970; Cutter, Schwab, and Nathan, 1970) have reported that when provided with "priming doses" of alcohol, either surreptitiously or openly, chronic alcoholics are not induced to continue drinking even when alcohol is easily available to them. It has also been demonstrated in laboratory studies that, after several days of alcohol consumption, many alcoholics voluntarily terminate drinking with no problem (McNamee, Mello, and Mendelson, 1968; Mello, 1972; Nathan and O'Brien, 1971; Gottheil, Corbett, Grasberger, and Cornelison, 1972).

Possibly the most convincing experimental test of the "loss of control" notion was reported by Marlatt, Demming, and Reid (1973). Via a taste rating task (see Chapter 2) alcoholics and social drinkers were provided with alcoholic beverages to consume. Half of the subjects in the groups were led to believe that the beverages contained alcohol while the other half were told that the drinks were nonalcoholic. Half of the subjects in each instructional condition were given alcoholic beverages and half nonalcoholic ones. Results indicated that the amount that alcoholics consumed was highly related to the instructional set and *not* to the actual content of the beverage. Thus, if they were told that they were drinking alcohol, regardless of whether they actually were or not, they consumed more of the beverages. Amount of beverage consumed was not influenced, even when alcohol was being consumed, if the subject believed that he was drinking a nonalcoholic beverage. The authors relate their findings to the importance of cognitive variables in determining "loss of control".

Certainly more studies, particularly ones examining drinking behavior of alcoholics over an extended period of time, are needed. Perhaps as Keller (1972) proposes, the "craving" or loss of control is not evidenced until certain levels of blood/alcohol concentration are reached. In this sense the "craving" (if this is a valid phenomenon) may be a response to the aversive physiological stimuli associated with a decreasing blood/alcohol level. In any event a complex of social, psychological, and physiological factors may be involved. It remains, however, not for the disease concept to be disproven, but for someone to present concrete evidence for its existence. At this point in time, it seems unwise to take a firm stand in favor of such a model when there is no evidence to support it, and indeed, an increasing number of reports refuting it.

Sociological Model

Cahalan, Cisin, and Crossley (1969) and Cahalan and Room (1974) have delineated a number of demographic variables that are related both to the use and abuse of alcoholic beverages. Generally, the highest rates of abuse are associated with low socioeconomic status, urban residence, history of broken home, Catholic or liberal Protestant religious affiliation, no church affiliation, and unmarried status (either single or divorced). Ethnic background is also related to drinking patterns in that some countries (e.g., Ireland, USA) exhibit a high rate of alcoholism while others (e.g., Israel) have a much lower rate.

In this context, Miller and Eisler (in press) describe three major factors related to substance abuse either within a social group or a larger culture. These include the availability of the drug, the context within which it is used, and the sanctions imposed on its abuse. Being a legal drug, alcohol is easily obtainable in our society. Even during Prohibition in the United States alcohol remained easily available. Since alcohol was available and so many consumers were willing to buy it, legal sanctions could not be consistently imposed and thus were ineffective. Such totally coercive methods, so characteristic of the manner in which our society attempts to solve its problems, have been repeatedly shown to have little lasting influence on behavior change (Skinner, 1971). In addition, sanctions of this nature that are not accepted by a large part of society may actually enhance the reinforcing properties of alcohol consumption since it becomes a "dangerous adventure".

Many social groups establish both specific contexts within which alcohol *use* is acceptable and negative sanctions for its abuse. These standards of behavior are often informally transmitted in a culture through the socialization process. Alcohol tends to be abused least when the norms for alcohol use are narrowly defined (e.g., for appetitive or religious reasons) and social punishment for abuse is strict. This is true among the Jews who typically place extensive social and religious censure on alcohol abuse. In contrast, when alcohol was introduced into the American Indian culture no norms for its use were established. This fact together with current economic and psychological deprivations endured by this group are probably responsible for their extremely high incidence of alcohol abuse.

There is also evidence to support the notion that patterns of abuse are transmitted within a family group by means of social role modeling (Bandura, 1969). The Criteria Committee of the National Council on Alcoholism (1972) reports that alcoholics most frequently come from families in which (a) one or both parents was an alcoholic or (b) the family was totally abstinent from alcohol. The reasons for this may be related to the fact that neither group of children were exposed to models of appropriate social drinking. Thus, neither the mechanics of moderate, responsible drinking nor its uses were learned.

Physiological Factors

While several physiological theories of the etiology of alcoholism have been proposed none has as yet been satisfactorily confirmed. One of the earliest theories of this nature was proposed by Williams (1946). He postulated that alcohol abuse is related to a basic nutritional deficiency which is genetically determined. This deficiency then leads to a "psychological need" for alcohol. This basic hypothesis, however, has not been supported by experimental evidence (Lester and Greenberg, 1952; Mardones, 1960).

Another popular theory of alcohol abuse is that it is an inherited disorder. Goodwin (1971) has recently reviewed the research literature in this area. A consistent finding is that alcoholism does run in families. If an individual has a parent or blood relative who is an alcoholic, he or she is more likely to abuse alcohol. Certainly social role modeling (Bandura, 1969) of the alcoholic drinking patterns of parents may account for these facts. On the other hand, in comparing adopted and nonadopted sons of alcoholics, Goodwin, Schulsinger, Moller, Hermansen, Winskur, and Guze (1974) concluded that environmental factors seem to contribute little to the development of alcoholism in sons of severe alcoholics. The evidence for a heredity theory of alcoholism is far from conclusive. It may be that rather than a direct genetic link there is an indirect one in terms of physiological predisposition. In this regard, an individual with low gastrointestinal tolerance for alcohol may be less likely to abuse alcohol. After one or two drinks this individual may experience slight discomfort or nausea and thus terminate drinking. The alcoholic may initially be able to tolerate more and hence obtain less negative physiological feedback.

Support for such an indirect genetic link in explaining the extremely low incidence of alcohol abuse among Orientals has been reported by Ewing, Rouse, and Pellizzari (1974). Heart rate, earlobe pulse pressure, and self-report measures of subjective feelings were obtained from twenty-four persons of European descent and twenty-four Orientals prior and subsequent to ingestion of standard amounts of synthetic alcohol. Effects of drinking by the Orientals differed significantly from those by the Europeans in that they experienced greater flushing of the face, increased capillary blood flow, increased heart rate, and more negative subjective physiological experiences (e.g., dizziness, muscle weakness, headaches). These concomitants of drinking were rare among the Europeans. The authors concluded that physiological factors seem related to the sensitivity of Orientals to alcohol.

Psychological Models

Within this category are included a wide range of interpretations of the etiology of alcohol abuse based upon psychodynamic or psychoanalytic theories of personality. Since it is beyond the scope of this book to describe these various approaches in detail, the reader is referred to comprehensive reviews by McCord and McCord (1960) and Emrick (1974). In the former paper the authors note that psychodynamic theories of alcohol abuse rest upon one or a combination of three assumptions:

(1) Alcoholism results from unconscious tendencies such as self-destruction, latent homosexuality, or fixation at the oral stage of development.
(2) Alcoholism represents a need for power and autonomy.
(3) Alcoholism is related to repressed hostility and/or dependency needs.

The evidence for these explanations is inconclusive at present partly due to a lack of prospective studies in which these factors are used to predict alcohol abuse before its onset. Otherwise, it may well be that alcohol abusers who exhibit dependent behavior, for example, are doing so as a *result* of a pattern of abusive drinking rather than as a cause.

Sutherland, Schroeder, and Tordella (1950) and Syme (1957) failed to demonstrate differences in personality traits between alcoholic and nonalcoholic populations. McCord and McCord (1960) evaluated the records of subjects who were initially subjected to comprehensive psychological and medical examinations as youngsters (via the Cambridge—Somerville Youth Study) and who subsequently exhibited abusive drinking patterns as adults. The early evaluations of this group were compared to a control group that did not evidence alcoholism. The results suggested that prior to the onset of abusive drinking these groups did not differ in nutritional or glandular functioning, inferiority feelings, oral tendencies or homosexual urges.

Behavioral—Empirical Model

The behavioral or social-learning approach to alcohol abuse has generally been grossly misunderstood and/or oversimplified. While investigators who are well acquainted with behavioral approaches have written excellent critical reviews in the area (Franks, 1958, 1963, 1966, 1970), these were necessarily limited in scope due to the paucity of clinical and research reports in the field at the time they were written.

In essence, behavioral approaches to alcoholism have relied on a simple conditioning (drive reduction) model derived from learning principles based on animal analogue data (Kingham, 1958; Conger, 1956). While others have attempted to expand this explanation (Kepner, 1964), emphasis was placed upon a mixture of psychodynamic and learning theory principles.

Such a simplistic approach does not represent the current status of behavioral approaches to alcohol abuse. Rather, this approach represents an empirical one stressing objective, observable assessment, systematic evaluation of clinical outcome, and the use of validated clinical procedures. While the result of this model has been the proliferation of treatment techniques based upon scientific knowledge of learning and behavior, its basic framework is a *methodological* one. That is, it provides a system of experimental methodology using objective assessment and evaluation to enhance knowledge in the field. Within this framework treatment strategies are empirically rather than theoretically based.

In discussing this orientation to the understanding of abusive drinking, Sobell and Sobell (1974) propose that current theories, with little evidence to support or refute them, have added little to the treatment or prevention of alcoholism. A more fruitful approach would involve investigations into current factors in an individual's environment which contribute to the maintenance of abusive drinking patterns. This functional analysis approach generates two general lines of research: (1) descriptive studies and (2) treatment evaluation studies. In descriptive analyses, specific factors (e.g., stress) thought to be contributing to the maintenance of excessive drinking are investigated through direct behavioral assessment. Direct observations of alcoholic drinking are systematically evaluated through controlled experimentation. Within the past 5 years behavioral researchers have made significant strides in both of these research areas.

The first step in determining factors which may be relevant to the maintenance of alcohol abuse consists of a functional analysis of specific antecedent and consequent events associated with this behavior pattern. Such an analysis would include a wide variety of social, situational, cognitive, physiological, and emotional factors such as those described in Figure 1.1. Any one or a combination of the antecedent factors may precipitate excessive drinking. Consequent events that increase the likelihood of excessive alcohol consumption may include an increase in positive experiences (e.g., attention from friends) or a reduction in an aversive antecedent cue (e.g., decreases in withdrawal symptoms). The exact combination of these factors necessary to initiate and maintain abusive drinking at any given time may be highly complex. Most behavioral studies have attempted to isolate one or two of these variables and investigate their influence on alcoholic drinking over time. Those factors for which empirical information is available are discussed below.

Factors Influencing Alcohol Consumption

Emotional Factors

The relationship between stress and excessive drinking has long been considered important in the etiology of alcoholism. It has generally been assumed that anxiety producing situations may serve as cues for abusive

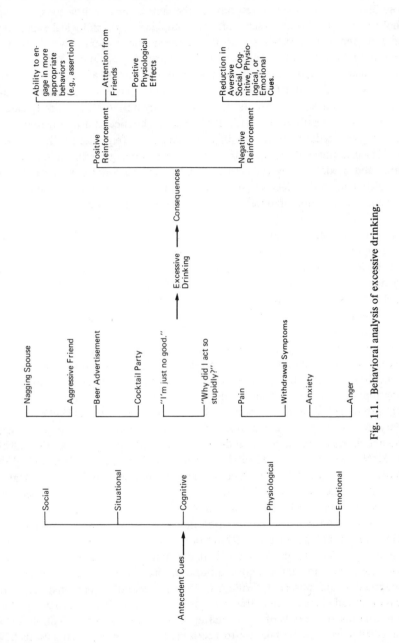

Fig. 1.1. Behavioral analysis of excessive drinking.

drinking. Supposedly, alcohol consumption results in decreases in anxiety and thus is more likely to occur again in response to the same or similar situations. Through alcohol the individual readily escapes from an unpleasant physiological experience. After repeated sequences of situational cue → anxiety → excessive drinking → anxiety reduction, the cue itself may elicit the drinking behavior. The individual gradually learns to avoid anxiety altogether by consuming alcohol early in this chain of events. Fort and Porterfield (1961) report that females and individuals raised by alcohol abstinent parents characteristically initiate their drinking careers in response to a stressful event. With little prior experience at drinking they often use alcohol as a sedative to deal with traumatic stress (e.g., the death of a loved one). This drinking pattern may then become a more generalized reaction to tensions and anxiety in everyday life. Finally, daily alcohol consumption may result although other factors such as avoidance of withdrawal symptoms may eventually become prepotent over anxiety reduction as a maintaining influence.

The major evidence to support or refute this "tension-reduction hypothesis" is based upon experiments with animals. Since these studies are so numerous a careful review of these findings is beyond the scope of this book. Cappell and Herman (1972), however, critically reviewed both the animal and human research in this area and concluded that much of the evidence was ". . . negative, equivocal and often contradictory" (p. 64). They note that the tension-reduction hypothesis may have outlived its usefulness and does not, at this point in time, offer a valid explanation of abusive drinking patterns.

Recent investigations in which hospitalized chronic alcoholics are provided with alcohol shed further light on this issue. In these studies self-report and observational assessments of an alcoholic's mood are accumulated before and during prolonged drinking episodes. Results of these studies indicate that, contrary to the popular assumption of tension reduction, alcoholics actually experience *increases* in anxiety and depression once drinking begins (Mendelson, 1964; McNamee, Mello, and Mendelson, 1968; Nathan and O'Brien, 1971). On the basis of the Mood Adjective Checklist and the Wittenborn Psychiatric Rating Scales Nathan and O'Brien (1971) found alcoholics to be more depressed, less active, and more pathological after drinking.

Interestingly, normal drinkers do not demonstrate increases in anxiety as a function of drinking. Mello (1972) notes that social drinkers generally experience *positive mood changes* when consuming alcohol. However, as the amount consumed increases (above 8 ounces), significant increases in anxiety and depression are observed (Williams, 1966). Alcoholics demonstrate these unpleasant mood changes even after low doses of alcohol (Mayfield, 1968).

In evaluating the results of these studies, characteristics of the alcoholics who served as subjects must be taken into account. Most of these investigations have utilized chronic Skid Row alcoholics. Drinking in these individuals may be maintained by factors that are quite different than factors associated with the alcohol consumption of less deteriorated alcoholics. Skid Row individuals drink daily as a way of life and their drinking is more likely to be influenced by environmental or physiological events (e.g., attention from drinking buddies or avoidance of withdrawal symptoms).

Another factor in the relationship between stress and alcohol involves the state of arousal of the individual prior to consumption of alcohol. Both Lienart and Traxel (1959) and Korn (1960) report that the tranquilizing and reinforcing properties of alcohol are enhanced under conditions of emotional arousal. It may be that the anxiety reducing properties of alcohol are important in the maintenance of excessive drinking *only* when emotional arousal precedes the drinking episode. The subjects in the above mentioned studies may have demonstrated a different pattern if they had been exposed to clinically relevant stress prior to alcohol consumption.

This issue has been recently examined in three separate analogue studies. Higgins and Marlatt (1974) investigated the relationship between emotional arousal and alcohol consumption in twenty alcoholics and twenty social drinkers. Alcohol consumption was measured via a taste rating test (see Chapter 2) during which subjects were requested to consume and rate the tastes of several alcoholic beverages. Presumably, subjects were unaware that the amount of alcohol consumed was to be recorded. Prior to this task subjects were randomly divided into two groups receiving either threat of painful electric shock or threat of nonpainful shock. In reality, none of the subjects was actually shocked. While the alcoholics tended to consume more alcohol than the social drinkers, no significant relationship was found between anxiety arousal and alcohol consumption for either group. This absence of a relationship between these two variables may have been related to a lack of potency of the rather artificial anxiety arousing manipulations utilized. Indeed, self-report anxiety ratings of subjects in the high threat condition did *not* present convincing evidence of the effectiveness of these conditions in arousing anxiety.

Contrary to these findings, Miller, Hersen, Eisler, and Hilsman (1974) found that clinically relevant social stress did significantly increase the drinking of alcoholic subjects. Stress was induced via exposure to a number of role-played social situations which required assertiveness on the part of the subject. Allman, Taylor, and Nathan (1972), however, suggest that this relationship between stress and alcohol consumption is very complex. It is apparently related to such factors as characteristics of the individual alcoholic, type of stress (e.g., interpersonal versus environmental), and the context within which stress occurs. Indeed, it would seem more productive to evaluate the nature of the specific situations which precede excessive alcohol consumption in individual alcoholic clients rather than examining responses to anxiety in general.

Social Factors

The influence of social-interpersonal cues on alcohol consumption has been investigated in a number of studies. To evaluate this relationship Nathan and O'Brien (1971) assessed the social behavior of four Skid Row alcoholics and four nonalcoholics during prolonged drinking in an experimental inpatient setting. Points earned by pressing an operant lever could be spent either on whiskey or to escape from social isolation. Social behavior was evaluated by number of points spent to obtain relief from isolation, a social distance measure, and ward observations. Alcoholics tended to be social isolates before, during, and after drinking episodes. Nonalcoholics engaged in more social behavior especially during and after alcohol consumption. The authors concluded that social isolation may serve as a cue for excessive alcohol consumption.

In direct contrast to these results Bigelow (1973) and Griffiths, Bigelow, and Liebson (1973, 1974a, 1974b) have repeatedly found that social interaction rather than isolation serves as a cue for excessive drinking in chronic alcoholics. In these studies alcoholics engaged in social interaction significantly more while drinking than while not drinking (Bigelow, 1973). In addition, during periods of drinking, alcoholics were more likely to choose opportunity to socialize over a small amount of money. Briddell and Nathan (1975) have postulated that the difference between Nathan's results and those of Bigelow, Griffiths, and Liebson may be due to the greater amount of alcohol consumed by the subjects in Nathan's study. Thus, while moderate amounts of alcohol may facilitate social interaction, larger amounts may have the reverse effect. In any event, there is convincing evidence to suggest that social interactions become more reinforcing to alcoholics after alcohol consumption.

A partial explanation for these findings may be found in the studies of Mendelson, Mello, and Solomon (1968), Steinglass, Weiner, and Mendelson (1971), and Weiner, Tamerin, Steinglass, and Mendelson (1971). These experimenters investigated the influence of excessive drinking on the social interaction of alcoholic pairs (father—son, and brothers). Results indicate that alcohol may allow an alcoholic to "engage in a series of dyadic and intergroup roles which are not available to him during periods of sobriety" (Mello, 1972, pp. 280–1). For example, Steinglass *et al.* (1971) observed the interactions of two alcoholic brothers during periods of experimentally induced intoxication. These subjects were voluntarily confined on a ward facility consisting of private bedrooms, a dayroom, and a variety of recreational resources. After 5 days of baseline during which the brothers became acquainted with the ward, up to one quart of 100 proof alcohol was available to them each day. This 14-day period of drinking was followed by a 5-day withdrawal period. Assessments during the drinking phase included daily blood samples, performance tasks to measure memory, and general behavioral observations. Observations indicated that interpersonal roles were more clearly defined during periods of one member's intoxication. Seldom did both brothers become excessively intoxicated at the same time. Rather, the more sober of the two maintained a passive-supportive role while the intoxicated brother assumed a more assertive behavior pattern. Much lability of behavior was observed in terms of one partner's alternating between criticizing the excessive drinking of his brother and assisting in obtaining more to drink. This pattern is often observed clinically in alcoholic marriages.

Social interactions may also direct influence on alcohol consumption via group pressure and social modeling. Goldman, Taylor, Carruth, and Nathan (1973) investigated the effects of group norms on alcohol consumption in four chronic alcoholics. As a group the subjects periodically decided when to begin drinking, how much to drink, and when to stop drinking. The individual drinking pattern of each group member was significantly influenced by the norms established by the group as a whole.

Similarly, Marlatt (1974) investigated the influence of one individual's drinking behavior on that of another. Specifically, the author hypothesized that, on a drinking task, subjects exposed to a heavy drinking model would drink significantly more than subjects exposed to either a light drinking model or no model. Forty-eight college students classified as "heavy social drinkers" were divided into three groups each receiving a different modeling condition: high consumption model, low consumption model, and a no model control condition. In addition, half of the subjects in each group were exposed to a "cold" argumentative social interaction with the model prior to the drinking task, while the other half interacted in a warm, friendly way with the model. All subjects then participated in a taste rating drinking task in which they were required to rate the taste of three burgundy wines. A total of 2100 ml. of wine was available to each subject. In the high consumption modeling condition, subjects performed the drinking task along with a subject (confederate) who drank a total of 700 ml. (one full bottle of wine) in a 15-minute time interval. In the low consumption modeling condition the model limited his drinking to 100 ml. Results indicated that subjects exposed to the high consumption model drank significantly more wine than subjects exposed to the low consumption model or no model conditions. The prior warm versus cold social interaction with the model had no effect on consumption.

These results may have important implications regarding both the development and treatment of alcoholism. Social modeling of excessive drinking patterns in others may be one significant factor in producing chronic alcohol abuse. Such social-learning phenomena may explain the high incidence of alcoholism among children of alcoholic parents. Similarly, the drinking behavior of the social group with which an individual interacts may significantly influence his drinking patterns. Clinically, this finding implies that replacement of an alcoholic's heavy drinking companions with friends who are moderate drinkers or abstainers may be an important aspect of therapeutic success.

Thus, studies of social factors related to alcohol abuse indicate that there appears to be a definite relationship between social interaction and alcohol consumption. Modeling or group pressure may significantly increase the amounts of alcohol that an individual consumes. In turn, drinking appears to enhance the rewarding properties of social interaction by explicitly defining roles and by allowing the individual to engage in behavior patterns (e.g., assertiveness) which are unavailable to him when sober. This enhanced behavioral repertoire may lead to increased social responsiveness from others. Indeed, Hersen, Miller, and Eisler (1973) present data to suggest that wives of alcoholic husbands tend to respond more positively in marital interactions when the husband is intoxicated.

Cognitive Factors

Few studies are available on the role of cognitive factors in alcoholism. It is often assumed, however, that alcoholics have a "poor self concept" which changes to a more positive one subsequent to alcohol consumption. Thus, thoughts of "I'm no damned good" or "I mess up everything I do" are presumably lessened by the effects of alcohol. Assessment of these patterns is difficult since experimenters must rely exclusively on self-report measures.

In an attempt to evaluate this factor Vanderpool (1969) administered the Gough Adjective Checklist and the Tennessee Self-Concept Scale to fifty intoxicated alcoholics and fifty sober alcoholics. Intoxicated subjects rated themselves *more negatively* on self-esteem, adequacy, estrangement and social worth, and tolerance to stress than did sober subjects. Thus, drinking tended to decrease thoughts regarding self-worth rather than increase them.

Situational Factors

It is often assumed that as a result of repeated associations between alcohol related cues in the environment (e.g., liquor advertisement or seeing other people drink) and intoxication, these cues serve to initiate drinking behavior. That is, the mere sight or smell of alcohol may increase the likelihood that an alcoholic will drink.

Miller, Hersen, Eisler, Epstein, and Wooten (1974) examined the relationship between alcohol cues and alcohol consumption in twenty alcoholics and twenty social drinkers. Alcoholic subjects were hospitalized patients with numerous arrests, job losses, and hospitalizations for alcoholism and a mean history of problem drinking of 12.4 years. Social drinkers were also hospitalized, but for nonalcohol related psychiatric problems. Subjects were matched on age and education. Subjects were asked to press a lever on an operant console for a 10-minute period of time. For every 50 lever presses a 5 cc squirt of alcohol mixed with water was dispensed into a shot glass in front of the subject. The subjects were instructed to drink the alcohol under the guise that they would be asked to rate its taste as part of a taste experiment. All subjects performed this task twice under two separate conditions of alcohol cue prominence. During the cue condition a variety of visual alcohol cues were placed directly in the subject's view. These cues included three bottles of bourbon (one full, one half full, and one nearly empty) and several pictures of people consuming alcoholic beverages. During the no cue responding the operant console remained free of extraneous stimuli. The total number of lever presses during the 10-minute period for both conditions was compared for all subjects. Social drinkers tended to respond significantly more under visual alcohol cue conditions while alcoholics did not respond differentially to the conditions. Visual alcohol cues may have little significance as antecedents to drinking in chronic alcoholics. Apparently chronic alcoholics often drink alone without the visual accessories of alcohol consumption. Social drinkers drink in situations that are highly discriminative in terms of visual alcohol cues (e.g., social gatherings with friends drinking, cocktail lounge with low lighting and rows of liquor bottles) and seldom drink when these cues are absent.

Results of this single analysis, however, must be considered preliminary. Perhaps the alcohol cues used in this study were not salient enough to affect consumption. More potent cues examined within a more naturalistic drinking environment may further delineate this relationship.

Physiological Factors

Clinically, it is frequently noted that the drinking of some chronic alcoholics is maintained by an avoidance of or escape from aversive physiological withdrawal symptoms which occur when excessive consumption is decreased or terminated. Nathan and O'Brien (1971) reported that decreases in blood/alcohol levels often served to precipitate drinking in their Skid Row alcoholic subjects.

Alleviation of pain may also serve to initiate and maintain excessive drinking. While clinically many alcoholics attribute their drinking to this factor, no experimental evidence is available.

Behavioral Treatment Procedures

Historically, due to the proliferation by early behaviorists of the notion that alcohol abuse was a function of simple conditioning factors, behavioral treatment of alcoholism has involved almost the exclusive use of aversion conditioning strategies. Currently, behavioral treatment goals have become more comprehensive in response to (a) the increasing number of research findings questioning a simple conditioning etiological model and (b) recent controlled evaluation studies questioning the efficacy of aversion procedures. A wide variety of non-aversive behavioral treatment strategies are now used to reduce excessive alcohol consumption and to enhance social, marital, and vocational functioning. Emphasis is placed upon initiating and then maintaining behavior patterns that are alternative to and incompatible with excessive alcohol consumption.

The remainder of this book will describe in detail the types of behavioral treatment strategies that are applicable to alcoholism treatment. The goal of these procedures is to modify the antecedent and consequent events associated with excessive drinking. The alcoholic is taught ways to either avoid certain antecedents or deal with them more effectively. Consequences can be rearranged either by the alcoholic himself through self-management procedures or through significant others in his or her environment. In this regard, the focus of treatment is highly dependent upon continuing descriptive research examining the influence of social, environmental, physiological and emotional variables on drinking.

A major emphasis of the behavioral approach is the necessity of careful evaluation of therapeutic efficacy. Thus, a variety of objective measures of drinking, marital, social, emotional, and vocational behaviors are accumulated concomitantly with treatment.

A comprehensive behavioral model of alcoholism treatment requires the use of a variety of techniques geared toward the individual needs of patients. The range of techniques currently in use is wide. Techniques which decrease the immediate reinforcing properties of alcohol are typically used. This has involved associating aversive or unpleasant stimuli with both the sequence of the drinking pattern (from urges to actual consumption) and the wide variety of environmental cues (e.g., sight or smell of alcohol, liquor advertisements, drinking "buddies") which elicit the behavior. This approach includes the use of self-control or self-management techniques to control urges and rearrangement of environmental stimuli associated with alcohol-approach behavior. In response to descriptive research studies, techniques designed to provide the alcoholic with social-emotional behaviors that are incompatible with alcohol abuse are being used. This includes learning alternative ways of dealing with stressful social, marital, and vocational situations. In addition, the use of operant conditioning strategies is increasing. Within this framework, significant persons in the environment are taught ways of reinforcing new, sober behavior patterns and of punishing or ignoring excessive alcohol consumption.

Goals of treatment tend to be more flexible than more traditional approaches. That is, controlled, moderate drinking as opposed to complete abstinence is frequently considered to be an acceptable therapeutic goal. Behavioral strategies have provided methods of teaching and maintaining these social drinking skills.

References

ABRAMSON, H. *Use of LSD in psychotherapy.* New York: Josiah Macy, Jr. Foundations, 1960.

Alcoholics Anonymous. New York: Cornwall Press, 1955.

ALLMAN, L. R., TAYLOR, H. A. and NATHAN, P. E. Group drinking during stress: Effects on drinking behavior, affect, and psychopathology. *American Journal of Psychiatry*, 1972, **129**, 669–78.

American Psychiatric Association. *Diagnostic and statistical manual of mental disorders* (2nd edition). Washington, D.C.: American Psychiatric Association, 1968.

BANDURA, A. *Principles of behavior modification.* New York: Holt, Rinehart, & Winston, Inc., 1969.

BIGELOW, G. Experimental analysis of human drug self-administration. Presented at Eastern Psychological Association, May, 1973.

BRIDDELL, D. W. and NATHAN, P. E. Behavior assessment and modification with alcoholics: Current status and future trends. In M. Hersen, R. M. Eisler, and P. M. Miller (Eds.) *Progress in Behavior Modification.* New York: Academic Press, 1975.

BRUNNER-ORNE, M. Group therapy of alcoholics. *Quarterly Journal of Studies on Alcohol*, 1958, **19**, 164–5.

CAHALAN, D., CISIN, I. H. and CROSSLEY, H. M. *American drinking practices: A national study of drinking behavior and attitudes.* Monograph No. 6. New Brunswick, N.J.: Rutgers Center of Alcohol Studies, 1969.

CAHALAN, D. and ROOM, R. *Problem drinking among American men.* Monograph No. 7. New Brunswick, N.J.: Rutgers Center of Alcohol Studies, 1974.

CAPPELL, H. and HERMAN, C. P. Alcohol and tension reduction: A review. *Quarterly Journal of Studies on Alcohol*, 1972, **33**, 33–64.

CONGER, J. J. Reinforcement theory and the dynamics of alcoholism. *Quarterly Journal of Studies on Alcohol*, 1956, **17**, 296–305.

Criteria Committee, National Council on Alcoholism. Criteria for the diagnosis of alcoholism. *American Journal of Psychiatry*, 1972, **2**, 127–35.

CUTTER, H. S., SCHWAB, E. L. and NATHAN, P. E. Effects of alcohol on its utility for alcoholics. *Quarterly Journal of Studies on Alcohol*, 1970, **30**, 369–78.

EMRICK, C. D. A review of psychologically oriented treatment of alcoholism. I. The use and interrelationships of outcome criteria and drinking behavior following treatment. *Quarterly Journal of Studies on Alcohol*, 1974, **35**, 523–49.

EWING, J. A., ROUSE, B. A. and PELLIZZARI, E. D. Alcohol sensitivity and ethnic background. *American Journal of Psychiatry*, 1974, **131**, 206–10.

FORT, T. and PORTERFIELD, A. L. Some backgrounds and types of alcoholism among women. *Journal of Health and Human Behavior*, 1961, **2**, 283–92.

FRANKS, C. M. Alcohol, alcoholism, and conditioning: A review of the literature and some theoretical considerations. *Journal of Mental Science*, 1958, **104**, 14–33.

FRANKS, C. M. Behavior therapy, the principles of conditioning and the treatment of the alcoholic. *Quarterly Journal of Studies on Alcohol*, 1963, **24**, 511–29.

FRANKS, C. M. Conditioning and conditioned aversion therapies in the treatment of the alcoholic. *International Journal of the Addictions*, 1966, **1**, 61–98.

FRANKS, C. M. Alcoholism. In C. G. Costello (Ed.) *Symptoms of psychopathology: A handbook.* New York: John T. Wiley and Sons, Inc., 1970, 448–80.

19

GERREIN, J. R., ROSENBERG, C. M. and MANOKAR, V. Disulfiram maintenance in outpatient treatment of alcoholism. *Archives of General Psychiatry*, 1973, 28, 798–802.

GOLDMAN, M., TAYLOR, A., CARRUTH, M. and NATHAN, P. E. Effects of group decision-making on group drinking by alcoholics. *Quarterly Journal of Studies on Alcohol*, 1973, 34, 807–22.

GOODWIN, D. W. Is alcoholism hereditary? A review and critique. *Archives of General Psychiatry*, 1971, 25, 545–9.

GOODWIN, D. W., SCHULSINGER, F., MOLLER, N., HERMANSON, L., WINOKUR, G. and GUZE, S. Drinking problems in adopted and nonadopted sons of alcoholics. *Archives of General Psychiatry*, 1974, 31, 164–9.

GOTTHEIL, E., CORBETT, L. O., GRASBERGER, J. C. and CORNELISON, F. S. Fixed interval drinking decisions. *Quarterly Journal of Studies on Alcohol*, 1972, 33, 311–24.

GRIFFITHS, R. R., BIGELOW, G. and LIEBSON, I. Alcohol self-administration and social interactions in alcoholics. Presented at American Psychological Association, Aug., 1973.

GRIFFITHS, R. R., BIGELOW, G. and LIEBSON, I. The effect of ethanol self-administration on relative reinforcing properties of money versus social interaction in alcoholics. Unpublished manuscript, Department of Psychiatry, Baltimore City Hospitals, 1974.

GRIFFITHS, R. R., BIGELOW, G. and LIEBSON, I. The use of contingent time-out from social interactions to suppress drinking in alcoholics. Unpublished manuscript, Department of Psychiatry, Baltimore City Hospitals, 1974.

HERSEN, M., MILLER, P. M. and EISLER, R. M. Interactions between alcoholics and their wives: A descriptive analysis of verbal and nonverbal behavior. *Quarterly Journal of Studies on Alcohol*, 1973. 34, 516–20.

HIGGINS, R. L. and MARLATT, G. A. The effects of anxiety arousal upon the consumption of alcohol by alcoholics and social drinkers. *Journal of Consulting and Clinical Psychology*, 1974, 41, 426–33.

JELLINEK, E. M. *The disease concept of alcoholism.* New Haven: College and University Press, 1960.

KELLER, M. On the loss-of-control phenomenon in alcoholism. *British Journal of the Addictions*, 1972, 67, 153–6.

KENDALL, L. The role of the nurse in the treatment of the alcoholic patient. In R. Fox (Ed.) *Alcoholism: Behavioral research, therapeutic approaches.* New York: Springer Publishing Co., Inc., 1967.

KEPNER, E. Application of learning theory to the etiology and treatment of alcoholism. *Quarterly Journal of Studies on Alcohol*, 1964, 25, 279–91.

KINGHAM, R. J. Alcoholism and the reinforcement theory of learning. *Quarterly Journal of Studies on Alcohol*, 1958, 19, 320–30.

KISSIN, B. and CHARNOFF, S. M. Clinical evaluation of tranquilizers and anti-depressant drugs in the long term treatment of chronic alcoholism. In R. Fox (Ed.) *Alcoholism: Behavioral research, therapeutic approaches.* New York: Springer Publishing Co., Inc., 1967.

KORN, S. J. The relationship between individual differences in the responsivity of rats to stress and intake of alcohol. *Quarterly Journal of Studies on Alcohol*, 1960, 21, 605–17.

LESTER, D. and GREENBERG, L. Nutrition and the etiology of alcoholism. The effect of sucrose, saccharin, and fat on the self-selection of ethyl alcohol by rats. *Quarterly Journal of Studies on Alcohol*, 1952, 13, 553–6.

LIENART, G. A. and TRAXEL, W. The effects of meprobamate and alcohol on galvanic skin response. *Journal of Psychology*, 1959, 48, 329–34.

LUNDWALL, L. and BAEKELAND, F. Disulfiram treatment of alcoholism: A review. *Journal of Nervous and Mental Disease*, 1971, 153, 381–92.

MARDONES, J. Experimentally induced changes in the free selection of ethanol. In C. C. Pfeiffer, J. R. Smythies (Eds.) *International Review of Neurobiology*, Vol. II, 1960, 41–76.

MARLATT, G. A. Modeling influences in social drinking: An experimental analogue. Paper presented at Association for Advancement of Behavior Therapy, Chicago, 1974.

MARLATT, G. A., DEMMING, B. and REID, J. B. Loss of control drinking in alcoholics: An experimental analogue. *Journal of Abnormal Psychology*, 1973, 81, 233–41.

MAYFIELD, D. Psychopharmacology of alcohol. I. Affective change with intoxication, drinking behavior and affective state. *Journal of Nervous and Mental Disease*, 1968, 146, 314–21.

McCORD, W. and McCORD, J. *Origins of alcoholism*. Stanford, California: Stanford University Press, 1960.

McNAMEE, H. B., MELLO, N. K. and MENDELSON, J. H. Experimental analysis of drinking patterns of alcoholics. Concurrent psychiatric observations. *American Journal of Psychiatry*, 1968, 124, 1063–9.

MELLO, N. K. Behavioral studies of alcoholism. In B. Kissin and H. Begleiter (Eds.) *The biology of alcoholism*. New York: Plenum Press, 1972.

MENDELSON, J. H. Experimentally induced chronic intoxication and withdrawal in alcoholics. *Quarterly Journal of Studies on Alcohol*, Supplement No. 2, 1964.

MERRY, J. The "loss of control" myth. *Lancet*, 1966, 1, 1267–8.

MILLER, P. M. and EISLER, R. M. Alcohol and drug abuse. In W. E. Craighead, A. E. Kazdin, and M. J. Mahoney (Eds.) *Behavior modification: principles, issues, and applications*. Boston: Houghton Mifflin, in press.

MILLER, P. M., HERSEN, M., EISLER, R. M., EPSTEIN, L. and WOOTEN, L. S. Relationship of alcohol cues to the drinking behavior of alcoholics and social drinkers: An analogue study. *Psychological Record*, 1974, 24, 61–6.

MILLER, P. M., HERSEN, M., EISLER, R. M. and HILSMAN, G. Effects of social stress on operant drinking of alcoholics and social drinkers. *Behavior Research and Therapy*, 1974, 12, 67–72.

NATHAN, P. E. and O'BRIEN, J. S. An experimental analysis of the behavior of alcoholics and nonalcoholics during prolonged experimental drinking. *Behavior Therapy*, 1971, 2, 455–76.

NATHAN, P. E., TITLER, N. A., LOWENSTEIN, L. M., SOLOMON, P. and ROSSI, A. M. Behavioral analysis of chronic alcoholism. *Archives of General Psychiatry*, 1970, 22, 419–30.

National Institute on Alcohol Abuse and Alcoholism. *Alcohol and health*, Washington, D.C.: U.S. Government Printing Office, 1970.

ROBINSON, D. The alcohologist's addiction: some implications of having lost control over the disease concept of alcoholism. *Quarterly Journal of Studies on Alcohol*, 1972, 33, 1028–42.

SILBER, A. Psychotherapy with alcoholics. *Journal of Nervous and Mental Disease*, 1959, 129, 477–85.

SKINNER, B. F. *Beyond freedom and dignity*. New York: Alfred A. Knopff, 1971.

SOBELL, L. C., SOBELL, M. B. and CHRISTELMAN, W. C. The myth of "one drink". *Behavior Research and Therapy*, 1972, 10, 119–23.

SOBELL, M. B. and SOBELL, L. C. The need for realism, relevance and operational assumptions in the study of substance dependence. Paper presented at International Symposium on Alcohol and Drug Research, Toronto, Oct., 1973.

STEINER, C. M. The alcoholic game. *Quarterly Journal of Studies on Alcohol*, 1969, 30, 920–38.

STEINGLASS, P., WEINER, S. and MENDELSON, J. H. Interactional issues as determinants of alcoholism. *American Journal of Psychiatry*, 1971, 128, 275–80.

SUTHERLAND, E. H., SCHROEDER, H. G. and TORDELLA, C. L. Personality traits and the alcoholic: A critique of existing studies. *Quarterly Journal of Studies on Alcohol*, 1950, 11, 547–61.

SYME, L. Personality characteristics and the alcoholic. A critique of current studies. *Quarterly Journal of Studies on Alcohol,* 1957, **18**, 288–301.

VANDERPOOL, J. A. Alcoholism and the self-concept. *Quarterly Journal of Studies on Alcohol,* 1969, **30**, 59–62.

WEINER, H. B. Psychodramatic treatment for the alcoholic. In R. Fox (Ed.) *Alcoholism: Behavioral research, therapeutic approaches.* New York: Springer Publishing Co., 1967.

WEINER, S., TAMERIN, J. S., STEINGLASS, P. and MENDELSON, J. H. Familial patterns in chronic alcoholism: A study of a father and son during experimental intoxication. *American Journal of Psychiatry,* 1971, **127**, 1646–57.

WILLIAMS, A. F. Social drinking, anxiety, and depression. *Journal of Personality and Psychology,* 1966, **3**, 689.

WILLIAMS, R. J. The etiology of alcoholism: A working hypothesis involving the interplay of hereditary and environmental factors. *Quarterly Journal of Studies on Alcohol,* 1946, **1**, 567–85.

WILLIAMS, T. K. The ethanol-induced loss of control concept in alcoholism. Ed.D. dissertation. Western Michigan University, 1970.

CHAPTER 2

Behavioral Assessment

Perhaps the major contribution of behavior modification to alcoholism treatment lies in its emphasis upon a scientific—evaluative approach to behavior change. Within this framework, objectivity of measurement is combined with the application of experimental methods to evaluate treatment effects. Techniques must undergo constant, scientific scrutiny. This allows the clinician to monitor therapeutic outcome empirically and thus improve treatment procedures. Historically, alcoholism treatment has been seriously hampered by a general disregard for systematic evaluation (Hill and Blane, 1967; Miller and Barlow, 1973). A major reason for this deficiency has been the lack of objective, quantitative measures of both alcoholic drinking and social, marital, emotional, and vocational behavior patterns.

Optimally, measures of behavior must be concise, communicable, and quantifiable. They must be based on factual data that can be observed with reliability by more than one individual. Many clinicians, for lack of better measures, succumb to the use of vague personality variables to assess therapeutic progress. Successful outcome may be based on "increased ego strength", "decreased dependency needs", "enhanced self-concept", "personal growth", or "self-realization". Such vague clinical judgements and inferred psychodynamic processes are influenced by obvious subjective biases. Due to their extremely low validity and reliability (Thorne, 1961), these assessment procedures are of little use in serious clinical evaluation endeavors.

Drinking Behavior

Traditional Measures

The ultimate criterion for successful outcome of alcoholism treatment is obviously the alteration of alcoholic drinking patterns. The most widely used clinical measure of drinking behavior is based upon the alcoholic's self-report. Certainly this is the easiest and most straightforward method of gathering information about an individual's behavior. Self-report data, however, have several obvious drawbacks. Simkins (1971) contends that such information may

23

be "more a function of the social approval contingencies that are programmed by some authority figure (e.g., behavior therapist, teacher, supervisor) than ... they are of the independent variables manipulated by the subject . . ." (p. 85). Thus, the alcoholic may provide the therapist with a verbal report that he thinks is expected of him. In addition, disclosure of drinking episodes to the therapist often results in social punishment in the form of termination of treatment due to the patient's "lack of motivation" to change, lectures on the evils of alcohol or withdrawal of acceptance and approval. Such reactions contingent upon reports of alcohol abuse are more likely to modify the patient's verbal behavior in the presence of the therapist than his actual drinking habits. Sobell and Sobell (1973a) argue that such contingencies "are frequently so severe as to possibly shape patients to be dishonest about their drinking behaviors during the course of treatment" (p. 237). They suggest that patients be praised for reporting drinking episodes, and therapists should respond to these reports in a very matter-of-fact manner.

Self-reports of drinking are also subject to the forgetfulness, misperception, or distortion of the alcoholic. Clinically, such reports are notoriously invalid. Alcoholics often have a long history of successfully avoiding the natural aversive consequences of their socially deviant behavior by distorting the truth. Summers (1970) gathered detailed drinking histories from fifteen male patients at the time of admission to an alcoholism treatment program. When requestioned about their drinking only 2 weeks later, more than 90% of these patients significantly changed their responses.

At times the alcoholic may feign a rapid improvement via faulty self-reports in order to avoid further treatment. When unpleasant treatment techniques such as confrontation therapy or aversion conditioning are used, self-reports are even more subject to underestimation. Relatives often unwittingly assist the alcoholic in his avoidance of treatment by readily accepting his reports of no drinking or his promises "never to touch another drop".

Whenever possible more objective data should be accumulated to substantiate self-reports. If reliance on self-report data is necessary, several methods may improve the scientific usefulness of this information. Instead of global reports, patients can be trained to record specific frequency counts, such as number of ounces of liquor consumed per day. Whenever possible such records should be accumulated before, during, and after treatment to allow for objective comparisons. For example, in the treatment of a 44-year-old heavy drinker, Miller (1972) instructed the patient to record on an index card the number of alcoholic beverages he consumed daily. A beverage was arbitrarily defined as 1½ ounces of alcohol either straight or mixed. By requesting the patient to maintain these records both during treatment and during a 2-week pretreatment phase, monitoring of therapeutic effects was facilitated. To objectively assess stability of therapeutic gains, the patient was recontacted for a 6-month follow-up and requested to record number of alcoholic beverages consumed during a 10-day period. Sobell and Sobell (1973a) have devised a more sophisticated self-monitoring technique in the form of an "Alcohol Intake Sheet". Episodes of alcoholic drinking are recorded by the patient in detail. Such information as date, type of drink, percent of alcohol content in liquor, time the drink was ordered, number of sips per drink, amount of the total drink consumed, and the environment where drinking occurred are recorded. Self-monitoring is not only used to objectify drinking behavior but also to enable the alcoholic to become more cognizant of the extent and nature of his drinking. While such complex systems are ideal for data collection, these detailed entries may become quite time-consuming and eventually aversive to the patient. Frequent recognition and praise by the counselor or therapist for such record-keeping would help to maintain this behavior.

In addition to detailed records, reliability of self-report data should be obtained through relatives, friends, and coworkers. Instructing these informants in the mechanisms of specific record-keeping as described above facilitates this process. Care must be taken to provide the alcoholic and the informants with the same criteria for recording drinking behavior. Since many alcoholics engage in secretive, solitary drinking, the *consequences* rather than the drinking itself might also be recorded. For example, the wife of an alcoholic could be instructed to record every instance in which her husband engages in "drunken" behavior such as staggering, and passing out, or in which she smells alcohol on his breath. Such data, however, are not easily definable and are more subject to distortion by the informant.

Alcoholics with no family or friends, no steady employment, and irregular living habits pose a problem in terms of reliability data. The best alternative in this case is the use of periodic blood/alcohol level determinations via a blood or breath test. These determinations would be easily obtainable and provide validation of self-reports of drinking behavior. The advantages of such assessment procedures for comprehensive outcome studies is discussed later in this chapter.

Even data reported by friends and relatives must be carefully scrutinized throughout treatment. Guze, Tuason, Stewart, and Pickens (1963) found that reports of relatives about the alcoholic's drinking frequently represented more of a distortion than self-reports by the patient himself. It would be advisable, then, to receive reports from a number of persons having contact with the abusive drinker. Separately kept records also prevent the alcoholic and his spouse from arguing over the veracity of reports of individual drinking episodes.

One other general consideration regarding self-reports should be mentioned briefly. A commonly used method of treatment evaluation involves obtaining follow-up reports of progress from patients or relatives via periodic telephone or written contacts. This data gathering procedure is even more open to question than the personal interview method. It would seem much easier for an alcoholic to report both abstinence and successful social and vocational functioning via impersonal communication. At least with periodic interviews or home visits the therapist has a chance to directly observe the alcoholic's current state of sobriety and personal appearance.

Another widely used procedure to evaluate efficacy of treatment does not assess drinking behavior directly but measures its correlates. Number of arrests for public intoxication or driving while intoxicated and number of hospitalizations for alcohol related problems comprise the measurement variables. These measures allow for independent, public reliability checks on other reports of drinking. With certain populations such as the chronic public inebriate (typically the Skid Row alcoholic), information regarding reduction in number of arrests would be essential since it represents one of the major goals of treatment intervention. These measures are most useful with alcoholics who have little environmental stability and are not likely to maintain contact with the treatment facility. A disadvantage of arrest and hospitalization data lies in the fact that they do not allow sufficient latitude to assess slight variations in drinking behavior during or subsequent to treatment. There is frequently a considerable time lag between onset of abusive drinking and eventual arrest or hospitalization. Also, many of the more affluent alcoholics are able to avoid the criminal justice system through their standing in the community. In general, this assessment information might be helpful when conducting long term follow-ups on large groups of treated and untreated alcoholics.

Behavioral Measures

Recently, more objective, quantitative measures of alcoholic drinking behavior have been developed in which the patient is actually given access to alcohol (Miller, 1973). While most are laboratory, analogue measures within an inpatient setting, they represent a major step forward in a "true" empirical assessment of the effects of various treatment strategies. Concern over the possibility of compounding the alcoholic's problem or inducing a drinking binge by providing him with alcohol in this manner may have hindered development and use of these measures. Experimental evidence (Sobell, Sobell and Christelman, 1972; Faillace, Flamer, Imber, and Ward, 1972; Gottheil, Murphy, Skoloda, and Corbett, 1972) demonstrates that there is no empirical basis for such concerns and that alcoholics are not impelled to continue drinking after receiving alcohol under controlled conditions.

These measures have been used mostly in gathering descriptive data on characteristic drinking patterns of alcoholics and concomitant social, emotional, and physiological effects of abusive drinking. Only very recently has their utility in the evaluation of clinical treatment procedures been fully realized. Such objective measures would allow continuous monitoring of treatment progress. Currently, clinicians must use their "best guesses" when deciding whether to continue a treatment regime or alter the therapeutic plan in some way.

Measures of this type can be divided into three general categories: operant analyses, "choice situation", and experimental bars.

Operant analyses. In an operant analysis, alcohol is used as reinforcement for a specific behavioral response. Alcohol is made contingent upon performance of either a simple motor task or a more complex set of ward, self-help behaviors in a hospital setting. Motivation for alcohol is measured quantitatively in terms of how much and how often subjects "work" for an alcohol "payoff". In a frequently reported procedure (Mello and Mendelson, 1965; Davidson and Wallach, 1970; Lawson, 1973; Miller, Hersen, Eisler, Epstein, and Wooten, 1974; Miller, Hersen, and Eisler, 1974) key or lever pressing responses are reinforced with alcohol dispensed automatically into a shot glass in front of the subject. One of the earliest reports utilizing such an analysis was conducted by Mello and Mendelson (1965). In their study two hospitalized alcoholics were given the opportunity to earn alcohol or money (subjects invariably chose alcohol) by pressing a translucent response key on which a series of colored lights was projected. Reinforcement (either 10 cc of bourbon or $.15 in cash) was made contingent upon changing the color of the lights as often as possible. Alcohol reinforcement was dispensed automatically into a glass in front of the subject. Frequency of correct responding together with frequency and duration of machine usage served as measures of alcohol drinking patterns. As the study progressed, one subject worked in short, frequent sessions while the other responded only occasionally for longer sessions (possibly equivalent to binge drinking in the natural environment).

Miller, Hersen, Eisler, Epstein, and Wooten (1974) and Miller, Hersen, and Eisler (1974) used a similar apparatus to evaluate the effects of a variety of environmental influences on drinking. The operant system (BRS-Lehigh Valley Modular Human Test System) consisted of a metal, paneled console which was located on a small table in front of the patient. An insert on the face of the console contained a 1½ ounce shot glass. A tube hanging above the glass was connected to a polyethylene bottle (containing a mixture of 30% bourbon and 70% water) inside the console. A manual electric switch attached to a separate relay rack delivered a 5 cc squirt of the alcohol mixture into the glass. A Lindsley-type manipulandum extended from the front of the console adjacent to the shot glass insert. Number of presses on the lever was recorded by a counter on the relay rack. Patients received alcohol reinforcement on a fixed ratio schedule of 50 responses for 1 reinforcement (FR 50). Patients were allowed 10 minutes of responding during each session. With some patients response rates exceeded 2500 in the 10-minute time period. Patients were usually allowed one or two sessions of responding to become accustomed to the equipment. After base-line rates of responding were established over a few days' time, treatment conditions were instituted and changes in operant response rates were recorded. Alcoholic patients in treatment readily drank under such conditions with little hesitation. The patient's perception of the purpose of this assessment procedure seems quite important. Some alcoholics in treatment feel that their self-control is being tested and they, therefore, respond at a very low rate. The initial instructions must convey to the patient the idea that he should respond in a natural manner in order to allow the clinician to obtain a better evaluation of his drinking patterns.

In a variation of this procedure, responding on a Lindsley-type manipulandum earns the patient points which in turn can be traded for alcohol. Rather than being dispensed immediately by the operant apparatus, alcohol can be purchased by the subject or patient via a vending machine or directly from the nurses' station in a hospital setting. This approach has been followed by Mello and Mendelson (1971); Nathan, Titler, Lowenstein, Solomon, and Rossi (1970); and Nathan and O'Brien (1972). Nathan and his colleagues at Rutgers University have used this approach more extensively than others. Their subjects are housed in a small inpatient unit equipped with individual bedrooms, a social area, and a bar area. Alcoholics earn points by pressing a lever on an operant panel located in their rooms (points are typically earned on an FR 150 schedule). Points can be spent on whiskey (20 points buys 30 cc or 1 "shot" of bourbon) via an alcohol dispenser or at specified times to escape from isolation (either by personal communication via closed circuit television or by unlocking the door to their rooms). Drinking patterns are measured by the frequency, duration, and distribution of each subject's use of his alcohol dispenser together with blood/alcohol levels (via the Breathalyzer) taken three times per day. Number of points spent to buy alcohol versus number spent to escape from social isolation are calculated to determine the relative rewarding value of these two situations. These measures not only differentiate Skid Row alcoholics from Skid Row nonalcoholics on a number of dimensions but also provide valuable descriptive information on the parameters of drinking behavior.

In a third variation of operant analysis, points used to purchase alcohol are earned, not on simple motor tasks, but by a complex set of behaviors via a token economy system (Cohen, Liebson, and Faillace, 1970). Thus, the alcoholic must engage in specified social, vocational, and self-help activities around the hospital or research setting in order to earn points to buy alcohol. While this procedure has not been extensively utilized, it has the advantage of representing a system with a high degree of similarity to the alcoholic's natural environment. This "mini-environment" might provide the most clinically relevant assessment of both alcohol abuse *per se* and its social and emotional concomitants. One would also expect modification of "alcohol purchases" in such a setting to generalize more readily to the real world.

One other related procedure involves simply providing the alcoholic with a fixed number of tokens or points each day and allowing him to use these to buy alcohol or providing him with free access to alcohol. While this approach has been used mainly as a measure to gather descriptive data on drinking (Mello and Mendelson, 1971), Gottheil, Corbett, Grasberger, and Cornelison (1972) and Cohen, Liebson, and Faillace (1970) have reported its use in evaluating treatment procedures.

Unfortunately, all of these operant systems of assessment have received only limited utilization. Subjects studied are usually Skid Row chronic alcoholics who participate on a paid basis. These subjects usually report that they have no desire to change their drinking patterns. Obviously, evaluation of operant data on more varied alcoholic populations, especially "motivated" patients in treatment settings, seems warranted.

"Choice situations". While operant analyses have been used primarily to gather descriptive data on the patterning of the alcoholic's drinking behavior, "choice situations" have offered a way of assessing progress in specific therapeutic procedures (predominantly aversion therapy). Choice measures present the alcoholic with the opportunity (usually within a hospital or laboratory setting) to choose from a variety of alcoholic and non-alcoholic beverages. Comparisons between percentage of choice of alcoholic versus non-alcoholic beverages before, during and after treatment are used to predict success of the therapeutic intervention.

Raymond (1964) reported use of a "choice reaction" to evaluate the effects of chemical aversion therapy (a technique in which the sight, smell, and taste of alcohol are repeatedly associated with nausea induced by an emetic). In Raymond's treatment, apomorphine was injected to produce nausea. After the patient began to express a distaste for alcohol, usually after several days of treatment, he was injected with 1 cc of saline solution instead of the apomorphine. When he was brought to the treatment room he found both alcoholic beverages and soft drinks, and was told to choose from among them. If the patient chose alcohol he was injected with apomorphine and the conditioning session occurred as usual. If a soft drink was chosen, the session was postponed and the therapist and staff talked with him in a relaxed manner. Thus, Raymond utilized these sessions both to assess progress and to reinforce non-alcoholic drinking.

During electrical aversion therapy in which alcoholics received electric shock to the leg following consumption of alcoholic beverages, Morosko and Baer (1970) presented patients with a series of two alcoholic and four non-alcoholic beverages in sequence. During alternate conditioning sessions patients were instructed to consume any five of the six beverages and to discard the sixth. Thus, 50% of the shocks could be avoided by discarding one of the alcoholic beverages. Eventually, patients were instructed to drink only four beverages and discard two, thereby avoiding all shocks. Measures of treatment success included: (1) percentage of sessions in which alcoholic beverages were discarded, (2) mean latencies for consumption of non-alcoholic beverages, and (3) mean latencies for discarding alcoholic beverages. While all three patients treated achieved 100% avoidance of shocks by the end of treatment, only one patient remained totally abstinent at a 19-month follow-up. Thus, the measure did not accurately predict long-range success.

Chapman, Burt, and Smith (1972) used a similar procedure to evaluate electrical aversion treatment effects with ten inpatient alcoholics. During a pretreatment baseline phase, patients were allowed twenty choices from a variety of alcoholic and non-alcoholic beverages. During forced choice conditioning, patients were instructed to choose fifteen alcoholic beverages. Electric shock to the forearm was made contingent upon sipping each beverage. In periodic free choice sessions, patients could choose freely and could avoid all shocks by choosing only non-alcoholic drinks. In seven of ten patients, percent of choice of non-alcoholic beverages increased from 30% during the initial baseline phase to 100% during the final free choice session. These patients remained abstinent from 8 to 9 months after treatment. The three patients who did not significantly change their choices on the drinking measure returned to heavy drinking. The choice measure, then, provided an objective method of evaluating therapeutic progress and predicting outcome in the natural environment.

One major disadvantage of these measures is that they are much too obvious to the patient. It would be very easy for alcoholics to discard alcoholic beverages to avoid immediate discomfort (e.g., shock) but readily consume such drinks when unpleasant consequences were no longer an immediate threat. Miller and Hersen (1972) and Miller, Hersen, Eisler, and Hemphill (1973) have developed a surreptitious "choice situation" which monitors quantitative changes in drinking behavior as a function of treatment. The "taste test" measurement system for quantifying alcohol consumption was adapted from a procedure used by Schachter (1971) in his studies of obesity. The subject is requested to participate in a "taste experiment". During the "experiment" the patient is seated before a table on which are placed six beverages with exactly 100 cc of liquid in each glass. Glasses are opaque in order to avoid making this constant amount conspicuous. Three of the beverages are alcoholic (30 cc of bourbon or vodka in 70 cc of water and 100 cc of beer), whereas three are non-alcoholic (Coke, ginger-ale, and water). The patient is presented with rating sheets and given the following instructions:

This is a taste experiment. We want you to judge each beverage on the taste dimensions (sweet, sour, etc.) listed on these sheets. Some of the drinks are alcoholic and some are non-alcoholic. Taste as little or as much as you want of each beverage in making your judgments. The important thing is that your ratings be as accurate as possible.

The patient is allowed 10 minutes to taste the beverages and complete a rating sheet for each drink. After he leaves the room, the exact amount of each beverage consumed is calculated and recorded. Order of presentation of the beverages is randomly rotated from session to session. The patient is not told that his consumption is being measured.

In order to measure attitude toward alcohol, the rating sheets are based on the semantic differential (Osgood, Suci, and Tannenbaum, 1957). The score on the evaluative scale provides a quantitative assessment of attitude toward each beverage. The relationship between amount consumed and attitude is currently being investigated. Thus far, it appears that attitude changes lag behind behavioral changes when using aversion therapy. It may be that change in both of these modalities is necessary for successful therapeutic outcome.

Marlatt, Demming, and Reid (1973) have devised a similar "taste rating task" during which the patient's drinking is observed via a one-way mirror. Data on the amount of each beverage consumed, sip rate, amount consumed per sip, and estimate of post-test blood/alcohol concentrations are accumulated.

As a measurement device the "taste test" is particularly amenable to single case design clinical research, as it allows for continuous monitoring of drinking behavior throughout treatment. It can be administered on a daily basis during treatment or given periodically as a probe measure of progress. When used in a group experimental design, three or four pre-treatment sessions are compared with the same number subsequent to treatment. It usually takes patients one session to become accustomed to the "test". Generally, patients drink very little initially and then increase rapidly and maintain a high, steady baseline consumption level. Another advantage of this measure is that any number or types of beverages may be used to evaluate generalization effects of treatment in multiple baseline designs. For example, aversion therapy using a particular type of alcoholic beverage may not generalize to other types of alcoholic drinks. The available clinical evidence of this phenomenon (Quinn and Henbest, 1967) could be experimentally substantiated using this assessment system.

Experimental bars. The ideal method of assessing alcoholic drinking behavior is to observe its occurrence in natural settings, such as bars, night clubs, living rooms, etc. Since this method is usually not feasible due to obvious practical problems, the next best approach consists of bringing a facsimile of the natural environment into the treatment setting. With this purpose in mind, Schaefer,

Sobell, and Mills (1971) and Mills, Sobell, and Schaefer (1971) converted a hospital dayroom into a cocktail lounge complete with padded bar, dimmed lighting, music, and bar-tender. While alcoholics and social drinkers are making appropriate use of these surroundings, staff members are either in the "bar" recording drinking behaviors or observing via closed-circuit television. Observers record (1) number of drinks ordered, (2) kinds of drinks ordered, and (3) magnitude of sips of drinks. Drinking measures such as these not only differentiate alcoholics from social drinkers but also effectively monitor changes in drinking patterns as a function of treatment.

Sobell and Sobell (1973b) later extended this idea of simulated natural drinking environments to include a living-room den "set-up". If this approach is to be used, a variety of settings must be available since alcoholics vary a great deal as to the location of their drinking behavior. Both the geographical location and the characteristics of the alcoholic population being treated often determine the drinking setting. Rural Southern alcoholics, for example, frequently report drinking at home watching television, driving in their cars, or while fishing or hunting. A middle-class alcoholic living in a large metropolitan area is more likely to drink in a local tavern or at a cocktail party. Obviously, the simulated environment must closely approximate relevant real world drinking situations.

In vivo *assessment*. The most clinically relevant assessment techniques are, of course, those taken directly in the natural environment. Since direct observation is frequently impractical, blood/alcohol concentrations appear to be an obvious means of objective measurement. Such data are most conveniently obtained via breath tests similar to the ones that law officers utilize to detect intoxicated motorists. Either the simple screening type which provides immediate estimates or the more complex collection device analyzed via gas chromatography can be obtained. While the screening device is prone to false-negative readings, the balloon-like collection apparatus correlates between 0.80 and 0.91 with actual blood alcohol analyses (Roberts and Fletcher, 1969; Nevada Safety Council, 1965).

Miller, Hersen, Eisler, and Watts (1974) successfully utilized such measures to monitor the effects of reinforcement contingencies on the drinking of a chronic Skid Row alcoholic. Breath/alcohol tests were administered bi-weekly on a random basis. A research assistant was sent to the patient's home and place of employment at these times. The patient was often called by telephone shortly before a visit to determine his whereabouts. Surprisingly, very few practical problems arose in administering the tests in this manner. Results of such blood/alcohol levels are almost immediate. In this case, a breath sample was accumulated at each visit and then taken back to the laboratory for analysis via a gas chromatograph. Within less than an hour an exact blood/alcohol concentration was recorded. In this study, time was of the essence since contingencies were placed upon certain levels of blood/alcohol concentrations and immediacy of reinforcement was essential.

If staff are not available for home visits, the alcoholic could be requested to report to the treatment location at specified times each week for a blood/alcohol test. At least one weekend measure should be obtained to avoid encouraging binge drinking on Saturday and Sunday and sobriety during the week. Without random measures alcoholics could very easily discriminate when it is "safe" to drink and when it is not.

In vivo blood/alcohol determinations could also serve to validate the analogue measures (operant, taste test) discussed previously. Single patients could be simultaneously monitored on the *in vivo* and analogue measures over a period of time. If high correlations are obtained, the analogue measures could then be used clinically to predict drinking in the natural environment. Administration of analogue measures at each follow-up visit would then provide a simple and economical method of objectively evaluating the patient's progress.

A related measurement problem in treatment programs is the determination of whether or not the alcoholic is regularly taking his disulfiram (Antabuse). While Antabuse maintenance can be an effective treatment regime, alcoholics seldom will take it daily as prescribed. The therapist must rely on the report of the alcoholic or his wife as to the regularity of his medicine taking. Alcoholics often claim they are taking Antabuse when they actually are not and they often hide tablets under their tongue and pretend to swallow when observed by relatives. Alcoholics have also been known to take Antabuse each day in the presence of a relative, friend, or boss only to expel the tablet shortly after its administration via self-induced vomiting. Either blood or urine samples taken at follow-up visits could be used to determine Antabuse levels. In this way there would be no doubt as to the veracity of the client's self-report. Such a measure could also allow for systematic reinforcement of Antabuse taking behavior.

Although this approach has not as yet been systematically utilized in the treatment of alcoholism using Antabuse, it has facilitated medication mainten- ance in psychiatric patients. A major example lies in the attempts to induce out-patient chronic schizophrenic patients to regularly take their phenothiazine medications. Such patients often stop taking their medicine soon after discharge from the hospital. This usually necessitates further inpatient treatment. Schizophrenic patients who take their medication regularly can be maintained in the community with very little professional intervention. Smith, Hersen, and Eisler (1973) utilized periodic blood tests to determine phenothiazine levels in chronic schizophrenic VA outpatients. Patients were reinforced for high blood/phenothiazine levels by means of VA canteen booklets (coupons exchangeable for cigarettes, clothing, food). Similar rewards made con- tingent upon progress reports from the patient would probably have little effect on daily medicine taking itself but increase the frequency of *reports* of such behavior.

Finally, the notion of actually observing drinking behaviors directly in the natural environment must be considered. In this approach personnel are sent to specific bars, night clubs, etc., to observe and record alcoholic drinking patterns. Number and kinds of drinks ordered, number of sips per drink, time between drinks, circumstances of drinking (solitary or with friends), and behavioral effects of drinking would all be observed for specific individuals. Such data would be important to establish norms of drinking behavior in groups of people or to evaluate changes in drinking of particular individuals as a function of therapeutic intervention. Observers could order drinks (perhaps non-alcoholic ones in order to maintain their objectivity) and be provided with simple recording devices (e.g., wrist counters) to allow them to remain as unobtrusive as possible. As a follow-up treatment procedure this method would be most useful with individuals who limit their drinking to certain public places. Observation in other more private settings (e.g., private homes, cars) either directly or via closed-circuit television would be practically and economically infeasible. Also, care must be taken so that the alcoholic does not learn to refrain from drinking while he is being observed and drink freely when he is alone. The possibility that the measurement method might promote a pattern of solitary, surreptitious drinking must be seriously considered.

In certain more controlled settings direct observations may be more easily obtainable. For example, in the military, servicemen frequently purchase alcoholic beverages either by the bottle (via the commissary) or by the drink (via clubs) on the premises of the military installation. Lowered costs of alcohol encourage drinking on the premises rather than in non-military bars. Under such circumstances direct observations of drinking are facilitated. Observers could periodically visit either the commissary or the officers' club to observe and record drinking. The ideal situation would consist of continuous monitoring of these facilities via closed-circuit television equipment. In this way even the alcohol consumption of individuals who drink alone could be assessed through package liquor store sales.

Another such restricted setting is the college campus. Increasing numbers of campuses now sell beer on the premises and a few (e.g., University of Wisconsin at Milwaukee) have fully stocked bars for the students. Observations obtained in such settings would provide valuable norms on the drinking patterns of this population. Such information may help to identify individuals who are abusing alcohol early enough in their lives so that intervention is possible. These data could help to predict individuals who may have alcoholism problems in the future. This setting would also be ideal for investigating the effects of stress (exams, failing grades) on alcoholic drinking behavior.

Direct observations in natural environmental settings raise the ethical issue of invasion of privacy. Ideally, individual alcoholics being monitored directly or via closed-circuit television should be apprised of the general assessment procedures being used. Thus, they have the choice of allowing such monitoring or not. The ultimate decision of whether to allow these observations or not should be the subject's. Military or college bars in which a number of customers are being observed should make it known (through written notice posted in clear view) that experimental observations are being obtained. The anonymity of those being observed should be stressed. Customers would then have the freedom to do business with other establishments.

One final naturalistic assessment technique is the establishment of an experimental bar for outpatient alcoholics. Entry cards would be issued to selected clients. The bar would serve both alcoholic and non-alcoholic beverages at reduced rates to encourage clients to use the facility. Clients' choices of beverages and drinking patterns would be observed and recorded. This setting is especially ideal when controlled, social drinking as opposed to abstinence is the goal of treatment (Shaeffer, Sobell, and Mills, 1971).

Social–Emotional Behavior Patterns

In addition to drinking behavior, a truly comprehensive assessment of therapeutic outcome includes measures of social, marital, emotional, and vocational behaviors. Unfortunately, evaluations of alcoholism treatment modalities including all sets of these data are scarce. While behavioral clinicians tend to evaluate outcome on the basis of drinking alone, most psychodynamically oriented therapists stress changes in social functioning and exclude objective assessment of alcohol consumption. Such uni-variable emphasis of either type represents a rather naive conception of the nature of alcohol abuse. Human behavior can seldom be dichotomized into distinct categories. Social, emotional, and vocational behaviors are intricately interrelated with drinking behavior. The interaction is reciprocal in that while alcohol abuse can affect social functioning, the manner in which an individual interacts with others may also affect how much he drinks.

Adequate functioning in social-emotional areas would be expected to increase the alcoholic's chances of maintaining sobriety. Indeed, clients' social characteristics are highly related to therapeutic outcome using either behavioral or more traditional, psychodynamic therapies. In an extensive 10½-year follow-up study evaluating the efficacy of chemical aversion therapy (see Chapter 3), Voegtlin and Broz (1949) found the factors of age, marital status, family discord, occupation, financial status, place of residence, conflict with the law, nervousness, physical deformity, delirium tremens, length of drinking history, and record of prior abstinence significantly related to outcome. For example, of patients who were married for the first time, 50% remained abstinent. Patients separated from their wives averaged only 25.6% abstinence, and those divorced, 32.4% abstinence. Occupationally, of those with a good work record with few job changes, 70.9% remained abstinent while of those frequently unemployed, only 21% remained abstinent. Patients who disassociated themselves from their past drinking companions and who developed friendships with abstainers also demonstrated a high (87%) success rate.

Along similar lines, McCance and McCance (1969) found that job stability, cooperation with treatment, living with a friend or relative, no criminal record, no history of delirium tremens, rural residence, "binge" as opposed to steady drinking, and whiskey or beer as opposed to wine drinking were more related to therapeutic outcome than type of treatment administered (either electrical aversion therapy, group therapy, or routine hospital care). Lunde and Vogler (1970) discuss the importance of considering these factors in treatment and suggest that they routinely be reported in clinical and research reports. Such a procedure would enable comparisons among studies evaluating similar treatment strategies.

The importance of these social-emotional factors indicates that they must be considered in the assessment of treatment. Attainment of these favorable characteristics often depends upon the presence of adequate social, marital, and vocational skills. Since many alcoholics do not possess such skills, new behavior patterns must be taught and subsequently evaluated as part of a comprehensive treatment program.

Analysis of Social–Emotional Functioning

Traditional Methods

Currently, the methods used to assess alcoholics' social-emotional functioning include clinical judgments, psychological test data, reports from the client, relatives, employers, or friends, and direct behavioral observations. The validity and reliability problems encountered with most of these measures have been discussed earlier in this chapter. The assumption of the behavioral approach is that direct observations of ongoing behavior provide the most useful information about the client. The further one departs from such observations the more one must rely on inference and "educated guesses".

Use of psychological tests and questionnaires to evaluate therapeutic outcome is widespread. However, for the most part, studies have indicated a marked discrepancy between predictions from test data and the actual behavior of the client using either objective (Hersen, 1973) or projective (Fulkerson and Barry, 1961) tests. Also, many tests assume that certain personality traits exist which are stable over a wide range of situations. Sufficient evidence exists to demonstrate that behavior at any one point in time is related not only to the individual's past experiences and behavior but also to the characteristics of the ongoing environmental circumstance (Skinner, 1972). For example, characteristics such as "passivity" or "dependency" are frequently used to describe alcoholics. Clinically, many alcoholics do respond in passive or dependent ways but certainly not in all situations. An alcoholic may be quite passive with his wife but appropriately assertive with friends or co-workers. His response in any one situation depends very much upon the behavior of those around him. Kanfer and Saslow (1969) discuss these issues at length and the reader is referred to this source for further elaboration. The major issue is that *direct behavioral analysis* of social, marital, emotional, and vocational functioning is a requisite of adequate therapeutic evaluation.

Behavioral Methods

Social and marital behaviors. Alcoholics often have difficulties with certain interpersonal relationships. Whether such problems are a cause or result of excessive drinking is frequently difficult to determine. Continued difficulties in these areas, however, can hinder the maintenance of sobriety. The possible range of social and marital interactions that might precipitate drinking episodes is diverse. Research evidence indicates that such events as social isolation (Nathan and O'Brien, 1971), social stress (Miller, Hersen, Eisler, and Hilsman, 1974), and certain responses from the wife in a marital pair (Hersen, Miller, and Eisler, 1973) may serve as cues for excessive consumption.

A simple way of analyzing social difficulties is in terms of *behavioral deficits* or *excesses* (Lindsley, 1967). A possible deficit behavior of the alcoholic is the lack of appropriate assertive skills necessary to stand up for his rights. Excesses would, of course, include drinking behavior. Initial assessment of interpersonal behavior is facilitated through the use of standard behavioral classification systems. By extending the excess-deficit notion, Kanfer and Saslow (1971) developed such a system which is presented below:

A. *Behavioral excess.* A class of related behaviors occurs and is described as problematic by the patient or an informant because of excess in (1) frequency, (2) intensity, (3) duration, or (4) occurrence under conditions when its socially sanctioned frequency approaches zero. Compulsive handwashing, combativeness, prolonged excitement, and sexual exhibitionism are examples of behavioral excesses along one or another of these four dimensions. Less obvious, because they often do not constitute the major presenting complaint and appear only in the course of the behavioral analysis, are examples of socially unacceptable solitary, affectionate, or other private behaviors. For instance, a housewife showing excessive solitary preoccupation can do so by excessive homemaking activities, (1) several hours a day, (2) seven days weekly for most of the waking day, (3) to the extent that phone calls or doorbells are unanswered and family needs are unattended. From this example it is clear that both duration and intensity values of the behavior may jointly determine the characterization of the behavior as excessive.

B. *Behavioral deficit.* A class of responses is described as problematic by someone because it fails to occur (1) with sufficient frequency, (2) with adequate intensity, (3) in appropriate form, or (4) under socially expected conditions. Examples are: reduced social responsiveness (withdrawal), amnesias, fatigue syndromes, and restrictions in sexual or somatic function (e.g., impotence, writer's cramp). Other examples of behavioral deficits can be found in depressed patients who have no appropriate behavior in a new social environment, e.g., after changes from a rural to an urban area, from marital to single status, or from one socioeconomic level to another. "Inadequate" persons often are also found to have large gaps in their social or intellectual repertoires which prevent appropriate actions.

C. *Behavioral asset.* Behavioral assets are nonproblematic behaviors. What does the patient do well? What are his adequate social behaviors? What are his special talents or assets? The content of life experiences which can be used to execute a therapeutic program is unlimited. Any segment of the patient's activities can be used as an arena for building up new behaviors. In fact, his natural work and play activities provide a better starting point for behavior change than can ever be provided in a synthetic activity or relationship. For example, a person with musical talent, skill in a craft, physical skill, or social appeal can be helped to use his strengths as vehicles for changing behavior relationships and for acquiring new behaviors in areas in which some successful outcomes are highly probable. While a therapeutic goal may ultimately be the acquisition of specific social or self-evaluative behaviors, the learning can be programmed with many different tasks and in areas in which the patient has already acquired competence.

(pp. 431–2)*

By listing specific excesses, deficits, and assets for each alcoholic, treatment goals can be easily expressed in terms of precise target behaviors which are to be increased or decreased in frequency. Traditionally, treatment goals are expressed in vague terms which are difficult to evaluate. A frequently stated goal is "to help the alcoholic truly recognize his problems and gain increased motivation to change". Use of such a global term as "motivation" does not significantly add to our knowledge of what exactly needs to be modified with this particular patient. Behavioral goals in this case might include:

1. Increase frequency of treatment-directed or change-directed statements (e.g., "I want to stop drinking", "I am an alcoholic").
2. Decrease frequency of denials regarding extent of alcohol consumption.
3. Decrease frequency of absences from treatment sessions.
4. Increase compliance to instructions from therapist (e.g., "Please ask your wife to come to your next appointment with you", "Make a list of situations which precipitate your drinking episodes", "Tell me how alcohol has affected your performance on the job.")

* From Behavioral diagnosis by Kanfer, F. H. and Saslow, G. In C. M. Franks (Ed.) *Behavior Therapy: Appraisal and Status.* Copyright 1971. Used with permission of McGraw-Hill Book Company.

Pinpointing goals in this manner allows for continuous evaluation of trends in behavior as treatment progresses. Other target goals relevant to alcoholism treatment might include decreasing alcoholic drinking, increasing amount of time spent with alcohol abstainers, increasing assertive behavior, increasing positive statements toward wife and children, decreasing complaints and self-reference statements, or increasing work productivity.

A comprehensive analysis of these behavior patterns is facilitated when the alcoholic is in a confined treatment setting such as a hospital. In such settings, specific interactional patterns can be continuously recorded by nursing personnel. Data on the patient's reactions to frustrating situations (e.g., denial of certain hospital privileges) or interactions with other patients can be accumulated. In a hospital-laboratory situation, Nathan and O'Brien (1971) objectively evaluated the value of social interaction to Skid Row alcoholics. Socially isolated patients could earn credits (points) to buy either time out of isolation or alcoholic beverages. Number of points used to purchase access to social interaction with other patients served as an objective measure of socialization behavior. Results indicated that these alcoholics tended to be social isolates (spending few points to be removed from isolation) before, during, and after drinking episodes. Non-alcoholics engaged in more social behavior especially during and after alcohol consumption. These investigators also used a Ward Sociogram in which the physical distances separating one patient from another were recorded six times each day. They assumed that physical and psychological distances between people are correlated.

Behavioral analysis of outpatients poses difficulties since the therapist usually observes only a miniscule sample (typically 1 hour per week) of the alcoholic's total behavior patterns. In such cases the use of staged or simulated mini-environments offers a simple means of evaluating the client's behavior. Eisler, Hersen, and Agras (1973) have developed a systematic procedure to assess interpersonal behavior in this manner. While they emphasized marital interactions, their technique can easily be applied to social interactions of all types. In a hospital setting, these investigators converted a research laboratory into a living room setting with appropriate furnishing. The room was monitored via a closed-circuit videotape television system which could be viewed in an adjacent room. Married couples were requested to sit on a sofa in this setting and discuss their marital problems. The authors felt that the presence of a therapist in the room distracted from the couples' natural style of interaction with one another. Couples readily adapted to the television equipment and reported that they felt very much at ease. Both verbal and non-verbal (smiling, looking, gesturing) behaviors were rated via videotape replays and quantitative interaction measures were obtained. When given such an unstructured task couples seem less likely to "cover up" their typical way of responding to one another. This situation allows for periodic monitoring of the alcoholic and his or her spouse.

Such probe measures taken periodically throughout treatment or follow-up can be used to substantiate the client's verbal report of the status of the marital relationship. The system can also be used therapeutically to train marital couples how to interact more effectively with one another. The details of such treatment are discussed further in Chapter 6.

Hersen, Eisler, and Miller (1973) discuss the use of a similar measurement technique to evaluate assertive behavior. Such behavior, which consists of the appropriate expression of rights and feelings (both positive and negative), is often deficient in alcoholics. In a study of general psychiatric patients (many of whom were alcoholics), Eisler, Miller, and Hersen (1973) identified the behavioral components of assertive behavior to be: pronounced affect, little or no compliance, requests for changes in the behavior of the interpersonal partner, lengthy responses, loud speech, and short latency of reply. A number of investigators (Eisler, Miller, and Hersen, 1973; Friedman, 1971; McFall and Marston, 1970) have utilized standard, contrived behavioral tasks to assess such behavior patterns. Eisler, Miller, and Hersen (1973) have developed the *Behavioral Assertiveness Test* which consists of a series of fourteen standard interpersonal situations requiring assertive responses. The situations are sequentially enacted with the client, using treatment personnel as role models (e.g., gas station attendant, wife) to prompt his responses. Videotaping these interactions allows for subsequent ratings of the client's behaviors on several verbal and non-verbal components of assertiveness. Such direct behavioral analysis is essential since there are contradicting findings with respect to the relationship between self-reports of assertiveness and overt indices of assertiveness. Clinically, discrepancies in this relationship seem to be even more evident with alcoholic patients since they do not readily acknowledge behavioral deficiencies.

Emotional behaviors. The term "emotional behavior" generally refers to the client's mood or feelings. Alcoholics often complain of anxiety, depression, agitation, and restlessness. Many report that such feelings often precipitate drinking episodes. Measurement and modification of these states might represent an important treatment goal.

Behaviorists have often been criticized for neglecting or at least deemphasizing emotional states in their clinical endeavors. However, emphasis of the behavioral approach is not necessarily on overt motor behavior but on *measurable behavior.* Thus, if emotional states can be objectively defined and quantitatively expressed, they certainly fall within the behavioral framework. Modern physiological monitoring equipment has opened up this area to more objective study. The growing interest in biofeedback has fostered increased technological sophistication in the measurement of physiological states.

Perhaps the most widely used method of clinically assessing anxiety or depression is through self-reports. Such reports can be either verbal or written via questionnaires and surveys. However, as with assertive behavior, there are often large discrepancies between the alcoholic's reports about his fears and his actual behavior in allegedly fearful situations. Hersen (1973) has suggested that an adequate clinical assessment of anxiety must include verbal, motor, and physiological components. In this regard, assessment of an alcoholic who reports that anxiety in social situations often leads to excessive drinking would include:

1. Administration of questionnaires (e.g., Fear Survey Schedule) designed to pinpoint the specific interpersonal situations eliciting anxiety.
2. Direct observations of the individual in various "real life" or simulated interpersonal situations. Both verbal (content of speech, tone of voice) and non-verbal (smiling, gesturing) behaviors would be assessed.
3. Exposure to real, imagined, or filmed interpersonal situations with concomitant physiological measures of heart rate, blood pressure, galvanic skin response, and respiration.

Another somewhat illusive correlate of excessive drinking is reported to be depression. Williams, Barlow, and Agras (1972) have developed an objective behavioral measurement system for depression. They attempted to avoid using observations of subtle behaviors, low frequency behaviors, verbal content, and affect since such categories are quite difficult to rate reliably. They desired a simple system that could be rated by personnel with little clinical experience and could provide a high degree of agreement among different observers. In a hospital setting, nurses rated psychiatric patients' behaviors at random intervals throughout the day. From 8 a.m. to 4 p.m., sixteen observations were made, averaging one per half hour. The following behaviors were rated:

1. *Talking* – Verbal behavior directed toward another person.
2. *Smiling* – Facial movement in which the corners of the mouth turn up. The teeth may or may not show.
3. *Motor Activity* – The following are activities:
   A. Patient in room with visitor or another patient.
   B. Patient at card table talking, reading, or sewing.
   C. Patient in TV lounge talking, reading, or sewing.
   D. Patient in room dressing or straightening up room.
   E. Patient taking shower.
   F. Patient in physical therapy, occupational therapy, or group therapy (or preparing to go).
   G. Patient sitting and watching TV.
   H. Patient at card table or in TV lounge with other patient or patients (even though patient is not actually talking at that particular minute observed).
   I. Patient drinking coffee on eighth floor.
   J. Patient alone in TV room, with set off, reading, sewing, or knitting.

The following are not activities:

    A. Patient in room alone — sitting, lying down, or looking out the window.
    B. Patient sitting alone in TV room, with set off.
  4. *Time Out of Room* — The patient is not inside the room at the time he is checked. (p. 331)*.

The authors discuss the use of the system to substantiate self-reports of depression as measured by the Beck Depression Inventory and the Hamilton Rating Scale.

Such behavioral dimensions could easily be rated by relatives in the alcoholic's home environment. Thus, the therapist could periodically assess depression during treatment or follow-up. If this behavior tends to precede episodes of drinking, such assessment would allow for preventive intervention.

Vocational behaviors. Vocational behaviors are perhaps easier to evaluate than social and emotional behaviors since they can be more precisely defined. Such dimensions as number of days worked per week, tardiness, or performance ratings from the immediate supervisor can be used to assess such behavior.

In hospital settings, token economy systems are often useful in assessing work behavior. Via a token economy, patients are required to purchase hospital privileges by earning points or credits through working, socializing, being responsible, or self-help behaviors. The notion is to provide incentives for behaviors in which the patient is deficient and for those that appear to be incompatible with excessive drinking. Points are awarded for showing up on time for work, job performance, number of hours worked, nature of work performed (patients are free to choose from various jobs). Number of points earned in each category serves as a simple, objective measure of vocational behavior.

In an outpatient setting, clients' work behavior could periodically be assessed by reports from employers. Therapists could provide employers or immediate supervisors with objective rating sheets to be filled in at regular intervals.

* From Williams, J. G., Barlow, D. H., and Agras, W. S. Behavioral measurement of severe depression. *Archives of General Psychiatry*, 1972, **27**, 330—3. Copyright 1972, American Medical Association.

References

CHAPMAN, R. F., BURT, D. W. and SMITH, J. W. Electrical aversion conditioning to alcohol: individual measurement. Paper presented at Western Psychological Association, Portland, Oregon, 1972.

COHEN, M., LIEBSON, I. A. and FAILLACE, L. A. The modification of drinking in chronic alcoholics. In N. K. Mello and J. H. Mendelson (Eds.) *Recent advances in studies of alcoholism: an interdisciplinary approach.* Washington, D.C.: U.S. Government Printing Office, 1970.

DAVIDSON, R. S. and WALLACH, E. S. Shock facilitation and suppression of alcohol and coke maintained behavior. Unpublished manuscript. Veterans Administration Hospital, Miami, Florida.

EISLER, R. M., HERSEN, M. and AGRAS, W. S. Effects of videotape and instructional feedback on nonverbal marital interaction: an analog study. *Behavior Therapy*, 1973, 4, 551–8.

EISLER, R. M., MILLER, P. M. and HERSEN, M. Components of assertive behavior. *Journal of Clinical Psychology*, 1973, 24, 295–9.

FAILLACE, L. A., FLAMER, R. N., IMBER, S. D. and WARD, R. F. Giving alcohol to alcoholics: an evaluation. *Quarterly Journal of Studies on Alcohol*, 1972, 33, 85–90.

FRIEDMAN, P. H. The effects of modeling and role playing on assertive behavior. In R. D. Rubin, H. Fensterheim, A. A. Lazarus, and C. M. Franks (Eds.) *Advances in Behavior Therapy*, New York: Academic Press, 1971, 149–69.

FULKERSON, S. E. and BARRY, J. R. Methodology and research on prognostic use of psychological tests. *Psychological Bulletin*, 1961, 58, 177–204.

GOTTHEIL, E., CORBETT, L. O., GRASBERGER, J. C. and CORNELISON, F. S. Fixed interval drinking decisions: I. A research and treatment model. *Quarterly Journal of Studies on Alcohol*, 1972, 33, 311–24.

GOTTHEIL, E., MURPHY, B. F., SKOLDA, T. E. and CORBETT, L. O. Fixed interval drinking decisions: II. Drinking and discomfort in 25 alcoholics. *Quarterly Journal of Studies on Alcohol*, 1972, 33, 325–40.

GUZE, S. B., TUASON, V. B., STEWART, M. A. and PICKEN, B. The drinking history: a comparison of reports by subjects and their relatives. *Quarterly Journal of Studies on Alcohol*, 1963, 24, 249–60.

HERSEN, M. Self-assessment of fear. *Behavior Therapy*, 1973, 4, 241–57.

HERSEN, M., EISLER, R. M. and MILLER, P. M. Development of assertive responses: clinical, measurement, and research considerations. *Behavior Research and Therapy*, 1973, 11, 505–22.

HERSEN, M., MILLER, P. M. and EISLER, R. M. Interactions between alcoholics and their wives: a descriptive analysis of verbal and nonverbal behavior. *Quarterly Journal of Studies on Alcohol*, 1973, 34, 516–20.

HILL, M. J. and BLANE, H. T. Evaluation of psychotherapy with alcoholics. *Quarterly Journal of Studies on Alcohol*, 1967, 28, 76–104.

KANFER, F. H. and SASLOW, G. Behavioral diagnosis, In C. M. Franks (Ed.) *Behavior Therapy: Appraisal and Status.* New York: McGraw-Hill, 1969, 417–44.

LAWSON, D. The effects of conditioned anxiety on the rate of acquisition of alcohol by excessive drinkers. Unpublished manuscript, McGill University, Montreal, 1973.

LINDSLEY, O. R. Theoretical basis of behavior modification. Paper presented at School of Education, University of Oregon, Eugene, Oregon, 1967.

43

LUNDE, S. E. and VOGLER, R. E. Generalization of results in studies of aversion conditioning with alcoholics. *Behavior Research and Therapy*, 1970, 8, 313–14.

MARLATT, G. A., DEMMING, B. and REID, J. B. Loss of control drinking in alcoholics: An experimental analogue. *Journal of Abnormal Psychology*, 1973, 81, 233–41.

McCANCE, C. and McCANCE, P. F. Alcoholism in North-East Scotland: Its treatment and outcome. *British Journal of Psychiatry*, 1969, 115, 189–98.

McFALL, R. M. and MARSTON, A. R. An experimental investigation of behavior reversal in assertive training. *Journal of Abnormal Psychology*, 1970, 76, 295–303.

MELLO, N. K. and MENDELSON, J. H. Operant analysis of drinking patterns of chronic alcoholics. *Nature*, 1965, 206, 43–6.

MELLO, N. K. and MENDELSON, J. H. A quantitative analysis of drinking patterns in alcoholics. *Archives of General Psychiatry*, 1971, 25, 527–39.

MILLER, P. M. The use of behavioral contracting in the treatment of alcoholism: A case study. *Behavior Therapy*, 1972, 3, 593–6.

MILLER, P. M. Behavioral assessment in alcoholism research and treatment: Current techniques. *International Journal of the Addictions*, 1973, 8, 825–33.

MILLER, P. M. and HERSEN, M. Quantitative changes in alcohol consumption as a function of electrical aversion conditioning. *Journal of Clinical Psychology*, 1972, 28, 590–3.

MILLER, P. M., HERSEN, M. and EISLER, R. M. Effects of instructions, agreements, and contracts on operant drinking of chronic alcoholics. Paper presented at Association for the Advancement of Behavior Therapy, Miami, 1973.

MILLER, P. M., HERSEN, M., EISLER, R. M., EPSTEIN, L. and WOOTEN, L. S. Relationship of alcohol cues to the drinking of alcoholics and social drinkers: An analogue study. *Psychological Record*, 1974, 24, 61–6.

MILLER, P. M., HERSEN, M., EISLER, R. M. and HEMPHILL, D. P. Electrical aversion therapy with alcoholics: An analogue study. *Behavior Research and Therapy*, 1973, 11, 491–8.

MILLER, P. M., HERSEN, M., EISLER, R. M. and HILSMAN, G. Effects of social stress on operant drinking of alcoholics and social drinkers. *Behavior Research and Therapy*, 1974, 12, 67–72.

MILLER, P. M., HERSEN, M., EISLER, R. M. and WATTS, J. G. Contingent reinforcement of lowered blood/alcohol levels in an outpatient chronic alcoholic. *Behavior Research and Therapy*, 1974, 12, 261–3.

MILLS, K. C., SOBELL, M. B. and SCHAEFER, H. H. Training social drinking as an alternative to abstinence for alcoholics. *Behavior Therapy*, 1971, 2, 18–27.

MOROSKO, T. E. and BAER, P. E. Avoidance conditioning of alcoholics. In R. Ulrich, T. Stachnich, and J. Mabry (Eds.) *Control of Human Behavior.* Glenview, Illinois: Scott, Foresman, and Co., 1970, 170–6.

NATHAN, P. E. and O'BRIEN, J. S. An experimental analysis of the behavior of alcoholics and nonalcoholics during prolonged experimental drinking: A necessary precursor to behavior therapy? *Behavior Therapy*, 1971, 2, 455–76.

Nevada Safety Councils. *Evaluating chemical tests for intoxication*, Chicago, 1953.

OSGOOD, C. E., SUCI, G. J. and TANNENBAUM, P. H. *The measurement of meaning.* Chicago: University of Illinois Press, 1967.

QUINN, J. T. and HENBEST, R. Partial failure of generalization in alcoholics following aversion therapy. *Quarterly Journal of Studies on Alcohol*, 1967, 28, 70–5.

RAYMOND, M. J. The treatment of addiction aversion conditioning with apomorphine. *Behavior Research and Therapy*, 1964, 1, 287–91.

ROBERTS, D. L. and FLETCHER, D. A. Comparative study of blood alcohol testing devices. *Rocky Mountain Medical Journal*, 1969, 66, 37–9.

SCHACHTER, S. Some extraordinary facts about obese humans and rats. *American Psychologist*, 1971, 26, 2, 129–44.

SCHAEFER, H. H., SOBELL, M. B. and MILLS, K. C. Baseline drinking behaviors in alcoholics and social drinkers: Kinds of sips and sip magnitude. *Behavior Research and Therapy*, 1971, 9, 23–7.

SIMKINS, L. The reliability of self-recorded behavior. *Behavior Therapy*, 1971, **2**, 83–7.

SKINNER, B. F. *Beyond freedom and dignity*. New York: Alfred A. Knopf, 1971.

SMITH, B. S., HERSEN, M. and EISLER, R. M. A contingent reinforcement approach for maintaining phenothiazine blood levels in outpatient chronic schizophrenics. Unpublished manuscript, Veterans Administration Center, Jackson, Mississippi, 1971.

SOBELL, L. C. and SOBELL, M. B. A self-feedback technique to monitor drinking behavior in alcoholics. *Behavior Research and Therapy*, 1973a, **11**, 237–8.

SOBELL, L. C., SOBELL, M. B. and CHRISTELMAN, W. C. The myth of "one drink". *Behavior Research and Therapy*, 1972, **10**, 119–23.

SOBELL, M. B. and SOBELL, L. C. Individualized behavior therapy for alcoholics. *Behavior Therapy*, 1973b, **4**, 49–72.

SUMMERS, T. Validity of alcoholics' self-reported drinking history. *Quarterly Journal of Studies on Alcohol*, 1970, **31**, 972–4.

THORNE, F. C. *Clinical judgement*. Brandon, Vermont: Clinical Psychology Publishing Company, 1961.

WILLIAMS, J. G., BARLOW, D. H. and AGRAS, W. S. Behavioral measurement of severe depression. *Archives of General Psychiatry*, 1972, **27**, 330–3.

CHAPTER 3

Aversion Therapy

Introduction

Aversion therapy is perhaps the earliest form of behavior modification that has been applied as a treatment for alcoholism. Table 3.1 traces the historical origins of its use. The first scientific report of its clinical application is attributed to Kantorovich (1929), a Russian investigator, who utilized *electrical* aversion procedures to treat twenty alcoholics. Although this applied use of conditioning methods with alcoholics was novel to the western world at that time, aversive techniques were apparently being routinely investigated at the Leningrad Psychiatric Hospital (Rachman and Teasdale, 1969). It is noteworthy that out of the myriad investigations of aversion therapy in the 44 years between 1929 and 1973, Kantorovich's study was one of the very few to utilize well controlled experimental procedures to objectively evaluate outcome data.

The earliest reported application of *chemical* aversion therapy is also of Russian origin (Sluchevsky and Friken, 1933). However, reports from England (Dent, 1934), France (Ichok, 1934), and Belgium (Ko, 1936) appeared shortly thereafter. The most extensive clinical investigations of chemical aversion therapy occurred between the late 1930s and 1950s at Shadel Sanitarium in Seattle, Washington under the supervision of Drs. Frederick Lemere and Walter L. Voegtlin. Between 1936 and 1950 this facility treated over 5000 patients using "conditioned aversion" techniques. Their detailed accounts of treatment procedures together with their extensive analysis of long-term follow-up data (up to 13 years in some cases) stand as exemplary models for present-day clinical researchers.

The development and utilization of *verbal* aversion methods was of much later historical origin. Although Cautela (1966) described the clinical use of this procedure in the United States in 1966, Strel'Chuk (1957), a Russian investigator, reported using a similar procedure with alcoholics almost 10 years earlier.

Often referred to as "conditioned reflex therapy", "conditioned aversion therapy", or "aversion conditioning", the term *aversion therapy* is used here since, as will become evident, the relationship between success in treatment and conditioning *per se* has never been established. During aversion therapy the

46

TABLE 3.1   Historical Origins of Aversion Therapy with Alcoholics
(Early applications)

Author	Aversive stimulus	Country	Year
Kantorovich	faradic shock	USSR	1929
Sluchevsky and Friken	apomorphine	USSR	1933
Markovnikov	apomorphine	USSR	1934
Dent	apomorphine	United Kingdom	1934
Ichok	apomorphine	France	1934
Galant	apomorphine	USSR	1936
Martimor and Maillefer	ipecac	France	1936
Ko	apomorphine	Belgium	1936
Fleming	apomorphine	United States	1937
Voegtlin	emetine	United States	1940
Voegtlin, Lemere and Broz	emetine	United States	1940
Strel'Chuk	verbal description of nausea	USSR	1957

sight, smell, and taste of alcoholic beverages are repeatedly associated with a noxious stimulus. Aversive stimuli most often used include nausea induced by an emetic (chemical aversion), faradic shock to the arm or leg (electrical aversion), and nausea induced by verbal descriptions and suggestions (verbal aversion or covert sensitization). Theoretically, after repeated pairings, alcohol acquires aversive properties and the patient's desire for alcohol diminishes.

Evaluation of the efficacy of aversion therapy has occurred in a very haphazard manner. Historically, investigators in this area were clinicians with little sophistication in experimental methodology. Thus, in the majority of clinical and research reports, little attention has been given to procedural or methodological details. Adequate descriptions of subject characteristics, instructions to the patient, exact timing and intensity of the aversive stimulus, and the specifics of adjunctive treatments are rarely provided. Seldom have control groups been included to allow for comparison of success rates with other treatment modalities or with no treatment.

Prior to examining the relevant clinical and experimental reports in this area, the basic conditioning paradigms upon which treatments are based must be reviewed. These descriptions are meant to provide the reader with procedural rather than theoretical information in order to better understand the rationale for the manner in which treatment sessions are conducted. Theoretical issues relevant to the aversion procedures will be discussed later as they relate to the specific technique being described. The basic concepts of conditioning in relation to aversion therapy with alcoholics have been extensively reviewed by Franks (1958, 1963, 1966, 1970) and Rachman and Teasdale (1969). Yates

(1970), Lovibond (1970), and Barlow (1972) have attempted to categorize the various types of classical and instrumental conditioning paradigms employed. These are all well-established conditioning procedures which have been repeatedly validated in experimental laboratory settings. Basically, these include:

1. *Classical conditioning.* The basic operation of classical conditioning is the association of two stimuli. One stimulus (conditioned stimulus or CS) is initially neutral in terms of eliciting a specified response. The other stimulus (unconditioned stimulus or UCS) is one which automatically elicits a particular response (unconditioned response or UCR) without prior learning. For example, some UCS-UCR pairs include: electric shock — increased heart rate, respiration, etc.; food (to a deprived organism) — salivation; emetic drug — nausea, vomiting. By *repeatedly* pairing these two stimuli in time and place, the CS comes to elicit a conditioned response (CR), a response similar to the UCR, in the absence of the UCS. In the conditioning process, the CS must precede the UCS with the optimum interstimulus interval being 0.05 second. In the case of alcoholism, the CS is alcohol (either the sight, smell, or taste) while the UCS is an aversive stimulus such as an emetic drug or electrical shock. Theoretically, after repeated pairings, alcohol will elicit a CR (either nausea or anxiety depending upon the UCS) which then should be incompatible with drinking.

2. *Punishment.* Punishment is an operant conditioning concept in which behavior is considered to be a function of its consequences. Punishment is defined empirically as any event which when presented decreases the probability of a response. Thus, an aversive event is contingent upon a response by the learner. In contrast to classical conditioning, the learner must be active and make a response before conditioning can occur. Thus, the act of picking up a glass of liquor or tasting it would be repeatedly followed by an aversive event (e.g., electric shock to the arm).

3. *Avoidance learning.* In this learning situation, the individual can avoid an aversive stimulus by engaging in a required behavior. For example, an alcoholic might be seated in front of a table containing two beverages, one alcoholic and one non-alcoholic. He is told that in 15 seconds he will receive a shock to his arm. However, if he pours the alcohol out into a receptacle and picks up the non-alcoholic beverage prior to that time, he will avoid the shock. This paradigm has been used infrequently with alcoholics.

4. *Escape learning.* In this paradigm, an aversive stimulus is presented and the learner must respond in a specified manner in order to terminate the stimulus. This represents a case of negative reinforcement whereby the probability of occurrence of a behavior is increased when its occurrence is consequated by cessation of an unpleasant event. This paradigm is most often combined with a

punishment model and used in electrical aversion therapy (Blake, 1965). The patient is instructed to sip an alcoholic beverage but not to swallow it. An electric shock is delivered to the forearm contiguously with the sip (punishment). Shock is terminated as soon as the patient spits the alcohol into a pan (escape learning).

The three major types of aversion therapy with alcoholics are: chemical, electrical, and verbal (known as covert sensitization). After reviewing the clinical and research studies of these procedures, the existing data will be evaluated on theoretical and procedural grounds.

Aversion Techniques are only temporary.

Chemical Aversion

Chemical aversion therapy refers to the repeated association between the sight, smell, and taste of alcohol and an unpleasant physiological response which is drug induced. The most widely employed drugs are (1) emetine, apomorphine, and ipecac which elicit nausea and vomiting and (2) succinylcholine chloride dehydrate (Anectine) which induces a state of complete muscular and respiratory paralysis. Aversive olfactory stimuli such as sulphurated potash can also be used. Choice of drug is many times determined by its side effects and specificity of action. For example, Voegtlin (1947) favored emetine over apomorphine as a conditioning drug since the latter tends to induce drowsiness as well as nausea. Such sedative effects often retard the conditioning process. Other possible contraindications of apomorphine include its rather ephemeral emetic action and its potentialities for inducing shock reactions. In spite of these factors, however, Raymond (1963) reported successful clinical results with apomorphine. The complete paralysis induced by Anectine is often considered unnecessarily severe by some clinicians particularly in light of reports of rather poor clinical results (e.g., Clancy, Vanderhoff, and Campbell, 1967) with this type of aversion therapy.

Rachman and Teasdale (1969) suggest that chemical aversion therapy is based upon a classical conditioning paradigm since the aversive consequences are not contingent upon any particular response as would be the case in an instrumental-punishment model. Their contention is also based upon the fact that many patients who have received chemical aversion therapy report that they actually experience nausea and vomiting at the sight, smell, and taste of alcoholic beverages. There is yet no experimental evidence to suggest that classical conditioning *per se* is a significant factor in success with this technique. Measures of physiological responses to alcohol before, during, and after chemical aversion therapy would certainly shed light on this issue.

Nausea Inducing Aversive Stimuli

The most widely used nausea inducing drugs in chemical aversion therapy are apomorphine and emetine. Perhaps the most extensive application of emetine in aversion therapy with alcoholics was performed by Voegtlin (1940) and his colleagues. In their procedure (Lemere, Voegtlin, Broz, O'Hollaren, and Tupper, 1942), the patient was told that he would receive a series of injections designed to "sensitize" his nervous system so that the true aversive characteristics of liquor would be more physiologically apparent. He was instructed never to taste or experiment with liquor once treatment was completed. The patient then drank 20 ounces of lukewarm saline solution containing 1½ grains of oral emetine. He was then given an injection of 3.25 grains of emetine hydrochloride, 1.65 grains of pilocarphine hydrochloride to produce sweating and salivation, and 1.5 grains of ephedrine sulphate. Prior to onset of nausea and vomiting (this time interval is often determined by prior observation of the injection – nausea interval), the patient was requested to take 1 ounce of whiskey into his mouth, swirl it around, and concentrate on the gustatory sensations. Two or three trials (alcohol-vomiting pairings) were held per session with each 45-minute session being held on alternate days. The average number of treatments was four to six and the course of treatment lasted about 10 days. After discharge from treatment, reconditioning sessions were scheduled at the end of 6 months and 1 year or at any time that the patient expressed a strong desire to drink.

These authors stress that exact attention to the details of the procedure must be maintained. In particular, it is essential that alcohol consumption immediately precede the onset of nausea and vomiting. Alcohol given too early in the sequence may produce sedative effects which might retard the conditioning process (Franks, 1966). To insure against such effects, Kant (1945) instructed his patients, in early conditioning sessions, to avoid swallowing the alcohol but to take it into their mouth and then spit it out. Alcohol given after the onset of nausea and vomiting would not adhere to the classical conditioning model in which the CS must precede the UCS. This procedure, known as "backward conditioning", usually does not lead to stable learning. Franks (1958) discusses this issue in light of the surprising number of early clinicians who were inadvertently using "backward conditioning" paradigms due to an apparent lack of familiarity with basic principle of learning.

In addition to this chemical aversion procedure, Voegtlin, Lemere, and their coworkers utilized adjunctive supportive techniques in their treatment program. Such methods as advising patients on problems of social functioning, vocational rehabilitation, family counseling, pentothal treatments, individual supportive psychotherapy, and Antabuse were used. While this provides a very comprehensive program for their patients, inclusion of these additional treatments makes it difficult to evaluate the specific effects of chemical aversion therapy.

Voegtlin and Broz (1949) and Lemere and Voegtlin (1950) reported follow-up information on over 4000 of their patients over a 13-year period. The methods used to accumulate this information are not entirely clear although it would seem that patients and their relatives were contacted by mail or telephone. Over the entire 13 years of follow-up, a total of 51% of the patients were totally abstinent from alcohol. This includes approximately 340 patients who relapsed and were successfully retreated. Results of treatment after 1 year yield an even higher rate of 60% total abstinence. This figure is important for comparative reasons since most studies evaluating such treatments report success rates in terms of 1-year follow-up data.

Treatment effects were also analyzed in terms of reconditioning or booster sessions. Voegtlin, Lemere, Broz, and O'Hollaren (1942) demonstrated that long-term treatment success was related to booster treatments. They reported that 90% of 130 patients who received these additional conditioning sessions remained abstinent at follow-up. The more booster sessions a patient received the better his chances were of maintaining sobriety.

As detailed in Chapter 2, effects of this treatment were related to socioeconomic, interpersonal, and vocational characteristics of the patients. In comparing these investigators' success rates with those obtained in other studies, the composition of their patient population must be considered. All of their patients were voluntary and paid between $450 and $750 each for 10 days of inpatient treatment. Thus, their group consisted of alcoholics who were economically and socially stable. In reference to these qualities of their patients as they relate to treatment outcome, Lemere and Voegtlin (1950) express the following:

> These circumstances indicate that we automatically get a high percentage of prognostically favorable patients for treatment and that the atmosphere of the institution is conducive to full cooperation on the part of the patient. We believe that the conditioned-reflex treatment is of value primarily for the advantageously circumstanced type of alcoholic patient. It probably does not offer much hope to the inadequate, skid-row type and is inapplicable to those alcoholics who do not admit their problem or, if they do, refuse to make an effort to help themselves.* (p. 200)

Although other clinical investigations of chemical aversion have not been nearly as extensive, they yield similar results (Edlin, Johnson, Hletko, and Heilbruun, 1945; Kant, 1945; Shanahan and Hornick, 1946; Thimann, 1949; Wallace, 1949). Abstinence rates for differing follow-up durations vary from 30% to 80%. Such discrepancies may be due to differences in populations studied, procedural differences, or adjunctive treatments used.

Raymond (1964) has devised some interesting procedural changes in the chemical aversion technique. Apomorphine is initially used and the dosage is

---

* Reprinted by permission from *Quarterly Journal of Studies on Alcohol*, Vol. 11, pp. 199–204, 1950. Copyright by Journal of Studies on Alcohol, Inc., New Brunswick, N.J. 08903.

kept to a minimum. The starting dose, 1/20 grain dissolved in 1 cc of normal saline (injected subcutaneously), is given to determine the exact time from injection to onset of nausea. Raymond contends that *nausea* and not vomiting is the desired response and is sufficient for treatment. He points out that even a small amount of nausea in the first session can be expanded upon in later sessions without increasing the dose. During treatment the patient is instructed to begin drinking just before nausea is expected to occur and to continue drinking during the earlier part of the nausea. Raymond warns against having the patient drink "through" the nausea so that the termination of nausea coincides with drinking. Also, the amount of alcohol should always be small so that intoxication does not occur. The alcoholic beverage first offered is the one least preferred by the patient. His favorite drink is the last to be offered on the assumption that aversion will be more easily conditioned through this hierarchical approach. After the nausea has passed the patient is given positive expectation about the treatment and the aversive consequences of his former drinking habits are discussed.

Another feature of this procedure is what Raymond calls the "choice reaction". After the patient begins to express a distaste for alcohol, usually in a week to 10 days, he is injected with 1 cc of normal saline instead of apomorphine, without his knowledge. When he is brought to the treatment room he finds the usual alcoholic beverage and also some soft drinks, and is told that he may choose his drink. Patients invariably choose a soft drink. At this point the therapist encourages a relaxed atmosphere. This procedure is then randomly interspersed among regular treatment sessions. The average length of treatment is 3 weeks. Upon release the patient is given Antabuse and is encouraged, with the help of a relative, to take it regularly.

Dent (1934) reports a rather unusual method of apomorphine-chemical aversion. For 2 or 3 days patients are administered injections of apomorphine and simultaneously encouraged to drink alcohol. Little reference is made to the precise order and timing of stimulus events. During the second treatment phase, apomorphine injections continue for 2 days in the absence of alcohol. The patient is then allowed to recuperate for a few days. In addition to this basic treatment, Dent devised a strategy for controlling "cravings" occurring periodically after treatment. The patient is required to take apomorphine orally every 2 hours for 3 consecutive days. During this time the patient is instructed to refrain from alcoholic beverages. Reportedly, as the days progress, the patient's urges gradually diminish. Dent's rationale for this approach lies in his assumption that apomorphine treatment is effective not because of conditioning factors, but because of the direct chemical action of the drug itself. In this respect he seems to equate the action of apomorphine with alcoholics to that of methadone for heroin addicts. Although Dent claims 60% to 70% total abstinence after 1 year, little evidence exists to support his rationale. The fact that he claims success using apomorphine alone without pairing it with alcohol might suggest the role of suggestion or "attention-placebo" factors in aversion therapy.

Thus far, all of the data presented on chemical aversion therapy has been clinical. That is, no matched control groups were included to determine if the results were due to the aversion treatment *per se*, additional supportive treatments, or merely a "placebo" effect. One of the few controlled experimental studies in this area was reported by Wallerstein (1957). He compared four treatment conditions — chemical aversion therapy, Antabuse, group hypnotherapy, and milieu therapy. The chemical aversion group received a 5-day course of conditioning followed by a "test" day in which liquor was provided in the absence of emetine. During this final day, 75% of the patients experienced nausea with 25% actually vomiting. Booster treatments were periodically administered. Effects of treatment were evaluated in terms of degree of abstinence, social adjustment, patients' self-assessment of feelings, changes in personality as analyzed by psychiatric observations, and psychological test data. On the basis of these criteria, patients were judged improved or unimproved after treatment. The following improvement percentages for the four groups at a 2-year follow-up were reported: Chemical aversion — 24%, Antabuse — 53%, hypnotherapy — 36%, milieu therapy — 28%. However, these percentages were calculated on the total number of patients in each group whether they were lost to follow-up or not. If one includes only those patients who were actually evaluated at follow-up, the improvement percentages become 41%, 62%, 50%, 42%, respectively for the four groups. Thus, Antabuse maintenance appears to be the most efficacious treatment procedure with chemical aversion rates being equivalent to the other treatments. These results, however, must be considered carefully in light of numerous methodological inadequacies present in this study. First, no statistical comparisons were calculated to determine the significance of group differences. Second, the groups were not adequately matched on such factors as age, education, length of problem drinking. Third, in two of the groups — conditioning and milieu therapy — no follow-up data were available on a substantial percentage of the patients (42% and 38%). Fourth, treatments were not discrete in that some groups were receiving other than the specified treatments. Fifth, the Antabuse group was administered "a series of carefully studied Antabuse-alcohol trials" (Wallerstein, 1957, p. 229) to regulate the dosage. These trials may have constituted "conditioning sessions" since alcohol was being paired with the aversive physiological reactions of the Antabuse.

Group Applications

An interesting procedural innovation has involved the application of chemical aversion to groups of alcoholics. Miller, Dvorak, and Turner (1960) treated groups of four alcoholics with a procedure quite similar to the Voegtlin and Lemere technique. One session was held each day for 2 weeks for a total of ten sessions. A mixture of emetine hydrochloride, pilocarpine hydrochloride, and ephedrine sulfate was injected after the patient drank two glasses of tepid water. Liquor bottles and beer were then opened and the four patients were instructed to smell and taste the beverages. Sessions lasted 30 to 45 minutes or until each patient reported a distaste for the alcoholic beverage. Of ten patients who were followed up for 8 months, two had relapsed to their former drinking habits only after "strenuous effort of holding down the first drink". Three patients had brief lapses of 1 to 3 days but stopped spontaneously.

A more extensive and economical use of the group procedure was conducted by Zvonikov (1968) in Russia, who treated over 1100 chronic alcoholics in groups of 40 to 45. In this procedure, although all patients received injections, only a few were given injections of apomorphine. The gagging and nausea produced in these few led to nausea and vomiting in the remaining patients. Different patients received apomorphine each day. The author reports that only 5 or 6 trials are needed and that because of "suggestion" the response established is more stable in the group procedure.

It is possible that group procedures may not only enhance the aversiveness of the session, but also provide mutual reinforcement for participation in therapy and maintenance of sobriety after treatment is complete. Also, since much drinking occurs in social settings, effects of treatment generalize more readily to the natural environment.

Paralysis-Inducing Aversive Stimuli

A second aversive stimulus employed in chemical aversion therapy is succinylcholine chloride dehydrate (Anectine). This stimulus was hypothesized to overcome the several disadvantages of emetic drugs, among these the relative unpredictability of the onset of nausea or vomiting. Anectine produces a nerve, muscle block through a curarizing effect at the motor endplate of the efferent neurons serving the skeletal muscles. While fully conscious, the patient experiences total respiratory paralysis. The effect lasts from 60 to 90 seconds. Only one conditioning trial is usually administered.

The initial impetus for the use of Anectine-chemical aversion therapy resulted from a report by Sanderson, Campbell, and Laverty (1963). After only one treatment session, 12 of 15 patients were reported to be abstinent from all alcoholic beverages. These results, however, were based on very short-term periods of sobriety.

In a report by Clancy, Vanderhoff, and Campbell (1967), patients were not specifically told of the details of the treatment beforehand, but were given vague indications that a reaction involving difficulty in breathing may or may not occur. Patients were instructed that they would not be able to drink alcohol in the future. During treatment a hypodermic needle was inserted into a vein in the arm and an Anectine drip attached. A syringe containing 10 mg of Anectine was inserted into the tube near the needle. When the drip was running and the Anectine was ready for injection, the patient was given a glass of his favorite alcoholic beverage. He was instructed to look at and smell it for approximately 20 seconds, and then give it back to the therapist. This procedure was repeated every minute. On the fourth repetition the patient was asked to taste the beverage and a signal was given to administer the Anectine. When apnea occurred (usually within seconds) the patient was ventilated with a breathing bag. The results of this procedure were in marked contrast to those of Sanderson, Campbell, and Laverty (1963). Despite the powerful aversive stimulus and the improvement in the temporal relationship of the CS-UCS event, very few long-lasting abstentions were noted. Clancy *et al.* (1967) reported no difference in percentage of patients abstinent between a group receiving Anectine treatment and a control group receiving the same procedure without Anectine. There was some trend for these two groups to do better than a third group receiving other forms of treatment such as psychotherapy or drug therapy. The fact that the control group did as well as the treatment group and better than a third group receiving another treatment suggests that an expectancy effect is an important therapeutic variable in this paradigm. Similar results were reported by Madill, Campbell, Laverty, Sanderson, and Vanderwater (1966).

The results obtained by Farrar, Powell, and Martin (1968) are noteworthy since they conducted the longest follow-up of any of these investigators. Of nine chronic alcoholics who received this treatment, only two remained abstinent at a 1-year follow-up contact.

While chemical aversion therapy employing Anectine has been the most carefully investigated form of aversion therapy with alcoholics, the disappointed results presented above would not support its clinical use. Nausea inducing agents as aversive stimuli, however, deserve more extensive experimental evaluation particularly in light of the more positive findings of Lemere and Voegtlin (1950).

Electrical Aversion

The most frequently used electrical aversion procedures follow a punishment-escape paradigm in which faradic shock is contingent upon alcohol sips, with shock being terminated when the patient spits out the alcohol. Shock is delivered through electrodes placed on the patient's forearm (ventral surface), leg, or fingers. Care is always taken to avoid placing electrodes in such a way that shock passes through the heart. Shock intensity varies considerably but most therapists administer between three to eight milliamps. Davidson and Wallach (1971) argue that such intensities may be too low to be aversive to chronic alcoholics since these patients frequently exhibit peripheral neuropathy. They utilize rather high shock levels, up to 20 to 30 milliamps. Intensity, however, must be individually determined by each patient's reports and reactions. Usually a pre-treatment test session is held to determine the range of shock intensities that are judged to be unpleasant but not extremely painful. Most therapists begin shocking the patient at low levels, presenting systematic increments until the patient reports pain. When electrodes are placed on the arm, the patient's arm flexion in response to shocks is used to corroborate self-reports of unpleasantness.

A number of shock generators that are safe and relatively easy to use are commercially available. Vogler, Lunde, and Martin (1970) suggest the use of the induction stimulator produced by the Harvard Apparatus Company. This apparatus is quite safe since it generates high voltage with a maximum of four to five milliamps. A similar generator is the Farrell AV-2 Shocker Control. The Grason—Stadler shock generator, model 700, allows more leeway in terms of shock intensities which vary from .001 milliamp to 30 milliamps. Pocket-sized portable shockers are also available to allow self-administered conditioning trials in the patient's natural environment. These are useful when patients are instructed to punish their urges and thoughts of alcohol in a self-control manner.

Procedural specifications of aversion therapy are highly variable. There are as yet no experimental data on the optimum number of alcohol-shock pairings or the spacing of conditioning sessions. A typical method in clinical use is to administer approximately 25 to 50 conditioning trials daily for 10 days. In this regard, information from studies on aversive control with animals together with reports of clinical experience of aversion therapists provide some useful guides to clinical applications. These procedural considerations include the following:

1. Generally, shock intensities should be high to be effective. While some animal experimental evidence indicates that shock levels should remain intense throughout treatment sessions, Lovibond (1970) suggests that varying shock intensities should be used within each session. He argues that maintenance of non-specific arousal by uncertainty increases the aversive properties of painful events. Concomitantly, he recommends varying the duration and time of onset of the shock together with the placement of the electrodes. The process of gradually increasing shock levels as treatment continues leads to rapid habituation, and is not usually recommended.

2. In a punishment paradigm, shock should be presented immediately after the response undergoing modification (e.g., sipping an alcoholic drink).

3. During early treatment sessions (acquisition) shock should be continuous,

that is, presented every time the response occurs. As sessions continue, intermittent shocks in which only some of the responses are punished should be used to insure resistance to extinction.

4. To insure generalization of results, electrical aversion sessions should take place in surroundings very similar to the situations in which the alcoholic drinks. Thus, settings with a variety of alcohol cues, such as a simulated bar, are desirable.

5. The entire chain of events from urges to actual consumption should be punished. Emphasis should be placed upon events occurring in the early parts of the drinking sequence (e.g., urges, sight of alcohol, pouring a drink).

6. An alternative response should be provided and then reinforced. While this procedure is well accepted in studies of punishment with animals, it has been noticeably disregarded in reports of aversion therapy.

These are certainly not all of the procedural considerations to be taken into account. Therapists are advised to keep abreast of the animal literature, where the parameters of aversive control have been investigated. For a more complete analysis of these parameters the reader is referred to Azrin and Holz (1966) and Lovibond (1970).

The range of reports on electrical aversion procedures includes clinical evaluations, controlled clinical experiments, and analogue or theoretical studies. An analysis of all three types of study provides an indication of the current applied clinical status of the technique.

Uncontrolled Clinical Evaluations

Evaluations of this type include reports of the clinical outcome of electrical aversion with either individual alcoholics or groups of patients. No control groups are included for comparison and thus only limited conclusions can be drawn from these results. For example, in those cases where success is attained, it is difficult to ascertain whether aversion therapy itself produced the changes or whether they were due to non-specific therapeutic influences.

Blake (1965, 1967) used an escape learning paradigm to treat twenty-five chronic alcoholics. In this procedure electrodes were initially attached to the patient's forearm with the placement varying from session to session. The patient chose and mixed his alcoholic beverage and was instructed to sip, but told not to swallow, the beverage. Concurrently, a shock previously judged by the patient to be unpleasant was administered. To terminate the shock the patient spit the alcohol into a bowl. Shock intensity was gradually increased across trials to prevent adaptation. A partial reinforcement schedule was used in that only 50% of the trials were actually shocked. In the remaining trials a green light signaled the patient to spit out the alcohol. The author reported that patients spit out the alcohol with the same eagerness during these trials as during shocked trials.

Twenty-five unselected patients were treated by this method in from three to thirty-six sessions, over 4 to 8 days. This group was compared to a group of thirty-seven unselected patients that received training in deep muscle relaxation in addition to electrical aversion. Although inclusion of this additional group provides information on the adjunctive effects of muscle relaxation to electrical aversion therapy, it does not constitute a "true" control group in which patients would not receive any treatment or in which they would be administered a placebo treatment. At a 12-month follow-up patients were described as abstinent, improved (only social drinking with marked improvement in general level of adjustment), or relapsed. In the aversion therapy alone group, 23% were totally abstinent, 27% improved, 27% relapsed, and 23% could not be followed. When relaxation was combined with aversion the figure rose to 46% abstinent, 13% improved, 30% relapsed, and 11% could not be followed.

MacCulloch, Feldman, Orford, and MacCulloch (1966) treated four alcoholics with an anticipatory avoidance learning paradigm previously used with success in the treatment of homosexuality. A hierarchy of stimulus situations consisting of photographs of various alcoholic beverages and also actual alcohol poured into a glass were presented in ascending order of attractiveness. Electric shock to the leg followed shortly after the presentation of each stimulus situation. Patients could avoid the shock by switching to photographs of orange squash and/or by actually drinking orange squash. Number of sessions per patient varied from ten to forty, and treatment was discontinued when the patient expressed a lack of interest in alcohol. Response latencies and pulse rate recordings indicated that none of the patients developed a stable conditioned avoidance response to alcohol. All of the patients have since relapsed. The investigators felt that their sample was too small for conclusive results. They attributed their failures to the patients' possible "pathological biochemical necessity" for alcohol or to the fact that more sensory modalities were not involved in the conditioning. No evidence for these explanations was offered.

Avoidance conditioning with alcoholics should not be completely dismissed, however, especially in light of the more optimistic findings of Morosko and Baer (1970) and Chapman, Burt, and Smith (1972) using a variant of this paradigm. Morosko and Baer (1970) alternated paired conditioning trials with avoidance trials in treating three outpatient alcoholics. During paired trials patients were instructed to drink a series of two alcoholic and four non-alcoholic beverages in sequence. Electric shock to the leg followed consumption of alcoholic beverages. During initial avoidance trials patients were instructed to consume any five of the six beverages and to discard the sixth. Thus, 50% of the shocks could be avoided by discarding one of the alcoholic beverages. Eventually, patients were instructed to drink only four beverages and discard two, thereby being able to avoid all shocks. Number of sessions per patient varied from six to nineteen with seventy-two trials during each session. Measures of success included percentage of avoidance trials on which alcoholic beverages were discarded and mean latencies for consumption of non-alcoholic beverages and discarding of alcoholic beverages. All patients showed marked changes on these measures as treatment progressed achieving 100% avoidance by the end of treatment. At a 19-month follow-up one patient was completely abstinent while the other two were drinking in moderation.

Chapman, Burt, and Smith (1972) used a similar procedure to evaluate treatment effectiveness with ten in-patient alcoholics. In this study patients were instructed not to swallow alcoholic beverages that they chose but to take a small amount into their mouth and then spit it out. A baseline phase consisted of twenty choices from a variety of alcoholic and non-alcoholic beverages. During forced choice conditioning, patients were instructed to choose 15 alcoholic beverages consecutively. Electric shock to the forearm was contingent upon sipping each beverage. In the free choice phase, patients were allowed to choose beverages freely and could avoid all shocks by choosing only non-alcoholic drinks. Each patient received five daily conditioning sessions lasting 60 to 70 minutes each along with booster sessions at 1- and 3-month intervals. In seven of ten patients treated, percent of choice of non-alcoholic beverages increased from 30% during baseline to 100% during the final free choice session. These patients have remained abstinent from 8 to 9 months after treatment. All of the three patients who did not significantly change their choices on the drinking measure have returned to heavy drinking. In addition to electrical aversion therapy all of the patients in this study received self-management training. In this procedure patients are taught to consequate urges to drink with an emotional reason for not drinking and the positive benefits resulting from abstinence. This training is combined with role playing regarding the refusal of drinks. This rather innovative self-control technique certainly deserves further investigation on its own.

Hsu (1965) also used an avoidance learning situation in which he requested patients to drink a series of alcoholic and non-alcoholic beverages. Severe electric shock (2 to 5 ma of 30-sec duration) to the head followed ingestion of alcoholic beverages while shock could be avoided by choosing non-alcoholic drinks. Treatment was administered for 5 days with booster sessions at 1 and 6 months after hospital discharge. This rather disagreeable treatment resulted in more than a 50% drop-out rate. Preliminary results indicated slightly less than 50% abstinent at varying follow-up visits. This success rate, which is quite similar to that reported with less severe aversive procedures, does not appear to justify subjecting patients to such extreme discomfort.

Controlled Clinical Experimentation

As was mentioned previously, the earliest controlled evaluation of the efficacy of electrical aversion was reported by Kantorovich (1929). In a treatment group containing twenty alcoholics, Kantorovich (1929) repeatedly paired the sight, smell, and taste of alcoholic beverages as well as cards displaying the printed name of the beverage, with shock in from five to eighteen sessions. Further details of this procedure are lacking, but the author reports that seventeen of the twenty patients acquired stable aversion reactions to alcohol. After a follow-up ranging from 3 weeks to 20 months, 70% of the treatment group remained abstinent. On the other hand, seven out of a control group of ten patients receiving hypnotic suggestion or medication reverted to their drinking pattern in a few days after release from hospital. Such results seem promising, but unfortunately, the absence of a precise procedural description hinders exact replication of this study.

Recently, a well controlled group study of electrical aversion was reported by Vogler, Lunde, Johnson, and Martin (1970). Subjects were assigned randomly to treatments of pseudoconditioning (random shock delivery), sham conditioning (no shock), routine hospital care, and aversive conditioning (contingent shock). An escape paradigm (Blake, 1965) was used for conditioning with two 45-minute sessions held daily for 10 days. Aversion conditioning subjects who returned for follow-up visits were given booster conditioning sessions. Results were based on fifty-one subjects with a median follow-up time of 8 months. Relapse took significantly longer for aversion conditioning subjects than for any of the controls. Proportion of relapses for the conditioning group did not differ significantly from the other groups (but was in the predicted direction). Booster sessions helped subjects maintain sobriety in that relapse took significantly longer for booster subjects than for "conditioning only" subjects. These data must be interpreted carefully, however, since subjects in the booster group were not matched with subjects in the "conditioning only" group. In fact, all subjects in the booster conditioning group voluntarily and routinely returned for follow-up treatments. Subjects in the conditioning alone group did not return for scheduled follow-up visits. This factor represents a major biasing variable in the conclusions on the efficacy of booster sessions.

Miller and Hersen (1973) demonstrated quantitative changes in alcohol consumption as a function of electrical aversion therapy. An A—B—A—B experimental single case design was used to evaluate drinking behavior of a chronic alcoholic, with a "taste test" system serving as the dependent measure. Escape conditioning (Blake, 1965) was used with alternating experimental phases of baseline electrical aversion, baseline, aversion. Aversion therapy was scheduled twice daily for 5 consecutive days. During baseline no treatment was administered. As a measure of progress the subject was requested to take part each day in a "taste experiment" in which he was to taste six beverages (three alcoholic and three non-alcoholic) and rate them on various taste dimensions. After completion of this task the experimenters calculated (without the subject's knowledge) the exact amount consumed from each glass. Conditioning sessions and "taste test" ratings were scheduled in different rooms and instructions were geared to minimize the possibility that the subject would associate the two procedures. Results indicated that during electrical aversion phases marked decreases in variability and absolute amount of alcohol consumption were noted. A follow-up "taste test" at 6 months revealed continuation of decreased alcohol consumption. Reports from the subject and from relatives also indicated that he had maintained complete sobriety.

Far too few experimental-clinical evaluations have been reported on electrical aversion therapy to allow for definitive conclusions as to its efficacy. A number of theoretical-analogue studies, however, have recently shed light on this issue.

Theoretical-Analogue Studies

Hallam, Rachman, and Falkowski (1971) examined attitudinal and physiological effects of electrical aversion therapy. Patients who maintained sobriety after treatment subjectively described their feeling toward alcohol as being one of repulsion or indifference rather than anxiety. In the second phase of this study the authors compared ten alcoholics who had received electrical aversion with eight who received general psychiatric care. On the basis of reactions of fantasies and photographic slides of alcohol, the aversion group showed no evidence of having developed heart rate or skin resistance responses to alcoholic stimuli. Successful cases (in terms of abstinence), regardless of type of treatment, showed a significant heart rate sensitivity to alcoholic stimuli and devalued these stimuli on semantic differential ratings. The authors concluded that these results fail to substantiate a classical conditioning model of electrical aversion therapy and stress a cognitive explanation for therapeutic success. They concluded that therapeutic success obtained as a function of electrical aversion was more likely related to elements common to a variety of treatments (including the non-behavioral ones), rather than to specific elements underlying electrical aversion. More detailed analysis of this issue is discussed in a recent article by Hallam and Rachman (1972).

Miller, Hersen, Eisler, and Hemphill (1973) evaluated the effects of electrical aversion therapy on alcohol consumption in an analogue group experimental study. Thirty chronic alcoholic patients were matched on age, education, and length of problem drinking and assigned to one of three treatment conditions. Group 1 received twenty sessions of electrical aversion therapy (escape paradigm) over a 10-day period (a total of 500 trials). Group 2 received the same aversion procedure with the exception of the aversive shock. In this pseudoconditioning group, shock intensities were kept constantly low so that they were barely perceptible. Finally, Group 3 patients received 6-hourly sessions of group therapy over the 10 days. Groups 2 and 3 were included to evaluate the influence of "attention placebo" and expectancy factors in therapeutic outcome. Pre-post measures of alcohol were obtained via the "taste test" assessment procedure previously described in detail. No significant differences in changes of alcohol consumption or attitudes toward alcohol were found among the groups. Trends in the data support Hallam, Rachman, and Falkowski's (1971) contention that the effects of electrical aversion may be more related to such factors as therapeutic instructions, specificity of the procedure, or therapeutic demand characteristics than to conditioning factors *per se.*

In a series of analogue studies, Wilson (1973) further assessed the efficacy of the traditional electrical aversion therapy model. Four inpatient chronic alcoholics were allowed free access to alcohol (up to 30 ounces in a 24-hour period) over 3 consecutive days. This was followed by the administration of thirty trials of either escape conditioning or backward conditioning over a 4-day period. Patients were then allowed access to alcohol once again. Using a crossover experimental design, results indicated that neither procedure significantly reduced alcohol consumption. When electric shock was used as punishment and applied directly to alcohol consumption in the free drinking situation, drinking behavior was significantly suppressed. However, as soon as punishment contingencies were removed, alcohol consumption increased to the initial baseline level. In the final phase of the study, the effects of self-administered shock were examined. Under these conditions, patients were instructed to deliver electric shock to themselves contingent upon alcohol consumption. Shock was gradually faded out completely. Alcohol consumption was significantly suppressed and remained so even in the absence of immediate threat of shock.

These are intriguing findings in light of the negative effects reported earlier. These data justify a more intensive evaluation of the parameters of electrical aversion therapy and also its use in a self-control manner. In the meantime, clinicians would be advised to make maximum use of positive instructional sets and therapeutic demand in applying electrical aversion rather than relying on "automatic" conditioning processes.

Covert Sensitization

The most recently developed clinical aversive procedure used with alcoholics is verbal aversion therapy or covert sensitization. This latter term was coined by Cautela (1966) who is perhaps the foremost advocate of the procedure. In this technique, imagined scenes of drinking are paired with imagined scenes of unpleasant events or feelings such as nausea and vomiting. Ten to twenty pairings are presented during each session with treatment continuing for several months. While the patient is in a relaxed state, scenes depicting drinking episodes from his own experience are described. Emphasis is placed upon early parts of the drinking sequence such as entering a bar or experiencing an urge to drink as opposed to actually consuming alcohol. The patient is instructed to imagine these situations as clearly as possible using all of his sense modalities. Typically, scenes of nausea and vomiting are then described for the patient to imagine.

An example scene follows:

> You are walking toward your refrigerator at home in order to get a beer. As you do, you get a sick feeling in the pit of your stomach. As you reach in for the beer, your stomach feels very queasy. When you pick up the beer you feel vomit coming into your throat. You try to swallow it back down but you can't. You vomit all over yourself and the beer. You open the beer and take a quick swallow. As you do, you vomit again all over yourself. You can smell vomit and beer mixed together and you feel miserable.

Relief scenes are frequently added in which imagined feelings of relaxation and well-being are paired with avoidance or rejection of alcohol. In addition to treatment sessions administered by the therapist, patients are instructed to practice these associations at home. The patient may be provided with tape-recordings of his covert sensitization treatments to aid in this process. Cautela (1970) also advocates the use of covert sensitization as a self-control procedure. Patients are advised to ward off urges and thoughts about alcohol by imagining the noxious scene in the presence of these events. At the sight of an alcoholic beverage in his community environment, the patient is told to imagine that the drink is covered with vomit.

Some alcoholics report that images of nausea and vomiting are not aversive to them since they have experienced these conditions so frequently in the past. In these cases, the Fear Inventory (Wolpe, 1973) provides a standard set of unpleasant situations which can be rated by the patient. Other than nausea and vomiting, imagined scenes of snakes, maggots, open wounds, death, or social rejection are frequently used with success. Therapists often utilize aversive scenes more relevant to abusive drinking consequences in the natural environment such as being arrested or losing a job.

Theoretical Analysis

Cautela's (1966) major assumption underlying covert treatment strategies is that imaginal events are subject to the same laws of learning as overt events. He initially modeled covert sensitization after the classical conditioning paradigm such as that used with chemical aversion therapies. Since then, however, he has developed a number of related treatment strategies (e.g., covert reinforcement, covert extinction) which are viewed from the operant framework. The issue of the exact nature of this conditioning process remains unclear partly because the imaginal nature of covert sensitization complicates objective investigations. Barlow, Leitenberg, and Agras (1969) and Miller and Hersen (1972) have experimentally demonstrated that the pairing of images with thoughts and feelings of nausea does seem to be the essential variable in the treatment process. Whether classical or operant conditioning mechanisms are involved is still open to question. It can probably be assumed, as with most aversive learning situations, that both types of conditioning processes may be present. Bandura (1969) and Rachman and Teasdale (1970) present more detailed analysis of these theoretical issues.

Clinical Reports

Cautela (1966) reported the use of covert sensitization to treat a 29-year-old female alcoholic. With only 8 to 10-weekly treatment sessions the patient reported decreased urges and abstinence from alcoholic beverages. At an 8-month follow-up the patient remained abstinent. Unfortunately, inclusion of systematic desensitization, assertive training, and anxiety relief through relaxation in the treatment program clouds the issue of the efficacy of the covert sensitization trials *per se*.

Miller (1959) reports the use of verbal aversion in combination with hypnosis. Strong suggestions of nausea and hangover symptoms were associated with the smell and taste of alcoholic beverages. These suggestions sometimes produced vomiting in the office. Patients were also advised that nausea would result from future alcohol drinking. Results indicated that 83% of twenty-four patients were completely abstinent at a 9-month follow-up. Strel'Chuk (1957), in Russia, reported similar success with this procedure.

Anant (1967) treated twenty-six patients using a *group* covert sensitization approach. After relaxation training, images of nausea were associated with images of alcohol-related scenes. After a minimum of five treatment sessions, 96% of these patients remained abstinent at follow-up contacts ranging from 8 to 15 months. However, in a later paper Anant (1968) reports that only three of fifteen patients, or 20%, remained abstinent at follow-up visits beyond the 8- to 15-month interval. Possibly, booster treatments administered at follow-up sessions may have produced better long-term results.

Controlled Experimental Studies

Ashem and Donner (1968) evaluated the effects of covert sensitization on twenty-three patients assigned to three treatment groups. Group 1 received nine sessions of standard covert sensitization over a 3-week period of time. Group 2 received a backward conditioning paradigm in which the aversive image preceded the image of drinking. Group 3 served as a no-treatment control. Groups 1 and 2 also received relaxation training and practice in self-control in which they would push alcohol away and then imagine feelings of adequacy and relaxation. As treatment progressed, Group 2 patients automatically associated the alcohol with nausea and vomiting despite the backward conditioning paradigm. Group 2 was therefore combined with Group 1 and compared with the no-treatment control. Six months after treatment a follow-up questionnaire was completed by the patient and one of his relatives. All of the eight control subjects were drinking to excess. Six out of fifteen patients, or 40%, who received covert sensitization remained abstinent at 6 months. It is unfortunate that a longer follow-up was not included since, after initial success, many alcoholics begin to relapse after 6 months of abstinence.

Using a single case experimental design (Barlow and Hersen, 1973), Miller and Hersen (1972) evaluated the effects of covert sensitization on alcohol consumption. The patient was a 30-year-old male with a 5-year history of alcohol abuse. Treatment was divided into four phases with alcohol available every other day (via a "taste test" measure) during each phase. Baseline drinking measures were accumulated during the first 5-day period during which no treatment was administered. During the next 5 days, covert sensitization was administered twice daily. The third phase of the study constituted an extinction condition during which the patient was instructed to imagine drinking scenes, but descriptions of nausea and vomiting were omitted. However, instructions were presented to sustain positive treatment expectancy. Covert sensitization, including use of the nausea scenes, was then reintroduced for 5 days in the final experimental phase.

Total amount (in cc) of alcoholic beverages consumed during each experimental phase is presented in Figure 3.1. During baseline, consumption

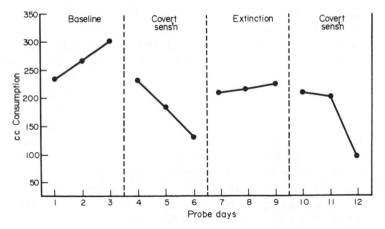

Fig. 3.1. Mean alcohol consumption (in cc) for probe measurement days during each experimental phase.

remained high with a steady increase from 233 cc to 300 cc. During the first covert sensitization phase, consumption decreased markedly to a low of 136 cc. When the scenes depicting nausea and vomiting were omitted in the extinction phase, alcohol consumption increased. Reintroduction of covert sensitization again resulted in decreased consumption. These results indicate that the changes in drinking were related to the covert sensitization pairings and not merely "attention-placebo" factors.

Covert sensitization, then, appears to be a viable aversion procedure. It has the advantage that patients can easily use it as a self-control technique in their natural environments. In addition, there are no medical contraindications for its use as with electrical and chemical aversion. Patients are also more likely to cooperate with treatment since covert sensitization is considerably less unpleasant than other aversive techniques.

Methodological Issues

Aversive Stimuli

The question of which aversive stimulus — chemical, electrical, or verbal — results in the most favorable therapeutic outcome is a relevant yet cloudy clinical issue. To date, there are no reports directly comparing the efficacy of the three major types of aversion therapy. Such a comparison is considered premature by some since so little is known about the particular factors *within* each technique that lead to therapeutic success.

With no comparative information available, choice of the aversive stimulus is frequently determined on procedural and theoretical grounds. Medical contraindications, possible negative side-effects, and ease of administration are taken into account. A major controversy in the literature has involved the relative merits of electrical versus chemical stimuli. Objections to the use of emetics include difficulty in controlling the timing between presentation of alcohol and onset of nausea, limitations on the number of conditioning trials per session due to the duration of side effects (e.g., drowsiness), diverse individual variations in response to drugs, and reluctance or refusal of some patients to participate in the treatment due to its unpleasantness. Although some of these same objections might apply to faradic shock, Rachman and Teasdale (1969) support the use of electrical aversion in that it allows for precise control and timing of conditioning events. Supposedly, such precision would not only increase the likelihood of adequate conditioning and subsequent therapeutic success, but also objectify experimental evaluation of the technique. These arguments have greatly influenced contemporary clinical applications of aversion therapy in favor of electrical shock. However, recent experimental studies on the nature of electrical aversion therapy (Hallam, Rachman, and Falkowski, 1971; Miller, Hersen, Eisler, and Hemphill, 1973) indicate that precision in the conditioning process may be of little importance in terms of therapeutic efficacy of the procedure. Furthermore, clinical studies of the aversion therapies reviewed in this chapter certainly do not provide evidence for the superiority of electrical aversion therapy. In fact, there is a trend for chemical aversion procedures to yield higher success rates.

From a theoretical standpoint, Wilson and Davison (1969) discuss the issue of the topological as opposed to the functional nature of aversive stimuli. They present results from animal learning studies to indicate that the aversive stimulus must be appropriate to the sense modality of the response being punished. For example, anxiety responses conditioned via electrical aversion therapy may condition only the visual attributes of alcohol and not the sensory or gustatory ones. Since alcohol cues vary greatly depending on the drinking setting, clinical effects of treatment would be very unstable. They suggest that chemical aversion therapy may be a more appropriate treatment for alcoholism.

A major disadvantage of both chemical and electrical aversion therapies is that they are often contraindicated by medical disorders of a gastrointestinal or cardiac nature. In this respect, covert sensitization has an obvious advantage. This procedure is also much less offensive to patients and can be administered easily without the need for expensive equipment or medical supervision. For this latter reason it can also be used to provide conditioning trials in the patient's home environment. A disadvantage of the procedure is that some patients report that they are unable to clearly imagine the described images. Also due to the covert nature of the procedure, it is difficult to experimentally investigate the ongoing *process* of treatment.

Bandura (1969) and Mavisakalian and Miller (1973) suggest a combination approach utilizing chemical aversion therapy and covert sensitization. A number of pairings between nausea (induced by an emetic) and descriptions and images of nausea during covert sensitization seems to enhance the ability of the patient to imagine nausea in the absence of the emetic. This procedure may enable the alcoholic to more effectively utilize aversion therapy in a self-control manner.

Booster Conditioning Sessions

In follow-up studies of both chemical (Voegtlin, Lemere, Broz, and O'Hollaren, 1942) and electrical (Vogler, Lunde, Johnson, and Martin, 1970) aversion therapy, inclusion of booster conditioning sessions during out-patient visits appears to enhance therapeutic effects. Generally, booster treatments are positively related to length of sobriety. When one examines the data more closely, however, the positive influences of booster sessions are not as readily apparent. In studies of this influence, patients who return for follow-up visits are given booster conditioning sessions, while those who fail to return for scheduled appointments are not. These groups are then compared for abstinence at varying follow-up intervals. Certainly the longer term sobriety of the booster group may be related to the fact that they received follow-up contact and the other group did not. Such factors as reinforcement and support from the therapist may have affected the changes.

Voegtlin *et al.* (1942) present data to illustrate the influence of the patient's attitude toward follow-up treatments as a significant variable influencing outcome. This relationship is described in Table 3.2. The data clearly indicate

TABLE 3.2   The Relation of the Patient's Attitude to the Prognosis

Attitude of patient	Number	Relapsed	Abstinent	Percent of abstinence
1. Patients originally accepting reinforcement program	130	13	117	90.0
2. Patients originally refusing reinforcement program	73	21	52	71.2
3. Patients approving reinforcement but prevented from accepting	25	0	25	100.0
4. Patients originally not offered reinforcement program	57	17	40	70.1

From: Voegtlin, W. L., Lemere, F., Broz, W. R., and O'Hollaren, P. Conditioned reflex therapy of chronic alcoholism. IV. A preliminary report of the value of reinforcement. Reprinted by permission from *Quarterly Journal of Studies on Alcohol*, Vol. 2, pp. 505–11, 1941. Copyright by Journal of Studies on Alcohol, Inc., New Brunswick, N.J. 08903.

that booster (reinforcement) conditioning sessions increased the percentage of patients who remained abstinent. However, of those patients approving booster treatments but prevented from accepting them due to distance from the hospital, 100% remained abstinent at follow-up. Thus, it appears that it may not be booster treatments *per se* that affect outcome but the patient's motivation for further treatments.

To clarify this issue aversion therapy studies should be conducted using at least two follow-up conditions. Half of the patients who attend scheduled follow-up sessions would receive an "attention-placebo" treatment. This treatment could include either a supportive, reassuring talk with a therapist or a sham conditioning session, with the noxious stimuli omitted but expectancy for success high. The other half of the subjects would receive regular booster conditioning sessions at follow-up visits. These groups could be compared both with each other and with a third group of patients who did not receive either follow-up (i.e., those failing to attend scheduled sessions).

Generalization of Results

There are two major aspects to the question of generalization in reference to aversion therapy. First, do the effects of aversion therapy to one type of alcoholic beverage (e.g., bourbon) generalize to other types of alcoholic beverages (e.g., beer and wine)? Second, do the effects of aversion therapy generalize from the treatment setting to the natural environment?

Various clinical observations have been reported regarding the first question. While results are variable from one patient to another, it appears that treatment involving one beverage does not necessarily generalize to other beverages. At follow-up visits some patients report that they no longer drink the beverage that was used in the aversion sessions, but drink other kinds of alcoholic beverages. The most specific report of this phenomenon was presented by Quinn and Henbest (1967). Using a chemical aversion procedure with apomorphine, they noted that specificity of aversion therapy only to one type of alcoholic beverage is quite common. Many of their patients who relapsed were abusing a different type of alcoholic beverage than the one that had been used in the conditioning. On the basis of reports such as these, it is often recommended that a variety of beverages (beer, bourbon, scotch, gin, vodka) be included in aversion therapy sessions.

It is unfortunate that there have been no experimental studies analyzing this issue. This could be accomplished easily by using a multiple baseline design experiment in which aversion therapy using only one beverage is evaluated by allowing patients a choice of a variety of beverages via an analogue drinking task. A "taste test" measure as described in Chapter 2 would seem well adapted to such an evaluation.

Generalization from the treatment setting to the patient's natural environment is a more complex problem. Generalization of treatment effects is enhanced when the treatment environment closely resembles the natural drinking environment. Many therapists take this fact into account and conduct aversion therapy sessions in simulated bar or living room settings. No comparison has as yet been reported between treatment under these conditions and treatment administered in settings dissimilar to the patient's home environment. Other methods of improving generalization effects would include the use of aversion therapy in a self-control manner. In this regard, covert sensitization might be most useful. Another advantage of covert sensitization is that the therapist is able to simulate the natural environment quite well (at least as well as the patient can imagine it). Aversion sessions might also be conducted periodically in the patient's home or in a favorite tavern. Inclusion of relatives, friends, and drinking buddies in these aversion sessions would also increase the likelihood of generalization.

Instructions and Expectancy

The expectations a patient has about the effects of a treatment procedure appear to influence therapeutic outcome. These expectations are . . . "induced in part by the instructions given about a particular situation and partly by prior experience with similar situations" . . . (Agras, 1972, p. 19). Barlow, Leitenberg, Agras, Callahan, and Moore (1972) investigated this factor by manipulating the therapeutic instructions given to patients receiving covert sensitization. Their data suggest that repeated pairings may not always be sufficient for behavior change and that positive therapeutic instructions (stressing the likelihood of success) contribute to treatment and facilitate successful outcome. The influence of instructional set on other therapeutic techniques has been reviewed by Agras (1972).

It is unfortunate that so few aversion therapists take these factors into account. It is interesting to note that in the series of clinical reports on chemical aversion therapy by Lemere, Voegtlin, and their colleagues, instructional set was an important aspect of treatment. Patients were told never to taste or experiment with liquor again. Instructions were geared to infer that conditioning effects were "automatic" and that alcohol would produce nausea and vomiting even after treatment had been discontinued. While the specific influence of instructions in this particular series of studies is difficult to evaluate, these investigators have reported one of the best abstinence rates using chemical aversive procedures. In another study reporting an impressive abstinence rate (83%) and using verbal aversion with hypnosis, Miller (1959) actually told his patients that they would definitely experience nausea and vomiting if they attempted to drink alcohol after treatment. It is impossible to analyze other reports along these lines since the majority do not include the specific instructions given to patients.

Clinicians administering aversion therapy would be advised to provide the patient with a positive instructional set regarding both the nature of the treatment and its long-term effects. An example set of instructions for chemical aversion therapy might include the following in addition to procedural explanations:

> This treatment you will be receiving has been found to be successful in the treatment of alcoholism. It has been used for many years with numerous reports of high success rates. We feel optimistic that this treatment will be effective in your case. After treatment is completed you will probably lose your desire to drink. You may very well experience nausea and possibly vomiting when exposed to alcohol. It is very important that you never attempt to drink alcohol after this treatment is completed.

Conclusions

It is highly doubtful that refinements in precision and timing of the conditioning process in search for the perfect means of establishing a conditioned response will significantly influence success rates of traditional aversion therapies. In view of research data on the effectiveness of instructional variables on classical conditioning, any analysis of aversion therapy as an "automatic" conditioning process appears to be rather naive. For example, Bridges and Mandel (1964) found that they could produce galvanic skin responses (GSR) to a previously neutral stimulus by using either electric shock or merely by the *threat* of electrical shock. Also, after conditioning cardiac rates, Notterman, Schoenfeld, and Bresch (1952) and Chatterjee and Erickson (1962) demonstrated that such responses extinguished almost immediately when subjects were told they would receive no more shocks. Subjects who were not given such instructions took longer to extinguish when shock had been discontinued. Gringer and Lockhart (1963) also reported this relationship and found it to be independent of either number of conditioning trials or intensity of the aversive stimulus.

On the basis of such evidence, Bandura (1969) postulates that aversion therapy, rather than being a counterconditioning process, serves to activate self-stimulation mechanisms which produce aversive reactions. He further contends that . . .

> after a person has repeatedly experienced strong nausea in conjunction with alcoholic beverages the mere sight or smell of alcohol leads him to revivify his past nauseous experiences. In this conceptualization aversive reactions are, in large part, self-induced rather than automatically evoked. If the aversive self-stimulation established through counterconditioning is potent enough, a person may be able to counteract the disposition to engage in deviant behavior by symbolically reinstating nauseous reactions whenever the need arises.*

In this respect, aversion therapy provides patients with self-control devices which allow them to imaginally consequate their own behavior with aversive stimuli. Most patients who have undergone aversion therapy do not experience nausea or anxiety when confronted with alcohol. They often report, however, that they avoid drinking alcohol when confronted with it by imagining the unpleasant experiences encountered during aversion therapy sessions. In this regard, the influence of aversion therapy may be similar to that of Antabuse with some patients. Many patients maintain long periods of sobriety via Antabuse even though they have never experienced an alcohol-Antabuse reaction. They refrain from using alcohol on the basis of the *threat* of an

* From Bandura, A. *Principles of behavior modification.* New York: Holt, Rinehart and Winston, 1969.

unpleasant physiological reaction. Thus, sight of alcoholic beverages leads to self-imposed images of the negative consequences of the alcohol consumption. Patients who have undergone aversion therapy may utilize a similar self-control technique.

Clinically, then, viewing aversion therapy as a method for temporarily suppressing alcohol abuse through self-control mechanisms seems useful. Positive instructions combined with covert sensitization and chemical aversion therapy may best accomplish this goal. While alcohol abuse is being suppressed through aversion therapy, patients can be taught and reinforced for alternative modes of responding that are incompatible with excessive drinking. Development of these new behavior patterns together with the rearrangement of environmental contingencies (via relatives, friends, coworkers) so that reinforcement is provided for sobriety and punishment for abusive drinking would be expected to maintain long-term abstinence more effectively. Aversion therapy is therefore viewed as one of a variety of techniques that must be combined into a total alcoholism treatment package.

References

AGRAS, W. S. *Behavior modification: principles and clinical applications.* Boston: Little, Brown and Company, 1972, pp. 19–20.

ANANT, S. S. A note on the treatment of alcoholics by a verbal aversion technique. *Canadian Journal of Psychology*, 1967, 8, 19–22.

ANANT, S. S. Treatment of alcoholics and drug addicts by verbal aversion techniques. *International Journal of the Addictions*, 1968, 3, 381–8.

ASHEM, B. and DONNER, L. Covert sensitization with alcoholics: A controlled replication. *Behavior Research and Therapy*, 1968, 6, 7–12.

AZRIN, N. H. and HOLZ, W. C. Punishment. In W. K. Honig (Ed.) *Operant Behavior.* New York: Appleton-Century-Crofts, 1966, pp. 380–447.

BANDURA, A. *Principles of behavior modification.* New York: Holt, Rinehart, and Winston, Inc., 1969.

BARLOW, D. H. Aversive procedures. In W. S. Agras (Ed.) *Behavior modification: principles and clinical applications*, 1972, pp. 87–126.

BARLOW, D. H. and HERSEN, M. Single-case experimental designs: Uses in applied clinical research. *Archives of General Psychiatry*, 1973, 29, 319–25.

BARLOW, D. H., LEITENBERG, H. and AGRAS, W. S. Experimental control of sexual deviation through manipulation of the noxious scene in covert sensitization. *Journal of Abnormal Psychology*, 1969, 74, 596.

BARLOW, D. H., LEITENBERG, H., AGRAS, W. S., CALLAHAN, E. J. and MOORE, R. C. The contribution of therapeutic instructions to covert sensitization. *Behavior Research and Therapy*, 1972, 10, 411–15.

BLAKE, B. G. The application of behavior therapy to the treatment of alcoholism. *Behavior Research and Therapy*, 1965, 3, 75–85.

BLAKE, B. G. A follow-up of alcoholics treated by behavior therapy. *Behavior Research and Therapy*, 1967, 5, 89–94.

BRIDGES, W. and MANDEL, I. A comparison of GSR fear responses produced by threat and electric shock. *Journal of Psychiatric Research*, 1964, 2, 31–40.

CAUTELA, J. R. Treatment of compulsive behavior by covert sensitization. *Psychological Record*, 1966, 16, 33–41.

CAUTELA, J. R. The treatment of alcoholism by covert sensitization. *Psychotherapy: Theory, Research, and Practice*, 1970, 7, 86–90.

CHAPMAN, R. F., BURT, D. W. and SMITH, J. W. Electrical aversion conditioning to alcohol: individual measurement. Paper presented at the Western Psychological Association, Portland, Oregon, April, 1972.

CHATTERJEE, B. and ERICKSON, C. Cognitive factors in heart rate conditioning. *Journal of Experimental Psychology*, 1962, 64, 272–9.

CLANCY, J., VANDERHOFF, E. and CAMPBELL, P. Evaluation of an aversive technique as a treatment of alcoholism: Controlled trial with succinylcholine-induced apnea. *Quarterly Journal of Studies on Alcohol*, 1967, 28, 476–85.

DAVIDSON, R. S. and WALLACH, E. S. Shock facilitation and suppression of alcohol and coke maintained behavior. Unpublished manuscript, Veterans Administration Hospital, Miami, 1971.

DENT, J. Y. Apomorphine in the treatment of anxiety states with special reference to alcoholism. *British Journal of Inebriation*, 1934, 43, 65–9.

EDLIN, J. V., JOHNSON, R. H., HLETKO, P. and HEILBRUUN, G. The conditioned aversion treatment in chronic alcoholism (preliminary report of 100 cases). *American Journal of Psychiatry*, 1945, **101**, 806–9.

FARRAR, C. H., POWELL, B. J. and MARTIN, L. K. Punishment of alcohol consumption by apneic paralysis. *Behavior Research and Therapy*, 1968, **6**, 13–16.

FLEMING, R. The management of chronic alcoholism in England, Scandinavia, and Central Europe. *New England Journal of Medicine*, 1937, **216**, 279–89.

FRANKS, C. M. Alcohol, alcoholism, and conditioning: a review of the literature and some theoretical considerations. *Journal of Mental Science*, 1958, **104**, 14–33.

FRANKS, C. M. Behavior therapy, the principles of conditioning and the treatment of the alcoholic. *Quarterly Journal of Studies on Alcohol*, 1963, **24**, 511–29.

FRANKS, C. M. Conditioning and conditioned aversion therapies in the treatment of the alcoholic. *International Journal of the Addictions*, 1966, **1**, 61–98.

FRANKS, C. M. Alcoholism. In C. G. Costello (Ed.) *Symptoms of Psychopathology*. New York: John Wiley and Sons, Inc., 1970, pp. 448–80.

GALANT, J. S. Apomorphine treatment of the alcoholic. *Psychiatric Neurology Wschr.*, 1936, **38**, 85–9.

GRINGER, W. and LOCKHART, R. Effects of "anxiety-lessening" instructions and differential set development on the extinction of GSR. *Journal of Experimental Psychology*, 1963, **66**, 292–9.

HALLAM, R. and RACHMAN, S. Theoretical problems of aversion therapy. *Behavior Research and Therapy*, 1972, **10**, 341–53.

HALLAM, R., RACHMAN, S. and FALKOWSKI, W. Subjective, attitudinal, and physiological effects of electrical aversion therapy. *Behavior Research and Therapy*, 1972, **10**, 1–13.

HSU, J. J. Electroconditioning therapy of alcoholics. A preliminary report. *Quarterly Journal of Studies on Alcohol*, 1965, **26**, 449–59.

ICHOK, G. Conditioned reflexes and the treatment of the alcoholic. *Progress in Medicine*, Paris, 1934, **45**, 1742–5.

KANT, F. The conditioned-reflex treatment in the light of our knowledge of alcohol addiction. *Quarterly Journal of Studies on Alcohol*, 1944, **5**, 371–7.

KANTOROVICH, N. V. An attempt at associative reflex therapy in alcoholism. *Novoye v Reflekologoii i Fiziologii Neronoy Sistemy*, 1929, **3**, 436 (*Psychological Abstracts*, 1930, No. 4282).

KO, S. In Voegtlin, W. L. and Lemere, F. The treatment of alcohol addiction: a review of the literature. *Quarterly Journal of Studies on Alcohol*, 1942, **2**, 717–803.

LEMERE, F. and VOEGTLIN, W. L. An evaluation of the aversion treatment of alcoholism. *Quarterly Journal of Studies on Alcohol*, 1950, **11**, 199–204.

LEMERE, F., VOEGTLIN, W. L., BROZ, W. R., O'HOLLAREN, P. and TUPPER, W. E. Conditioned reflex treatment of chronic alcoholism: VII technic. *Diseases of the Nervous System*, 1942, **3**, 243–7.

LOVIBOND, S. H. Aversive control of behavior. *Behavior Therapy*, 1970, **1**, 80–91.

MacCULLOCH, M. J., FELDMAN, M. P., ORFORD, J. F. and MacCULLOCH, M. L. Anticipatory avoidance learning in the treatment of alcoholism: a record of therapeutic failure. *Behavior Research and Therapy*, 1966, **4**, 187–96.

MADILL, M. F., CAMPBELL, D., LAVERTY, S. G., SANDERSON, R. E. and VANDERWATER, S. L. Aversion treatment of alcoholics by succinylcholine-induced apneic paralysis. *Quarterly Journal of Studies on Alcohol*, 1966, **27**, 483–509.

MARKOVINKOV, A. Therapy by combination of persuasion with development of conditioned reflex of vomiting after swallowing alcohol. *Soviet Vrach Gazett*, 1934, 807–11.

MARTIMOR, E. and MAILLEFER, J. In Voegtlin, W. L. and Lemere, F. The treatment of alcohol addiction: a review of the literature. *Quarterly Journal of Studies on Alcohol*, 1942, **2**, 717–803.

MAVISAKALIAN, M. and MILLER, P. M. Apomorphine-chemical aversion therapy with alcoholics. Unpublished data. Veterans Administration Center, Jackson, Mississippi, 1973.

MILLER, E. C., DVORAK, B. A. and TURNER, D. W. A method of creating aversion to alcohol by reflex conditioning in a group setting. *Quarterly Journal of Studies on Alcohol*, 1960, **21**, 424–31.

MILLER, M. M. Treatment of chronic alcoholism by hypnotic aversion. *Journal of the American Medical Association*, 1959, **171**, 1492.

MILLER, P. M. and HERSEN, M. A quantitative measurement system for alcoholism treatment and research. Paper presented at Association for the Advancement of Behavior Therapy, New York, 1972.

MILLER, P. M. and HERSEN, M. Quantitative changes in alcohol consumption as a function of electrical aversion conditioning. *Journal of Clinical Psychology*, 1972, **28**, 590–3.

MILLER, P. M., HERSEN, M., EISLER, R. M. and HEMPHILL, D. P. Electrical aversion therapy with alcoholics: an analogue study. *Behavior Research and Therapy*, 1973, **11**, 491–8.

MOROSKO, T. E. and BAER, P. E. Avoidance conditioning of alcoholics. In R. Ulrich, T. Stachnich, and J. Mabry (Eds.) *Control of Human Behavior*. Glenview, Illinois: Scott, Foresman, and Co., 1970, pp. 170–6.

NOTTERMAN, J., SCHOENFELD, W. and BERSH, P. Conditioned heart rate responses in human beings during experimental anxiety. *Journal of Comparative and Psychological Psychology*, 1952, **45**, 1–8.

QUINN, J. T. and HENBEST, R. Partial failure of generalization in alcoholics following aversion therapy. *Quarterly Journal of Studies on Alcohol*, 1967, **28**, 70–5.

RACHMAN, S. and TEASDALE, J. *Aversion therapy and behavior disorders: an analysis.* Coral Gables, Florida: University of Miami Press, 1969.

RAYMOND, M. J. The treatment of addiction by aversion conditioning with apomorphine. *Behavior Research and Therapy*, 1964, **1**, 287–91.

SANDERSON, R. E., CAMPBELL, D. and LAVERTY, S. G. An investigation of a new aversive conditioning treatment for alcoholism. *Quarterly Journal of Studies on Alcohol*, 1963, **24**, 261–75.

SHANAHAN, W. M. and HORNICK, E. J. Aversion treatment of alcoholism. *Hawaii Medical Journal*, 1946, **6**, 19–21.

SLUCHEVSKY, I. F. and FRIKEN. In Voegtlin, W. L. and Lemere, F. The treatment of alcohol addiction: a review of the literature. *Quarterly Journal of Studies on Alcohol*, 1942, **2**, 717–803.

STREL'CHUK, I. V. New contemporary methods of treating patients with alcoholism. *Soviet Medicine*, 1957, **21**, 26–33.

THIMANN, J. Conditioned reflex treatment of alcoholism. II. The risks of its application, its indications, contraindications, and psychotherapeutic aspects. *New England Journal of Medicine*, 1949, **241**, 406–10.

VOEGTLIN, W. L. The treatment of alcoholism by establishing a conditioned reflex. *American Journal of Medical Science*, 1940, **199**, 802–9.

VOEGTLIN, W. L. Conditioned reflex therapy of chronic alcoholism: ten years' experience with the method. *Rocky Mountain Medical Journal*, 1947, **44**, 807–11.

VOEGTLIN, W. L. and BROZ, W. R. The conditioned reflex treatment of chronic alcoholism: X. An analysis of 3,125 admissions over a period of ten and a half years. *Annals of Internal Medicine*, 1949, **30**, 580–97.

VOEGTLIN, W. L., LEMERE, F., BROZ, W. R. and O'HOLLAREN, P. Conditioned reflex therapy of alcoholic addiction: VI. Follow-up report of 1,042 cases. *American Journal of Medical Science*, 1942, **203**, 525–8.

VOGLER, R. E., LUNDE, S. E., JOHNSON, G. R. and MARTIN, P. L. Electrical aversion conditioning with chronic alcoholics. *Journal of Consulting and Clinical Psychology*, 1970, **34**, 302–7.

WALLERSTEIN, R. S. (Ed.) *Hospital treatment of alcoholism: a comparative, experimental study*. New York: Basic Books, 1957.

WILSON, G. T. Aversive control of drinking by chronic alcoholics in a controlled laboratory setting. Paper presented at Association for Advancement of Behavior Therapy, Miami, 1973.

WILSON, G. T. and DAVISON, G. C. Aversion techniques in behavior therapy: some theoretical and metatheoretical considerations. *Journal of Consulting and Clinical Psychology*, 1969, 33, 327.

WOLPE, J. *The practice of behavior therapy.* New York: Pergamon Press, 1973.

YATES, A. J. *Behavior therapy.* New York: John Wiley & Sons, 1970.

ZVONIKOV, M. Z. A modification of the technique of conducting conditioned reflex apomorphine and suggestive therapy of alcoholism. *Zhurnal Nevropatologii i Psikhiatrii*, 1968, 68, 596.

CHAPTER 4

Teaching Alternative Behaviors: Assertiveness, Relaxation, Self-Control

Introduction

A major goal in the behavioral treatment of alcohol abuse consists of teaching patterns that are incompatible with excessive drinking. In situations which serve as cues for abusive drinking, the alcoholic must develop more appropriate alternative responses. Thus, if binges are preceded by situations in which he feels angry but does not express this feeling appropriately, then an alternative to drinking would be to respond more openly and assertively. If anxiety in response to stressful situations precipitates drinking, the client might be taught a different emotional response, namely, relaxation. In addition, alcoholics might be taught alternatives to the entire chain of events that lead up to excessive drinking. Instead of socializing with heavy drinking friends, for example, he might lessen the likelihood of his own drinking by avoiding these "friends" and socializing with social drinkers and/or abstainers.

These new ways of responding not only allow the individual to avoid excessive drinking but also to obtain more satisfaction from a sober life on the basis of utilizing more adaptive coping skills. Thus, prescribing Antabuse, administering aversion therapy, and/or providing direct environmental punishment to suppress excessive drinking is an insufficient treatment. Without providing new behavior patterns, prognosis for success is poor.

This therapeutic aim has the additional advantage of providing the individual, himself, with *control* over his drinking patterns and his life in general. Other behavioral techniques, particularly the aversion therapies and operant approaches, rely on external control so that others are "doing something" to the client to alter his behavior. In some cases such control is perceived as demeaning by the individual and he tends to resist therapeutic endeavors of this nature. Also, since much of his problem behavior may occur in the absence of a "controlling other", long-term therapeutic success probably depends on the eventual development of self-control.

The issue of internal versus external control of one's behavior is an interesting theoretical and empirical question (Thoresen and Mahoney, 1974). The alcoholic's "lack of motivation to change" along with chronic relapses to drinking

77

is, by definition, lack of internal control of his behavior. Thus, initial stages of treatment must often involve external control to initiate behavior changes. This might include (1) coercion by the law, family or employer to initiate the treatment process, (2) a planned reinforcement program to induce Antabuse taking, and/or (3) systematic rewards and punishment from the environment to change behavior (see chapter on operant approaches). The ultimate and optimum goal is to very gradually replace external control and "motivation" with internal control. That is, the patient, himself, assumes prime responsibility for his behavior.

The types of behaviors that clients can use in this manner are varied. However, three major alternative responses have been the focus of behavioral alcoholism treatment. These are assertiveness, relaxation, and self-management skills.

Assertive Training

Assertive behavior refers to the ability to appropriately express personal rights and feelings (both positive and negative) in the presence of others (Hersen, Eisler, and Miller, 1973). This involves a wide variety of responses including the expression of differences of opinion, anger, love and affection, negative replies to unreasonable requests by others, and dissatisfaction with infringement of one's rights. Deficits in this behavior often serve as a source of interpersonal problems which in turn engender a variety of maladaptive responses (e.g., depression, social withdrawal, chronic resentment, alcohol and drug abuse, social phobias). They become clinically significant in the treatment of alcoholism since an individual's inability to handle situations requiring assertive behavior often sets the occasion for episodes of excessive drinking.

Rimm and Masters (1974) have delineated several ways in which deficits in assertive behavior can produce stress. These will be described here in the context of the alcoholic. First, certain interpersonal situations may elicit severe anxiety which in turn inhibits assertive responding. In this case the individual knows *how* to respond appropriately but is unable to do so. Thus, an alcoholic may be so intimidated by his overbearing employer that his anxiety prevents him from requesting a well-deserved raise. He may find that after consuming a few alcoholic beverages his anxiety is lessened to the point that he is able to respond as he would like to. However, under the influence of alcohol his behavior is often disrupted and he subsequently responds inappropriately. Often his behavior is overreactive under these circumstances and he may become hostile and demanding rather than appropriately assertive.

Anxiety in interpersonal situations also frequently leads to avoidance responses. Since the individual is unable to respond to certain interpersonal encounters he may begin to isolate himself from all social interactions. Avoidance can be accomplished physically or psychologically through the use of alcohol. By socially isolating himself he is avoiding situations which may be potentially satisfying and thus narrows the range of social reinforcements available to him.

Some individuals may exhibit deficits in assertive behavior, not because of anxiety but because of poor social skills. They have not developed skills appropriate to social interactions. Inappropriate responses include a variety of reactions that are either too passive or too aggressive. This may be true both in regard to positive assertiveness in which one individual expresses a statement of love, affection, or compliment to another or negative assertiveness in which one's rights are being infringed upon. Two example stimulus situations are presented below.

Example 1.
A husband comes home from work late one evening and is in a hurry to get ready for an important club meeting. His wife has supper on the table and has a change of clothes ready for him. She greets her husband with an affectionate hug and says: "I knew you'd be in a hurry tonight, dear, so I got everything ready."

An appropriate assertive response might be one in which the husband returns his wife's affection and responds with "Gee, honey, I really appreciate what you've done. You're a great wife. Leave the dishes and I'll wash them after I get home from the meeting."

Since the wife went to so much trouble, an inappropriate response might be one in which he simply smiles and says "Thanks" in a very unenthusiastic manner. In the extreme he may say nothing or even provide a negative comment such as "It's about time you did something around this house." Many of these inappropriate responses are related to an insensitivity to the reciprocal nature of interpersonal relationships. Perhaps this is due to lack of appropriate models for this behavior earlier in life or insufficient feedback from others.

Example 2.
Ms. Brown is at a weekly meeting of her office staff. An important issue affecting all of the employees is being discussed. A number of the more assertive management level individuals are strongly presenting and elaborating their position. Ms. Brown strongly disagrees with their ideas since the position they are taking may negatively affect her status in the company. Just before a vote on the matter, the presiding member of the meeting says "Would any one else like to express an opinion on this matter?"

Even though Ms. Brown disagrees strongly she may be unable to express her true feelings on the matter. At times the individual may lack the verbal skills necessary to forcefully get a point across.

Assertive Deficits and Alcohol Consumption

Clinically, it is often observed that interpersonal situations that require assertive responding often set the occasion for a drinking episode. While most of the evidence for the relationship between these situations and excessive drinking is based upon anecdotal information, Miller, Hersen, Eisler, and Hilsman (1974) directly examined the influence of exposure to interpersonal situations requiring assertiveness and excessive drinking. Eight alcoholics and eight social drinkers matched on age and education were each exposed to two experimental conditions prior to responding on an alcohol drinking task. The first condition constituted a social stress phase in which subjects were individually exposed to a series of staged interpersonal encounters requiring assertive behaviors. An example scene follows:

> Narration: You take your car to a service station to have a new tire put on. The mechanic tells you that your car will be ready in an hour. When you return to the station you find that instead of one new tire they have replaced two tires and have given your car a major tune-up. The cashier says:
>
> Prompt: "You owe us $150.00. Will that be cash or charge?"

After the prompt, delivered by one of the experimenters, the subject was instructed to respond as he normally would. His reply was countered with an antagonistic reply from the role model. During the second or no-stress condition the experimenters spent an equal amount of time with the subject discussing favorite hobbies and spare-time activities. Pulse rates were taken before and after the stress and no-stress conditions. Immediately subsequent to the experimental and control conditions, subjects' drinking was measured via 10 minutes of operant responding whereby lever pressing earned alcohol reinforcement on an FR-50 schedule. The results indicated that the alcoholics significantly increased their drinking following stress conditions while social drinkers did not. In fact, social drinkers tended to decrease their consumption slightly following stress conditions. In terms of autonomic arousal, both groups were equally stressed.

The authors noted that these data support the contention that alcoholics do not seem to have a lower tolerance for socially stressful encounters (Coppersmith and Woodrow, 1967). Rather, the alcoholic has learned to respond to these situations by means of excessive alcohol consumption, whereas the social drinker has learned more adaptive responses (e.g., being appropriately assertive).

In a similar analysis, Marlatt and Kosturn (1973) deliberately angered and annoyed heavy drinking college students to examine effects on drinking. Subjects were randomly assigned to three conditions: insult, insult with opportunity to retaliate; no-insult and no retaliation. In the insult condition subjects were annoyed and criticized while working an anagram task. Retaliation consisted of the opportunity to deliver electric shocks (supposedly as part of a learning experiment) to the confederate subject who initially delivered the insults. Alcohol consumption was assessed via a taste rating task (Marlatt, Demming, and Reid, 1973) in which subjects were requested to rate the tastes of three different wines. Subjects who were angered with no opportunity to retaliate demonstrated the greatest alcohol consumption. Subjects who were allowed to retaliate, however, drank significantly less than the insult or the control group. Thus, exposure to anger-provoking situations that require assertive responding led to excessive drinking. One might infer from this study that retaliation in real life in the form of assertiveness would also decrease the likelihood of excessive drinking.

In a rather detailed descriptive analysis of both alcoholics and non-alcoholics, Eisler, Hersen, Miller, and Blanchard (1975) examined both positive and negative assertiveness via self-report measures and direct behavioral observations. On self-report measures of assertiveness alcoholics rated themselves as being significantly more assertive than non-alcoholic psychiatric patients (excluding psychotic diagnoses). On videotaped behavioral ratings of responses to role played situations, however, there were no significant differences between the alcoholics and non-alcoholics. Both groups were equally low in assertiveness. Thus alcoholics are more likely to perceive themselves as being more assertive than they actually are. In addition, alcoholics had less difficulty in being positively assertive (e.g., giving compliments) than in being negatively assertive (e.g., disagreeing). Finally, the less assertive an alcoholic was behaviorally, the more alcohol he consumed on an analogue drinking task. That is, a statistically significant negative correlation (0.63) was obtained between negative assertiveness and alcohol consumption.

Thus, this evidence suggests that alcoholics may have difficulty in dealing with certain assertive situations, especially those in which negative emotions (e.g., anger) are being expressed. Furthermore, the lack of ability in this area seems directly related to excessive consumption of alcohol.

Definition and Assessment of Assertiveness

Since comprehensive reviews on the definition and assessment of assertive behavior together with techniques of assertive training are available (Alberti and Emmons, 1974; Hersen, Eisler, and Miller, 1973), only a brief discussion of these areas will be necessary here. Although the components of assertive behavior have recently been specified (Eisler, Miller and Hersen, 1973), assertiveness is not easily defined since it is highly situation specific and at times qualitative in nature. In essence, the appropriateness of an individual's response to a provoking situation may vary greatly depending on the circumstances. Alberti and Emmons (1974) note that assertiveness might be *inappropriate* when: (a) you are wrong,

(b) you are dealing with an overly sensitive individual, (c) the person who has provoked your response has already apologized, and (d) when understanding rather than assertiveness is required. Lazarus (1973) discusses this latter issue in the context of the case of a rude sales person. Rather than asserting one's rights about being waited on more courteously, an alternative and at times more appropriate response might be, "You seem to be having a difficult day. Is there anything that I can do to help?" Indeed, this may lead to more courtesy and cooperation from the sales person than would have resulted from an "assertive" response.

Eisler, Miller, and Hersen (1973) and Eisler, Hersen, and Miller (1974) have illustrated an objective means of behaviorally defining and assessing assertiveness. They engage the client in a series of role played interpersonal situations requiring assertive responses (i.e., either the expression of negative feelings, a differing opinion, personal rights, or positive and complimentary feelings). Some of these situations are standard while some are idiosyncratic and derived from life problems of the individual client. Responses are videotaped and subsequently rated on various verbal (e.g., affect, speech duration, loudness) and nonverbal (e.g., eye contact, facial expressions) components. This allows for a detailed assessment of the client's specific deficits in various situations. Eisler, Hersen, Miller, and Blanchard (1975) stress the importance of role playing a wide range of interpersonal situations (e.g., those including males versus females, familiar versus unfamiliar role models, and positive versus negative assertiveness). In this sense, assertiveness is not a global trait but varies greatly within each individual depending on the situation.

An example scene that might be role-played would be:

Situation: You've been working very diligently on a special project that must be completed by the end of the day. Your co-workers, who are supposed to be helping you, have been standing around talking to one another about a football game for almost an hour. As you get up from your desk to get a cup of coffee your supervisor comes over to you and says . . .

Prompt from role model: "Say, stop fooling around and get this job done."

The ways in which the client responds allows the therapist to assess his assertiveness.

Other means of evaluating assertive behavior include (a) self-report questionnaires and (b) reports from relatives and/or friends. The Wolpe and Lazarus Assertiveness Questionnaire (Wolpe and Lazarus, 1966) and the Rathus Assertiveness Scale (Rathus, 1973) consist of a series of questions regarding ways in which a client usually responds to a variety of situations calling for assertive behavior. Relatives, friends, co-workers, bosses can be trained to record the client's response to particular day-to-day situations.

Techniques of Assertive Training

The techniques and procedures of assertive training have been investigated under controlled conditions in numerous studies. Most experimental studies have indicated that (a) the components of assertive behavior (e.g., eye contact, voice inflections, gestures, etc.) must be taught one at a time (Eisler, Hersen, and Miller, 1974) and (b) therapist modeling and instructions together with behavioral rehearsal are the most effective techniques to teach assertiveness (Hersen, Eisler, Miller, Johnson, and Pinkston, 1973).

In a well-written and easily readable manual designed for both professionals and laymen alike, Alberti and Emmons (1974) present a step-by-step analysis of the process of assertive training. Their book provides a useful manual including rationale of assertiveness and numerous examples and practice situations which can be used as an adjunct to treatment. They present seven steps in the assertive training process similar to the following:

1. Identify the situation in which the client is deficient.
2. Write out the scene.
3. Present the situation for covert rehearsal of correct responding.
4. Model appropriate assertiveness.
5. Analyze the correct assertive reponse for the client.
6. Repeat step 3.
7. Rehearse again.
8. Go over performance.
9. Repeat steps 4 through 8 if necessary.
10. Encourage the client to test the new response in the real situation.
11. Review performance.

In the actual clinical situation the training process is not always as systematic as this list might imply. Frequently, the client is quite hesitant to engage in assertive behaviors for fear of hurting other's feelings or eliciting anger from them. A few initial sessions are required to alleviate the client's anxiety by describing in detail the rationale of assertive training, particularly in reference to the differences between *assertiveness* and *aggressiveness*. It is also helpful to illustrate the specific relationship between the client's lack of assertiveness and drinking episodes. In many instances cognitive and attitudinal changes along these lines occur subsequent to the acquisition and successful use of assertiveness.

While the behavioral components of assertiveness are learned quickly, generalization of this newly acquired response pattern to the natural environment is a more complex problem. Generalization must be programmed as part of therapy and cannot be left to chance. One method of accomplishing this is through frequent outpatient follow-up sessions in which (a) the client reports on specific recent instances in which he was or should have been assertive, (b) feedback is provided on the appropriateness of the client's response and possible alternatives, (c) training is provided on those components of assertiveness which are in need of improvement, and (d) responses to situations which are likely to occur before the next appointment are rehearsed. In addition the client must be taught many of the subtleties of assertiveness including the ability to judge when it is appropriate. Newly trained clients are often too assertive in many situations. As they become more adept at this behavior they are able to utilize a variety of alternative assertive responses based upon the nature of the situation they are confronted with. The ultimate goal, then, is to teach not the specific skill of assertiveness, but rather more general social-interactional skills.

Applications to Alcoholics

Unfortunately, few systematic analyses of the effects of assertive training with alcoholics are available. In a recent study Martorano (1974) evaluated the effects of assertive training on four chronic Skid Row alcoholics in a controlled laboratory atmosphere. While the training period was quite short (only 6 days), subjects rated themselves as being less tense and aggressive, more active, more socially attractive, more friendly and vigorous as a result of assertive training. Once subjects were allowed to consume alcohol under these conditions, however, they were rated by the staff as being more angry, tense, depressed, confused, less friendly and active. Subjects tended to drink to higher blood/alcohol levels *after* assertive training. The author suggests that while assertive training may be beneficial to an alcoholic during periods of sobriety, it may lead to more negative behavior during drinking episodes.

Unfortunately, two factors seriously limit the conclusions of this study. First, Skid Row individuals are a special population of alcoholics and probably in need of more comprehensive treatments to significantly modify their behavior. Secondly, 6 days of assertive training seem far too little to change long-standing ways of dealing with interpersonal situations. Clinically, during initial stages of assertive training the client's behavior often becomes disrupted and at times overly aggressive until he learns the subtleties of assertiveness and the judgement involved in how and when to use it appropriately. This may explain why drinking actually increased subsequent to assertive training. In spite of the limitations, however, the study does illustrate some immediate benefits of assertive training during sobriety. Studies using pre-post measures of responses to specific assertive situations may provide a more clear-cut analysis of the effects of this treatment.

Two case studies by Eisler, Miller, and Hersen (1973) and Eisler, Hersen, and Miller (1974) provide illustrative examples of this procedure. The former study involved a marital couple and is described later in Chapter 6. Briefly, it was found that increased assertiveness on the part of an alcoholic husband led to decreases in drinking behavior and modifications in his marital interactions.

In the second case, Eisler, Hersen, and Miller (1974) described the treatment of a 34-year-old chronic alcoholic whose drinking episodes were precipitated by stressful situations related to his job as a motel manager. These included:

(1) his inability to confront subordinates regarding their inadequate job performance,
(2) his tendency to comply with unreasonable requests issued by his employer, the motel owner,
(3) his inability to refuse unnecessary purchases from salesmen, and
(4) his inability to effectively handle unreasonable complaints from motel guests.

Six interpersonal encounters relating to these deficit behaviors were constructed and role-played before and after treatment as an index of improvement.

Analysis of the pre-treatment videotape revealed that the patient responded in a generally passive, compliant manner. He failed to look at the role model when delivering his response, sounded very apologetic and uncertain, and failed to ask the other person in these situations to modify his or her behavior. Using instructions and videotape feedback the patient was trained to increase his eye contact, decrease compliance, increase assertive affect, and increase behavioral requests. A total of ninety-six behavioral rehearsals were used over a series of training sessions. In order to investigate generalization of the results the patient was trained on scenes that were different from those that were being evaluated. Significant increases were observed in duration of eye contact, quality of his affect, frequency of his requesting a change in behavior from the role model, and in ratings of his overall assertiveness. Frequency of compliance decreased drastically so that the patient did not comply in any scene. Unfortunately this patient failed to report for continued treatment sessions and no follow-up was obtained.

Relaxation Training and Systematic Desensitization

The relationship between physiological stress and alcohol abuse is an extremely complex one that has yet to be delineated on the basis of present experimental information (Allman, Taylor, and Nathan, 1972; Higgins and Marlatt, 1974; Miller, Hersen, Eisler, and Hilsman, 1974). Some alcoholics, possibly the younger, less chronic ones, may drink excessively in an attempt to relieve tension and anxiety. Using the Fear Survey Schedule developed by Wolpe and Lazarus (1966), Wisocki (1969) found that alcoholics subjectively report anxiety in relation to anger, failure, making mistakes, feeling disapproved of, and feeling rejected. In turn, they report that these emotional states serve as cues which typically elicit excessive drinking.

Relaxation training and systematic desensitization have been used to provide the alcoholic with an alternative response to anxiety producing events. Training patients with anxiety problems in deep muscle relaxation is not new (Jacobson, 1938). Relaxation training involves a process whereby, over a series of sessions, the client is taught complete muscular and cognitive relaxation. Muscle groups (e.g., facial muscles, biceps, triceps, back and neck muscles, leg muscles) are individually tensed and then gradually relaxed. Suggestion, encouragement, and verbal reinforcement are used by the therapist to foster the notion that the client is able to control and relax his muscles as much as he wants. Concomitantly, the client is asked to imagine either a specific cue word such as "relax" or "calm" or to imagine a pleasant scene described by the therapist. Clients are then urged to practice this relaxation at home and to use it to avoid or suppress tension and anxiety.

As discussed earlier, Blake (1967) examined the therapeutic efficacy of combining electrical aversion therapy with relaxation training. Relaxation training lasted up to twenty-eight sessions and reportedly resulted in an ability to control tenseness, enabling many patients to discontinue their tranquilizing medication. Apparently, these patients were taught to use relaxation in a self-control manner to deal with stress in their environment. As noted earlier, this combined technique resulted in a higher rate of abstinence (46%) than the use of electrical aversion therapy alone (23%).

Nathan (in press) describes some interesting investigations by Steffen (1974) on the relationship between relaxation and drinking behavior. Using a crossover design study a total of four subjects were exposed to the following conditions: free access drinking period (12 days), electromyographically induced relaxation training or an attention placebo condition (6 days), free access drinking period (4 days). Measures accumulated throughout the study included blood/alcohol concentrations, electromyographic tension levels from the frontalis muscle, and subjective reports of anxiety. Relaxation training resulted in decreased blood/alcohol levels (i.e., less drinking), lower muscle tension levels, and less subjective anxiety. In addition, increasing blood/alcohol levels were associated with increased muscle tension as measured physiologically but with decreased subjective reports of anxiety. Thus, as the alcoholic drinks to excess he is reporting more relaxation even though he is physiologically more tense.

More typically, however, relaxation training is not used alone but as part of the procedure of systematic desensitization. Systematic desensitization (Wolpe, 1973) consists of associating anxiety producing situations, either imaginally or in *vivo,* with relaxation. Treatment is guided by a list of anxiety producing situations, graded in hierarchical order from least to most anxiety provoking. Each situation is then associated with relaxation imaginally or *in vivo* repeatedly until the client can experience the situation with little or no discomfort.

Although few reports of the use of the technique with alcoholics are available, Kraft (1969) and Kraft and Al-Issa (1967, 1968) have reported a number of successful case studies. Relaxation was initially induced by hypnosis or methohexitone sodium. Hierarchies involved social settings with increasing numbers of people. Out of eight young alcoholic patients treated, all were reported to be improved or to be drinking socially in moderation.

In more controlled experimentation, Lanyon, Primo, Terrell, and Wener (1972) compared the effects of "interpersonal aversion": combined with systematic desensitization, "interpersonal aversion": alone, and a group discussion condition on 21 Skid Row alcoholics. Interpersonal aversion consisted of abusive confrontation by two therapists and observation of videotaped self-deprecating statements by the patient himself. Results indicated that 71% of the aversion-desensitization patients remained abstinent at a 9-month follow-up as compared to 14% in the aversion alone group and 25% in the discussion group. The fact that follow-up data were accumulated by mail with only some of the original patients responding seriously limits the conclusions of this study. As with Blake's (1967) results with an aversion-relaxation combination, however, there is a trend for systematic desensitization to add to treatment effects.

Self-Management Behaviors

Another set of behaviors that serve as alternatives to excessive drinking are incorporated under the general heading of self-control or self-management techniques. In essence, these are responses made by the alcoholic that decrease the likelihood of his excessive drinking. They do not merely serve as alternatives to alcohol abuse since they often occur either before or after the time during which drinking is likely or actually occurs. For example, Thoresen and Mahoney (1974) note that by taking Antabuse each day the alcoholic has exhibited self-control over his environment so that he or she has prearranged the consequences of alcohol consumption.

According to Goldfried and Merbaum (1973) self-control is "a process through which an individual becomes the principle agent in guiding, directing, and regulating those features of his own behavior that might eventually lead to desired positive consequences".* While a number of self-management strategies

* From Goldfried, M. R. and Merbaum, M. (Eds.) *Behavior change through self-control*, p. 11. Holt, Rinehart and Winston, 1973.

have been developed, two basic forms are *stimulus control* and *behavioral programming* (Thoresen and Mahoney, 1974).

Stimulus control involves rearranging environmental cues or sequences to decrease the probability of one's drinking. Let us assume that an alcoholic businessman's excessive drinking occurs most frequently in the time interval between the end of his work day and the evening meal. On the basis of his past behavior he is much less likely to drink at work during the daytime or after he has eaten his evening meal. His typical pattern is to stop in a bar on the way home, have four or five drinks, and on his arrival home, prior to dinner, have four or five more. Two stimulus control maneuvers he might use would be to (1) never carry money with him on his way home from work, and (2) arrange to have his evening meal the minute he arrives home from work.

The author treated a 49-year-old traveling salesman who only drank to excess when he was away from home on business trips. These trips often precipitated drinking binges that lasted several days. This pattern had resulted in severe marital difficulties and the threat of job loss. A functional analysis of his behavior revealed that excessive drinking occurred most frequently (1) when he was alone in his motel room during the time he arrived in the town in the afternoon until the evening or the next morning when he would call on his customers and (2) when he was with a customer or group of customers at dinner and they were ordering drinks and encouraging him to do the same. The client agreed to the following self-control strategies:

(1) He was to arrange his schedule so that he would arrive for a business meeting very close to the time that the meeting was scheduled. Thus, if the meeting was in the morning, he was to arrive early that morning rather than the previous evening. Since much of his traveling was within a statewide area, he could arrange to awake early and drive to his destination.

(2) Whenever possible he was to conclude his business in one day and return home that same evening.

(3) Whenever possible he was to arrange to excuse himself from cocktail gatherings on the basis of further work or meetings.

(4) When in a bar or restaurant with business customers who would be ordering alcoholic beverages, he was to always order first and was to order coffee or a Coke. The client reported that when others with him ordered alcoholic beverages before he had a chance to order, he was more likely to order one also.

(5) He was to practice (with the aid of the therapist) and use various prepared verbal statements in response to questions regarding his ordering of non-alcoholic beverages or encouragement to order an alcoholic beverage.

Through modeling and behavioral rehearsal with the therapist the client acquired a repertoire of such statements as "No thanks. My doctor advises me against it", or "I don't believe so. I have to watch my weight." With some customers that the client knew well and felt comfortable with he was less vague and would say "I'd better not have one. I have a tendency to overdo it and I'm trying to control my drinking."

In relation to this final point, Mertens (1964) discusses the self-control advantages of an individual making public the fact that he is an alcoholic and is not able to drink. Once he has made this statement he sets the occasion for negative social consequences if he does drink. Kanfer, Cox, Griener, and Karoly (1974) have demonstrated experimentally that individuals are much more likely to abide by an agreement to change their own behavior if the conditions of that agreement are made public.

Abusive drinkers may also lessen the likelihood of drinking by:

(1) Keeping liquor supplies low or inaccessible.
(2) Scheduling specific activities such a special work project, reading the newspaper, playing with the children, or going for a walk at times when drinking is most likely.
(3) Breaking up chains of behavior that set the occasion for excessive drinking by rescheduling daily activities.
(4) Socializing with abstainers or moderate social drinkers.

When alcohol is inaccessible the chain of behavior necessary to obtain it is lengthened and the individual is less likely to drink. In dealing with a 55-year-old unmarried chronic alcoholic, the author utilized such a procedure. The client's pattern was to work for a week or two to save enough money for a binge and then stay drunk for 2 to 3 weeks. He usually ran out of money quickly and would then use money he had deposited in a local bank that he had saved from pension checks. Since accessible money set the occasion for binges, the client agreed to deposit all of his pension into a bank that was located in a small town 20 miles from the city in which he was living. He also deposited it into an account that required 90 days' notice for a withdrawal. Money he earned through working was also deposited into this account directly by his employer. He kept enough money with him for food, rent, and daily living expenses. This system made it very difficult for the client to go on a long, drinking binge. Although he continues to drink, he usually runs out of funds quickly (in 1 or 2 days) and terminates his drinking.

This same technique can be quite effective when controlled, social drinking as opposed to abstinence is the treatment goal. An analogous approach is observed in the treatment of obesity using behavioral approaches (Stunkard, 1972). Since overweight individuals eat in a wide variety of situations (watching television, standing up, sitting down, etc.) each of these situations serves as a stimulus cue for eating. Treatment involves narrowing the range of cues that are associated with eating so that more specific events such as time since last meal, sitting at the kitchen table, or sitting in a restaurant lead to eating but other cues do not.

In relation to excessive drinking, Miller, Hersen, Eisler, Epstein, and Wooten (1974) demonstrated that the drinking of social drinkers is associated with highly specific cues (bottles of alcohol, low lighting in a bar atmosphere, cocktail parties) but that alcoholics' drinking is cued by a variety of non-alcohol related cues such as social isolation or boredom. In order to gain increased control over drinking the individual would be advised to drink only in specified locations. He could drink at parties, in a bar, with his family at home but never in his car, garage, or at work. He might also be asked to agree to drink only when others are present or only between the hours of 5 p.m. and 10 p.m. In order to promote controlled drinking at a party he might always:

(1) Mix his own drink
(2) Always use a shot glass to measure alcohol
(3) Mix weak drinks
(4) Take small sips
(5) Fix himself a non-alcohol beverage for the first drink
(6) Eat a meal before drinking will occur
(7) Record and chart number of drinks consumed

Ultimate Aversive Consequences

In their behavioral treatment of obesity, Ferster, Nurnberger, and Levitt (1962) discuss the concept of the "ultimate aversive consequences" of a behavior and how they can be used in a self-control manner. For the alcoholic, these consequences might include a hangover, loss of family or loss of employment. Unfortunately, behavior is controlled by immediate aversive consequences and these long-range ones occur too long after drinking behavior *per se* to affect its frequency and/or amount. One method of using these factors to an advantage is to request the client to list (1) those aversive consequences that will occur if he continues excessive drinking and (2) positive consequences which would result from his abstinence or moderate drinking. Table 4.1 illustrates such lists derived from several cases.

The client is requested to write these consequences on an index card and read them to himself whenever he feels a "need" for a drink. Vividly picturing these consequences along with their accompanying emotions (as is the case of covert sensitization) enhances the self-controlling power of these factors. At times, clients may be advised to read these lists at specified times during the day whether or not they want a drink.

TABLE 4.1   Consequences of Behavior as Self-Control Techniques

Aversive consequences of alcohol abuse	Positive consequences for abstinence or moderate drinking
1. Loss of spouse and children	1. More satisfying family life
2. Loss of employment	2. Children and spouse proud
3. Loss of friends	3. Possible promotion at work
4. Cirrhosis of liver	4. Good health — feeling well physically
5. Confinement in State Hospital	5. Recognition and approval of others
6. Death due to automobile accident while intoxicated	6. Feelings of accomplishment
7. Causing the death of another while driving in an intoxicated state	

In one of the few applications of this approach with alcoholics, Mertens (1964) described an operant learning approach aimed at increasing self-control and promoting behaviors which are incompatible with alcohol abuse. State hospital alcoholics attended classroom sessions in which a learning approach to drinking behavior was discussed. Two manuals (Mertens and Fuller, 1964a, 1964b) — one for the therapist and one for the patient — aided in the dissemination of this information. In order to develop self-control, patients were encouraged to rearrange alcohol cues in the environment by making them less prominent and to utilize thoughts of ultimate aversive consequences of drinking as a self-control device. Alternative ways of handling problem situations were taught through the use of relaxation training and role playing. Craft and music training were encouraged as spare-time, non-drinking activities. Reinforcement for active participation in the program and desired behavior changes was provided both by the approval and recognition of staff members and by reductions in the length of hospitalization. The report of this program was descriptive in nature with no post-treatment follow-up data presented.

Behavioral Programing

According to Thoresen and Mahoney (1974) the concept of behavioral programing refers to an individual's rearranging the consequences of his own behavior. Basically this is similar to operant approaches in which reinforcement is made contingent upon abstinence or moderate drinking and punishment or withdrawal of reinforcement is contingent upon excessive drinking. In this sense, however, the individual himself is arranging for and providing himself with these contingencies. Self-reinforcements and punishments may be either covert or overt in nature.

Covert Contingency Management

Cautela and Upper (1975) have devised a number of strategies by which covert events can be arranged to consequate drinking behavior. Covert sensitization, as a type of aversion therapy, is basically a self-punishment procedure. Whenever the alcoholic is confronted with the opportunity to drink, he punishes himself covertly by imagining an unpleasant experience such as nausea or vomiting. On the other hand, successfully avoiding excessive use of alcohol can be consequated by a pleasurable thought such as sitting by a fireplace with a loved one feeling secure and relaxed. This procedure, known as *covert reinforcement,* is usually preceded by a series of sessions in which the client is requested to imagine refusing an alcoholic drink and/or choosing a non-alcoholic beverage in association with a pleasant imagined scene. This technique is often used in combination with covert sensitization. Cautela and Kastenbaum (1967) have developed a Reinforcement Survey Schedule, listing a variety of potentially reinforcing situations. This questionnaire assists the client in specifying pleasurable scenes to imagine.

One other technique, *covert extinction,* is based upon the principle that withholding reinforcement for a behavior leads to a gradual decrease in the occurrence of that behavior. In this procedure, an alcoholic would be asked to repeatedly imagine consuming alcoholic beverages but experiencing no positive or intoxicating feelings from this consumption. While results of this technique have not been reported in alcoholism treatment, Götestam and Melin (1974) report its use with four female amphetamine addicts ranging in age from 16 to 46 years. Initially, recordings describing circumstances under which each patient injected herself were played. Each of the patients received approximately 100 pairings of the injection scene with the extinction scene over a number of sessions. Three patients remained drug-free at a 9-month follow-up while the fourth relapsed after 2½ months. It is interesting to note that during hospital treatment two of these patients left the hospital for a brief period of time and injected amphetamines. Both reported, however, that they experienced no euphoria or positive feelings from this injection as they had in the past.

While further analysis of the efficacy of these techniques is warranted, the imaginal nature of the process provides difficulties in objective evaluation. For example, one must rely on the client's self-reports as to whether or not he is complying with therapeutic instructions.

Overt Contingency Management

An individual may also consequate his behavior with external reinforcing or punishing events. An excellent step-by-step analysis of the ways in which this can be accomplished has been presented by Watson and Tharpe (1972). While

McGuire and Vallance (1964) and Wilson, Leaf, and Nathan (1975) have demonstrated that self-administration of electric shock contingent upon "urges" or actual consumption can decrease drinking, the self-management procedures discussed here involve more naturally occurring consequences. A patient might schedule various favorite activities so that they occur only if he has remained sober for a certain length of time. These activities would be withheld if he were to drink excessively. Excessive drinking episodes could be punished by the client's tearing up a dollar or 5-dollar bill or sending a check for a substantial amount of money to a highly disfavored political organization.

The Premack principle in which opportunity to engage in a high probability behavior serves to reinforce a low probability behavior is frequently used. In this sense an individual would not allow himself to engage in behaviors that he frequently engages in (e.g., smoking, reading, watching television, meeting with friends) unless he has remained abstinent for that day or limited his drinking in a specified manner. The alcoholic may also arrange with others to reinforce or punish him contingent upon his drinking behavior.

Maintenance of Self-Management Behaviors

An obvious problem in the area of self-management relates to the ways in which the therapist initiates and maintains these patterns in the alcoholic client. How does one develop self-control or self-discipline skills in an individual who appears to be so dependent on the external environment? This is an especially relevant question since the alcoholic is supposedly lacking in self-motivation and "will power". As Thoresen and Mahoney (1974) note, however, these are rather nebulous terms which add little to our ability to predict and modify behavior. Rather than being a trait that someone has or does not have, self-control refers to the ability to distinguish and then manipulate variables (either covert or overt) influencing excessive drinking. This is a skill that an individual can learn. In fact it may be that individuals with chronic behavioral problems have never learned such skills and therefore their behavior is determined mainly by haphazard contingencies in their interpersonal and/or physical environment. A simple laboratory task in which alcoholics and social drinkers are requested to reward correct responses with points and to fine themselves points for incorrect responses could experimentally validate the notion that perhaps alcoholics are deficient in self-managing behaviors.

Initiation of these behavior patterns is certainly less of a problem than maintenance. Thus, it is relatively easy to determine contingencies influencing an individual's likelihood of drinking or abstaining and to instruct him in ways to rearrange or control these contingencies. It is difficult, however, to ensure that he reinforces or punishes himself according to schedule in his everyday life. One complicating factor involves the therapist's inability to reliably evaluate whether the client is engaging in these behaviors.

A number of methods are available to assist the therapist in accomplishing this task. Cooperation by the client is enhanced when the behaviors to be modified together with the contingencies to be arranged are highly specific. In this way the client will always be certain when he is to reward or punish his behavior. Depending on the treatment goal, positive contingencies might be placed on (1) total abstinence from all alcoholic beverages for a 24-hour period of time or (2) drinking no more than 3 ounces of whiskey or three cans of beer within a 24-hour time period.

Written contracts, specifying the consequences for behaviors and the manner in which they will be scheduled, seem useful. In this sense, the client actually makes a written agreement with himself, signs it, and keeps it in an accessible place. The contract itself serves as a cue to engage in self-management behavior. Kanfer and Karoly (1972) speculate that contract fulfillment may be a function of such factors as its explicitness, presence of self-monitoring and evaluation, the client's past experience with contracts, and the mutuality of control between the therapist and the client. This latter point stresses the fact that external control (e.g., reinforcement from the therapist) may be necessary to maintain the client's efforts at self-control. Thus, the therapist does not socially reinforce or punish drinking behavior *per se* but rather the client's efforts to control it using the techniques he has learned. Focusing on the reinforcement of self-management behaviors in this manner has been demonstrated to prolong the maintenance of self-control over time (Mahoney, 1974).

Instructing the client to self-monitor his behavior assists the therapist in evaluating and thus reinforcing successful applications of self-control. The client would record (in written form) not only drinking episodes and/or number and kinds of drinks but also occasions in which he had the opportunity to reward or punish himself and whether he actually implemented these consequences. Self-monitoring also serves as a self-control device which may lessen the likelihood of excessive drinking.

One additional factor involved in whether or not a client will engage in self-control behaviors is related to competing responses. Epstein, Miller, and Webster (in press), for example, demonstrated that self-monitoring by subjects was less likely if they were being rewarded for a competing response. If after one too many drinks an alcoholic has a choice between self-punishment and consuming another drink he will most probably engage in the most immediately rewarding behavior, i.e., alcohol consumption. Therefore, potent external contingencies may initially have to be imposed on the alcoholic with the notion of fading these out and replacing them with his own control.

Miscellaneous Alternative Behaviors

Certainly some alcoholics have individual deficit behaviors other than the ability to be assertive, relax, and implement self-control techniques. Occupational skills, for example, are often an essential alternative to excessive drinking. Training in specific job skills, increasing basic educational attainment, placement in an employment position compatible with the individual's capabilities and interests, and training in interpersonal skills related to job interviewing may be necessary with many clients. Other areas that may warrant modification include recreational and spare-time behaviors, more general interpersonal and social skills behaviors (Hersen and Eisler, in press), and marital and family skills (e.g., parenting abilities). Gary and Guthrie (1972) reported improvement in alcoholics' self-esteem, sleeping patterns, and cardiovascular functioning as a function of a daily physical fitness program in which they jogged a mile per day. Indeed, strenuous physical exercise may serve as a response which is incompatible with excessive drinking.

References

ALBERTI, R. E. and EMMONS, M. L. *Your perfect right.* San Luis Obispo, California: Impact, 1970.

ALLMAN, L. R., TAYLOR, H. A., NATHAN, P. E. Group drinking during stress: Effects on drinking behavior, affect, and psychopathology. *American Journal of Psychiatry*, 1972, **129**, 669–78.

BLAKE, B. G. A follow-up of alcoholics treated by behavior therapy. *Behavior Research and Therapy*, 1967, **5**, 89–94.

CAUTELA, J. R. and KASTENBAUM, R. A reinforcement survey schedule for use in therapy, training, and research. *Psychological Reports*, 1967, **20**, 1115–30.

CAUTELA, J. R. and UPPER, D. The process of individual behavior therapy. In M. Hersen, R. M. Eisler, and P. M. Miller (Eds.) *Progress in Behavior Modification.* New York: Academic Press, 1975, 276–301.

COOPERSMITH, S. and WOODROW, K. Basal conductance levels of normals and alcoholics. *Quarterly Journal of Studies on Alcohol*, 1967, **28**, 27–32.

EISLER, R. M., HERSEN, M. and MILLER, P. M. Shaping components of assertive behavior with instructions and feedback. *American Journal of Psychiatry*, 1974, **30**, 643–9.

EISLER, R. M., HERSEN, M., MILLER, P. M. and BLANCHARD, E. B. Situational determinants of assertive behaviors. *Journal of Consulting and Clinical Psychology*, 1975, **43**, 330–40.

EISLER, R. M., MILLER, P. M. and HERSEN, M. Components of assertive behavior. *Journal of Clinical Psychology*, 1973, **29**, 295–9.

EISLER, R. M., MILLER, P. M., HERSEN, M. and ALFORD, H. Effects of assertive training on marital interaction. *Archives of General Psychiatry*, 1974, **30**, 643–9.

EPSTEIN, L. H., MILLER, P. M. and WEBSTER, J. S. The effects of reinforcing concurrent behavior on self-monitoring. *Behavior Therapy*, (in press).

FERSTER, C. B., NURNBERGER, J. I. and LEVITT, C. B. The control of eating. *Journal of Mathematics*, 1962, **1**, 87–109.

GARY, V. and GUTHRIE, D. The effect of jogging on physical fitness and self-concept in hospitalized alcoholics. *Quarterly Journal of Studies on Alcohol*, 1972, **33**, 1073–8.

GOLDFRIED, M. R. and MERBAUM, M. (Eds.) *Behavior change through self-control.* New York: Holt, Rinehart, and Winston, Inc., 1973.

GÖTESTAM, K. G. and MELIN, L. Covert extinction of amphetamine addiction. *Behavior Therapy*, 1974, **5**, 90–2.

HERSEN, M., EISLER, R. M. and MILLER, P. M. Development of assertive responses: Clinical, measurement, and research considerations. *Behavior Research and Therapy*, 1973, **11**, 505–21.

HERSEN, M., EISLER, R. M., MILLER, P. M., JOHNSON, M. B. and PINKSTON, S. G. Effects of practice, instructions, and modeling on components of assertive behavior. *Behavior Research and Therapy*, 1973, **11**, 443–51.

HIGGINS, R. L. and MARLATT, G. A. The effects of anxiety arousal upon the consumption of alcohol by alcoholics and social drinkers. *Journal of Consulting and Clinical Psychology*, in press.

JACOBSEN, E. *Progressive relaxation.* Chicago: University of Chicago Press, 1938.

KANFER, F. H., COX, L. E., GRIENER, J. M. and KAROLY, P. Contracts, demand characteristics, and self-control. *Journal of Consulting and Clinical Psychology*, 1974, **30**, 605–19.

KANFER, F. H. and KAROLY, P. Self-control: A behavioristic excursion into the lion's den. *Behavior Therapy*, 1972, 3, 398–416.

KRAFT, T. Alcoholism treated by systematic desensitization: A follow-up of eight cases. *Journal of the Royal College of General Practice*, 1969, 18, 336–40.

KRAFT, T. and AL-ISSA, I. Alcoholism treated by desensitization: A case study. *Behavioral Research and Therapy*, 1967, 5, 69–70.

LANYON, R. I., PRIMO, R. V., TERRELL, F. and WENER, A. An aversion-desensitization treatment for alcoholism. *Journal of Consulting and Clinical Psychology*, 1972, 38, 394–8.

LAZARUS, A. On assertive behavior: A brief note. *Behavior Therapy*, 1973, 4, 697–9.

MAHONEY, M. J. Self-reward and self-monitoring techniques for weight control. *Behavior Therapy*, 1974, 5, 48–57.

MARLATT, G. A., DEMMING, B. and REID, J. B. Loss of control drinking in alcoholics: An experimental analogue. *Journal of Abnormal Behavior*, 1973, 81, 233–41.

MARLATT, G. A. and KOSTURN, C. F. Elicitation of anger and opportunity for retaliation as determinants of alcohol consumption. Unpublished manuscript. University of Washington, 1973.

MARTORANO, R. D. Mood and social perception in four alcoholics: Effects of drinking and assertion training. *Quarterly Journal of Studies on Alcohol*, 1974, 35, 445–57.

McFALL, R. M. and MARSTON, A. R. An experimental investigation of behavior rehearsal in assertive training. *Journal of Abnormal Psychology*, 1970, 76, 295–303.

McGUIRE, R. J. and VALLANCE, M. Aversion therapy by electric shock: A simple technique. *British Medical Journal*, 1964, 1, 151–3.

MERTENS, G. C. An operant approach to self-control for alcoholics. Paper presented at symposium on "Alcoholism and Conditioning Therapy" at the American Psychological Association, Sept., 1964.

MERTENS, G. C. and FULLER, G. B. *The manual for the alcoholic*. Willmar, Minnesota: Willmar State Hospital, 1964a.

MERTENS, G. C. and FULLER, G. B. *The therapist's manual*. Willmar, Minnesota: Willmar State Hospital, 1964b.

MILLER, P. M., HERSEN, M., EISLER, R. M. and HILSMAN, G. Effects of social stress on operant drinking of alcoholics and social drinkers. *Behavior Research and Therapy*, 1974, 12, 67–72.

MILLER, P. M., HERSEN, M., EISLER, R. M., EPSTEIN, L., and WOOTEN, L. Relationship of alcohol cues to the drinking behavior of alcoholics and social drinkers: An analogue study. *Psychological Record*, 1974, 24, 61–6.

NATHAN, P. E. Alcoholism. In H. Leitenberg (Ed.) *Handbook of behavior modification*. New York: Appleton-Century-Crofts, in press.

RATHUS, S. A. An experimental investigation of assertive training in a group setting. *Journal of Behavior Therapy and Experimental Psychiatry*, 1972, 3, 81–6.

RATHUS, S. A. Instigation of assertive behavior through videotape-mediated models and directed practice. *Behavior Research and Therapy*, 1973, 11, 57–65.

RATHUS, S. A. A 30-item schedule for assessing assertive behavior. *Behavior Therapy*, 1973, in press.

RIMM, D. C. and MASTERS, J. C. *Behavior Therapy: Techniques and empirical findings*. New York: Academic Press, 1974.

STEFFEN, J. J. Tension-reducing effects of alcohol: Further evidence and some methodological corrections. Unpublished manuscript, 1974.

STUNKARD, A. New therapies for the eating disorders: Behavior modification of obesity and anorexia nervosa. *Archives of General Psychiatry*, 1972, 26, 391–8.

THORESEN, C. E. and MAHONEY, M. J. *Behavioral self-control*. New York: Holt, Rinehart, and Winston, Inc., 1974.

WATSON, D. L. and THARPE, R. G. *Self-directed behavior: Self-modification for personal adjustment*. Monterey, California: Brooks/Cole Publishing Co., 1972.

WILSON, T., LEAF, R. and NATHAN, P. E. The aversive control of excessive drinking by chronic alcoholics in the laboratory setting. *Journal of Applied Behavior Analysis*, 1975, 2, 13–26.

WISOCKI, P. A. A comparison of the responses of alcoholics to the Fear Survey Schedule and the reinforcement survey schedule. Unpublished manuscript, Boston College, Chestnut Hill, Mass., 1969.

WOLPE, J. *Psychotherapy by reciprocal inhibition.* Stanford: Stanford University Press, 1958.

WOLPE, J. *The practice of behavior therapy.* New York: Pergamon Press, Inc., 1973.

WOLPE, J. and LAZARUS, A. A. *Behavior therapy techniques.* New York: Pergamon Press, 1966.

CHAPTER 5

Operant Approaches

Within an operant conditioning framework, alcohol abuse is viewed as being determined by its consequences. Such consequences may be social, environmental, physiological, or cognitive. The mechanisms of operant conditioning as they relate to the initiation and maintenance of behavior have been well established through laboratory investigations. Numerous references present a detailed account of the empirical underpinnings of this approach (Skinner, 1953, 1969, 1971; Krasner, 1971). Clinically, operant conditioning strategies have been used mostly with patients whose environment can be easily manipulated. These include children, chronic psychotics, and the mentally retarded. More recently, however, operant treatment procedures have been adapted for use with more varied clinical and social problems such as drug abuse (Boudin, 1972), alcoholism (Miller and Barlow, 1973), unemployment (Jones and Azrin, 1973), depression (Lewinsohn, 1975), and racial integration (Hauserman, Whalen, and Behling, 1973). The widening utilization of this approach is in part related to more creative and innovative formulations of the basic laws of conditioning such as self-management and biofeedback procedures.

Positive Reinforcers

In relation to alcohol abuse, certain consequences (referred to as *positive reinforcers*) of excessive drinking tend to increase the probability that such drinking will occur again. For example, increased recognition and attention from friends repeatedly contingent upon intoxication may reinforce and thus serve to maintain this behavior. Obviously, human behavior is very complex and no one single operant factor, such as social reinforcement, could explain chronic alcohol abuse. There are certainly numerous other consequences of behavior which may be difficult to identify. The behavior modifier must attempt to tease out these factors and manipulate them (or assist the patient to manipulate them) to the advantage of the alcoholic. Consequences related to the maintenance of abusive drinking must be determined *empirically*. That is, positive reinforcers may not be judged to be "positive" or "pleasant" events at face value. Certainly, the old adage "What is one man's meat is another man's poison" applies here. Let's

99

assume that John Smith consistently arrives home late and intoxicated approximately 4 nights each week. His wife's response to this behavior is to become very upset to the point of crying and lecturing him. If we observe that this pattern either maintains or increases the frequency of his behavior, we may assume that the wife's becoming upset may serve as a positive reinforcer. We could validate this notion further by instructing her to completely ignore his late intoxicated arrivals and observing subsequent decreases in the frequency of his behavior. On the other hand, we may notice a similar relationship between Bill Jones and his wife. In this case, however, the wife's behavior may result in Mr. Jones' arriving home sober more frequently. Thus, her being upset serves as a punishment since it decreased his intoxicated arrivals. Each case, then, must be analyzed individually with significant functional consequent relationships being determined on a purely empirical basis.

Negative Reinforcers

A behavior pattern which leads to the termination of an upleasant or aversive event is thereby more likely to occur under similar circumstances. This *removal* of an aversive event is known as *negative reinforcement*. A classical example of this from the author's experience relates to the interaction between a 50-year-old chronic alcoholic and his wife. Over the years the wife had developed a pattern of frequent critical comments and nagging directed toward her husband. This behavior occurred most frequently when her husband was either abstinent or drinking in moderation. As the husband consumed more alcohol, the intensity and frequency of his wife's nagging significantly decreased. When he finally became intoxicated, she would "feel sorry for him", terminate all nagging, and attend to his wishes. In this case the husband's excessive drinking served to "turn off" the aversive nagging and hence was being negatively reinforced.

Another example of negative reinforcement is observed in the very chronic alcoholic. Termination of an episode of heavy drinking generally results in the beginning of withdrawal symptoms (i.e., hangover). If the individual has consumed a great deal of alcohol these symptoms can be quite unpleasant consisting of agitation, shaking, sweating, heart palpitations, hallucinations. Consuming alcohol the "morning after" in the presence of these "shakes" will alleviate withdrawal symptoms. This type of drinking would be negatively reinforced through this process.

Such conditioning of drinking habits can occur either through *escape* or *avoidance learning*. The examples discussed above illustrate drinking to escape from an aversive event. The alcoholic may come to anticipate aversive situations due to past experience and drink to avoid them. Confrontation with a difficult business or interpersonal situation may be avoided through intoxication. While the long-term consequences of this behavior may also be unpleasant (e.g., being fired), immediate reinforcing consequences have the most powerful influence over behavior.

Consequences Which Decrease Behavior

While certain consequences tend to maintain abusive drinking patterns, others serve to decrease drinking. Two factors which decrease the likelihood of the occurrence of a behavior are *punishment* and *extinction*. As with reinforcers, punishment is defined empirically in terms of its effects on behavior and includes a wide variety of aversive events. These might include social censure, loss of reinforcement (job loss, separation from wife and children), isolation from all reinforcement (jailing), aversive physiological events (nausea), or aversive mood changes (increased depression, anxiety). Such consequences frequently have little influence on alcoholics' behavior since they usually occur long after drinking has begun. In this regard, Vogel-Sprott and Banks (1965) examined the effects of punishment on a rewarded response in alcoholics and non-alcoholics. Their experimental apparatus consisted of a three-button response panel, a money reward dispenser, and a shock generator. Both money reward and shock punishment were made contingent upon the operant response of button pressing. Both immediate and delayed punishment were found to be less effective in suppressing the response of alcoholics than of non-alcoholics. Thus, punishment may not serve as an effective treatment modality for abusive drinking.

In a similar study, Okulitch and Marlatt (1972) further investigated this phenomenon. They examined the effects of simultaneous contingent reward and intermittent punishment on alcoholics' operant responses. They assumed that these contingencies were most like what occurs in the natural environment when alcoholics drink to excess. Through money reinforcement alcoholics and non-alcoholics acquired a simple operant pushbutton response. Subjects were then switched to one of three extinction conditions: no reward, reward (money) and punishment (electric shock delivered to the fingers), or punishment alone. Number of responses to extinction (suppression of the button-pressing response) were calculated for all subjects. Results indicated that alcoholics in the punishment and reward-punishment condition failed to suppress their response to the same extent as the controls. The latter condition produced the greatest resistance to extinction in all subjects but more significantly with the alcoholics. No significant differences were found between the groups on the non-reward condition. The authors hypothesized that in light of these findings perhaps non-aversive reinforcement contingencies would be more effective in altering alcoholic drinking patterns. These findings must be considered inconclusive for a number of reasons. First, and foremost, if an aversive stimulus does not decrease behavior, it is not, by definition, punishment. Second, the mean aversive shock intensity used for alcoholics was 2.37 ma. This is a very low intensity when compared to the levels used in other studies. Third, chronic alcoholics frequently develop peripheral neuropathy in which they lose feelings and sensation in their extremities. Low-intensity shocks to the fingers of alcoholics could hardly be an aversive stimulus strong enough to compete with reinforcement. In addition, due to this physical degeneration in the extremities, one would expect such unpleasant stimuli to be less aversive to alcoholics than non-alcoholics and thus less effective in altering their behavior. It is quite possible that other events (e.g., response cost, social censure) more akin to natural environmental phenomena may be equally effective for alcoholics and non-alcoholics. Since both reinforcing and punishing events typically occur concomitantly with excessive drinking, the behavior will be most influenced by whichever event is most potent at the time. The presence of alcohol in the body tends to reduce the probability that certain stimuli will serve as punishers. Vogel-Sprott (1967) illustrated that even low doses of alcohol reduce anxiety and concern regarding avoidance of aversive stimuli.

Experimental evidence indicates that punishment must occur frequently, intensely, and immediately to be most effective. The social punishment received by an alcoholic in his natural environment is highly erratic and far from immediate. In addition, Nathan and O'Brien (1971) point out that since the chronic alcoholic usually experiences loss of memory during prolonged drinking episodes, he is not affected by the aversive mood changes (increases in anxiety and depression) which occur as a consequnce of such drinking. They feel that if these "blackout" periods could be disrupted, natural aversive events would more likely serve as effective punishers.

Another operant method of eliminating unacceptable behavior is *extinction*. Extinction is merely the removal or withholding of reinforcement. Thus, if friends tend to laugh and joke with Bill when he begins to drink heavily, extinction would be the process whereby they might choose to completely ignore his drinking. Systematic withholding of reinforcers in this manner tends to gradually decrease the frequency of a behavior. However, the initial withdrawal of reinforcement usually leads to a temporary increase in behavior known as "extinction burst". In a sense this is similar to "testing the limits" of the system. The reasoning would be, "If one drinking episode doesn't get what I want, maybe ten will." The individual, of course, is seldom aware of these functional relationships maintaining his behavior.

Extinction is also problematic with alcoholics since it is often difficult to control the wide variety of reinforcers that maintain drinking behavior. Removal of one or two reinforcers may have little effect on a behavior that is being maintained by numerous consequences.

One of the most important aspects of both punishment and extinction is the reinforcement of alternative behaviors. Suppose that an alcoholic frequently drinks to excess in response to stressful interpersonal encounters. His drinking relieves his anxiety and helps him to escape from the situation. If we simply arrange to systematically punish his drinking, we still have not solved his basic problem. While punishment is suppressing his excessive drinking, systematic reinforcement would be provided to him for more appropriate ways of coping with stressful social situations. If he lacks the necessary social skills, training must necessarily precede reinforcement. The combination of punishment or extinction together with reinforcement of an alternative behavior seems to be a powerful therapeutic package.

Schedules of Reinforcement

The plan or schedule by which reinforcement occurs is also relevant to behavior change. Reinforcement can occur every time a behavior occurs (continuous reinforcement) or only after the behavior has occurred a number of times (partial reinforcement). Reinforcement can also occur after a fixed number (fixed ratio schedule) of behavioral responses or a variable number (variable ratio). Reinforcement on a time schedule occurs after either a fixed amount of time has elapsed since the last response (fixed interval) or after a varying amount of time (variable interval). In general, human behavior is more likely to be a function of variable schedules of reinforcement. For example, it is unlikely that an alcoholic would receive attention from others every time he is intoxicated. Schedules of reinforcement for excessive drinking are often complex. At the beginning of a drinking episode, the alcoholic seems to be on a schedule known as DRH (differential reinforcement of high rate responding). That is, he is reinforced for frequent and large sips, since this pattern results in rapid intoxication. Social drinkers probably are on a DRL (differential reinforcement of low rate responding) schedule in that they pace their sips to avoid intoxication.

Setting Events

While operant conditioning is primarily concerned with the consequences of behavior, the concept of *setting events* or *stimulus cues* is relevant to alcoholic behavior. Setting events are environmental stimuli which set the occasion for a behavior to occur. These events, such as the presence of "drinking buddies", have been so frequently associated with the reinforcement derived from excessive drinking that they assume secondary reinforcing properties. Thus, the mere presence of these cues serves to initiate the drinking response. Once initiated the environment tends to reinforce it. Cues can also serve as discriminative stimuli. That is while certain sets of circumstances are associated with excessive drinking, others are associated with abstinence or moderate drinking. Since the alcoholic drinks in a wide variety of circumstances (while driving, in the basement, alone, with friends, at work) more stimulus cues for alcohol consumption exist for him. Along these lines, the social drinker drinks in more narrowed, specific situations (e.g., before a meal, at a cocktail party). Excessive drinking of alcoholics may be a function of other types of external cues (e.g., social isolation, social stress) or internal cues (e.g., increased heart rate and respiration, decreasing blood/alcohol level). The aim of treatment, then, may be to initially narrow the range of cues that are associated with alcohol consumption so that fewer environmental and physiological events are associated with the drinking response. When controlled drinking is the desired goal, the alcoholic must be taught to discriminate situations in which drinking is appropriate (e.g., cocktail party) from situations in which it is not appropriate (e.g., in his office at 8.00 a.m.). Alterations in stimulus cue situations is often accomplished through self-management procedures (see Chapter 4).

Operant technologies have proven useful both in the assessment and treatment of alcoholics. Since operant assessment systems have been discussed in detail in an earlier chapter, this chapter will emphasize operant therapeutic strategies.

Therapeutic Intervention

A comprehensive treatment approach to alcohol abuse via an operant orientation involves a number of elements:

1. Removal of reinforcers for abusive drinking.
2. Systematic, frequent, and varied social punishment for abusive drinking.
3. Reinforcement of behaviors incompatible with excessive drinking.
4. Rearrangement of environmental cues which set the occasion for abusive drinking.

While these elements have not as yet been combined into a total treatment package, several of them have been evaluated in both inpatient and outpatient settings.

Inpatient Applications

Operant strategies applied to inpatient alcoholic populations include token economy procedures, contingency management, and alterations in schedules of reinforcement.

Token economy systems. The systematic application of operant conditioning to hospitalized psychiatric patients is often accomplished through a token economy system. While token economies have been used with a variety of populations (Kazdin and Bootzin, 1972), only a few studies report its use with alcoholic patients. Basically, the token economy is a system in which patients earn credits or points for appropriate behaviors and lose credits or fail to earn them for inappropriate, maladaptive behaviors. Points are then used to purchase reinforcers in the form of hospital privileges, passes, more desirable living accommodations (e.g., private room as opposed to a ward). This system serves to foster adaptive behaviors which are then useful to the patient when he leaves the hospital. Although the token economy has been criticized for being a mechanical, routine environment which puts patients into a child-like position, it actually fosters independence and responsibility. The patient is free to decide to engage in certain behaviors or not. Whatever reinforcers he obtains from the environment are determined solely by his own behavior. In this sense, the token economy is a replica of the real world and constitutes a mini-environment. The lesson being taught is that you only get out of something what you put into it.

The first major application of a token economy system to alcoholics was reported by Narrol (1967). His goal was to increase work behavior in hospitalized alcoholics. Patients were paid 100 points per hour for on- and off-ward work assignments. Out of these earnings patients were required to pay for room and board, ground privileges, clothing maintenance, and recreation. Voluntary purchases included passes, Antabuse, Alcoholics Anonymous meetings, group therapy, and individual therapy. Through increasing payments, patients could gradually advance from a drab, closed ward to a more pleasant open ward. Patients on this token economy unit averaged 8 hours of work per day compared with 4 hours a day for a group not on token economy. No post-hospitalization follow-up was included since the goal of the project was simply to increase hospital work behavior.

Rozynko, Flint, Hammer, Swift, Kline, and King (1971) report the use of a token economy with alcoholics in a State hospital setting. The goal of the program was to reinforce responses incompatible with drinking alcohol. Through "credit slips" which were exchangeable for money at a weekly payday, patients were reinforced for attending didactic classes, systematic desensitization, and assertive training sessions. Credits were also accumulated by demonstrating desired behavior changes. Changes were recorded on the basis of terminal behavior measures taken at various stages of the program. Specific goal behaviors required included responding in a neutral manner (as determined by respiration, movements, etc.) to specific systematic desensitization hierarchies, emitting verbal behavior (in a short interview) consistent with a positive, learning approach to the drinking problem, and engaging in more appropriate, assertive social behavior (defined in terms of eye contact, talking and listening more).

Patients also received "credit slips" for jobs around the hospital. In addition to money, reinforcement was provided in terms of varying work schedules and approval and recognition from the staff. Patients spent an average of 76 days in the program with active participation during treatment ranging from 29.70 to 33.95 hours per week. This comprehensive and innovative approach is currently being evaluated under controlled conditions.

Miller, Stanford, and Hemphill (1974) have described a similar system for alcoholic VA inpatients. Aversion therapy, relaxation training, systematic desensitization, assertive training, group behavioral rehearsal, and marital counseling (via contingency contracting) are used within a token economy system. Patients are reinforced with points for a wide variety of personal-social (personal hygiene, reporting on time to scheduled activities, appropriately handling interpersonal conflicts) and vocational (work assignment in hospital, job interviews) activities. Point fines are also imposed for breaking ward rules (e.g., smoking in room, physical violence) and for irresponsible behavior (e.g., failure to carry out job assignment, failure to attend treatment session). If the patient returns from a pass in an intoxicated state he is fined heavily and loses all privileges for 3 days. Points earned and lost are tallied each morning at "Banking Hours" and traded in for privileges (eating in main mess hall, 1 hour in room during the day, extended bed time, and day, evening, or weekend passes). The system fosters motivation to actively participate in treatment and development of more responsible, mature behaviors which help to maintain sobriety outside of the hospital. The program also places contingencies (in terms of fines and loss of privileges) on drinking *per se*.

Cohen, Liebson, and Faillace (1971) utilized an innovative *group* fine approach along with a monetary based token economy. Alcoholic patients either earned or lost money based upon their ward behavior. Sixty dollars was deposited in each patient's account upon entering the ward. Fines were deducted from this amount. Under the group fine conditions, whenever a patient was fined for inappropriate behavior, all other patients on the ward were fined a similar amount. While this condition seemed to make no difference for minor infractions ($1 and $5 fines), major ward infractions ($10) were reduced to one-fourth the level previously observed under individual-only fine conditions. This system puts the patient into a position in which he is accountable to others which in turn places increased social pressure on him to behave appropriately. This also assists the alcoholic in learning the functional relationship between his own misconduct and its effect on others.

Contingency management. Contingency management refers to the systematic scheduling of both positive and negative consequences of behavior. Excessive drinking, then, is either punished or ignored while sobriety is being reinforced.

A research group at Baltimore City Hospital and affiliated with Johns Hopkins University has pioneered inpatient work in this area. In one of their earlier reports, Cohen, Liebson, and Faillace (1971) describe a series of experiments using a 39-year-old chronic alcoholic (10-year history of alcohol abuse) who was hospitalized on the Alcohol Research Unit during the study. A free operant drinking situation was used in which the subject had access to 24 ounces of 95 proof ethanol each day. During contingent reinforcement weeks if the subject drank 5 ounces of alcohol or less on a particular day, he was placed in an enriched ward environment. This environment provided opportunity to work for money, private telephone, recreation room, and television. If the subject drank over 5 ounces he was placed in an impoverished environment (loss of all privileges) for the rest of the day. During control conditions no contingencies were placed on drinking. The results of an ABABA experimental single case design indicated that controlled drinking (under 5 ounces per day) was maintained during contingent phases with reversal to excessive drinking during non-contingent phases. Other experiments in this series demonstrated that these findings were unrelated to type of evironment during non-contingent weeks or total amount of alcohol available. When contingencies were maintained for as long as 5 successive weeks, the subject drank moderately on all but 2 days.

Similar results have been demonstrated using other reinforcements such as money (Cohen, Liebson, and Faillace, 1971; Cohen, Liebson, Faillace and Speers, 1971) and opportunity to visit a girlfriend outside of the hospital (Bigelow, Liebson, and Griffiths, 1973). In a more recent study Liebson, Bigelow, and Flamer (1973) established an experimental contingency such that methadone would reinforce the taking of Antabuse in alcoholic ex-heroin addicts.

A more formal method of scheduling behavioral consequences is through the use of *contingency* or *behavioral contracting*. Behavioral contracts are written agreements delineating behaviors to be changed and contingencies applied to fulfillment or nonfulfillment of the agreement. While this technique has been used clinically with marital problems (Stuart, 1969), juvenile delinquency (Stuart, 1971; Stuart and Lott, 1972) and drug abuse (Boudin, 1972), few experimental investigations of its efficacy are available. The clinical use of behavioral contracts with alcoholics and their wives is discussed at length in Chapter 6.

In an inpatient analogue study Miller, Hersen, and Eisler (1974) investigated each of the three basic components of contracting as they apply to alcohol abuse. These included instructions to reduce alcohol consumption, a written agreement signed by the patient and therapist agreeing to these instructions, and the contingencies attached to the patient's compliance or non-compliance with the agreement. Forty chronic alcoholic inpatients matched on age, education, length of problem drinking, and number of operant responses to obtain alcohol were used. An operant task in which lever pressing during a 10-minute interval to obtain alcohol on an FR 50 schedule of reinforcement was used to assess results. Four separate 10-minute operant sessions were scheduled for each subject. Based upon the mean number of responses for these sessions, a drinking goal was established for each subject by calculating one-half of his mean number of drinks during this pre-test. Subjects were then assigned to one of four groups with ten subjects in each group: (1) verbal instructions to limit responding to the goal level, (2) written agreement signed by the subject and experimenter, (3) verbal instructions plus reinforcement for compliance, and (4) written agreement plus reinforcement for compliance. Reinforcement consisted of 15 points after each operant session in which drinking was at or below the goal level and a loss of 30 points for non-compliance. Points could be exchanged for hospital canteen booklets at the rate of one dollar's worth for every 15 points. Subjects were then scheduled for four post-test operant sessions. Results were calculated in terms of difference between each subject's goal and his actual performance, and the percentage of trials of fulfilled agreement. Number of subjects in each group who did and who did not respond at or below their drinking goal is presented in Table 5.1.

TABLE 5.1   Number of Subjects Attaining Drinking Goal
(Miller, Hersen, and Eisler, 1974)

Group	1	2	3	4	Total
Attained goal	2	4	9	9	24
Did not attain goal	8	6	1	1	16
Total	10	10	10	10	40

(Table 2 from Miller, P. M., Hersen, M., and Eisler, R. M. Relative effectiveness of instructions, agreements, and reinforcement in behavioral contracts with alcoholics. *J. of Abnor. Psychol.* 1974, 548–53. Copyright 1974 by the American Psychol. Assoc. Reprinted by permission.)

The results indicated that reinforcement contingencies seem to be the major therapeutic ingredient in behavioral contracts with alcoholics. As clinicians have frequently observed, instructions had little influence on alcohol consumption. Signed written agreements appeared to have only a slight influence. The authors discuss the fact that elaborately written and mutually signed agreements may not be necessary in behavioral contracting with alcoholics. It may be sufficient to simply ensure the implementation of contingencies for specified reductions in drinking.

Although inpatient studies in the area of operant conditioning with alcoholics are relatively few, they provide valuable information regarding clinical applications. The advantages of experimental control and direct assessment of alcohol consumption obtained in inpatient settings allows for the refinement of techniques prior to their clinical application. These studies suggest that operant technologies may provide a viable treatment strategy for alcohol abuse. In the natural environment, contingencies would be much more complex and varied and could possibly be applied via friends, relatives, halfway houses, courts, or community treatment facilities.

Reinforcement schedules. Another method of modifying drinking patterns is through variations in the scheduling of reinforcement. In this regard, Bigelow and Liebson (1972) investigated the effects of varying fixed-ratio schedules of reinforcement on simple motor responses of two male, Skid Row alcoholics. The subjects were housed on a research ward and could earn alcohol by operating a lever. Lever pressing, at any time of the day, initiated a tone which was a cue for the nursing staff to dispense a drink (1 oz. of 95 proof ethanol in 2 oz. of orange juice) to the subject. A fixed ratio schedule requires the subject to press the lever a specific number of times to obtain reinforcement (alcohol). The number of responses required to obtain reinforcement varied in the following manner: FR 100 (1 day), FR 3000 (4 days), FR 1000 (4 days), FR 100 (2 days), FR 5000 (3 days). Mean number of drinks earned under the FR 100 and FR 1000 conditions tended to be high, i.e., 16 per day. However, drinking was decreased to about half in the FR 3000 condition. At FR 5000 drinking was very moderate, with both subjects choosing to abstain rather than exert that much effort.

Outpatient Application

Systematic applications of operant strategies to the clinical treatment of alcoholics in outpatient settings are rare. Such treatment usually involves concentrated efforts to involve community agents (friends, relatives, courts) to provide reinforcers or punishers at specified times. These agents must receive both extensive training in these applications together with reinforcement from the therapist for their efforts.

Frequently, social reinforcement from relatives or friends can serve as a powerful influence on drinking behavior. In attempting to rearrange social reinforcers in a alcoholic's environment, Sulzer (1965) made peer companionship and spouse attention contingent upon non-alcoholic drinking behavior. The patient's friends were instructed to periodically meet him for a "drink". If he ordered an alcoholic beverage at this meeting, the friends were to immediately leave his presence. If he ordered a non-alcoholic beverage, they were to remain and provide social reinforcement in the form of friendly conversation and increased attention. Sobriety was also reinforced by positive comments from the wife and the therapist. Reportedly, the patient discontinued the use of alcohol and was functioning more efficiently. Unfortunately, no long-term follow-up was provided.

With most alcoholics, however, more potent reinforcers must be used in conjunction with social reinforcers. In a single case study, Miller, Hersen, Eisler, and Watts (1974) demonstrated *experimental* control of alcohol abuse via monetary contingencies. The subject was a 49-year-old chronic alcoholic who lived with his mother. Although he worked sporadically, he was usually in need of money. He had a history of numerous hospitalizations for alcohol abuse and at least twenty-five public drunkenness arrests. He reported drinking from one pint to one-fifth of whiskey together with wine and beer on a daily basis. An ABCB experimental single case design (Barlow and Hersen, 1973) was used in which contingent reinforcement of a zero blood/alcohol concentration was systematically introduced, removed, and then reintroduced. The study was divided into four phases with 3 weeks in each phase. During the first phase bi-weekly blood/alcohol levels were accumulated via breath tests. These tests were administered randomly in the subject's home or place of employment. During the next 3 weeks the subject received 3 dollars in coupon booklets (exchangeable for meals, cigarettes, clothing, etc., at the VA Hospital commissary) contingent upon each blood/alcohol concentration of 0.00. Breath samples were analyzed within an hour after collection to provide for immediate reinforcement. During the third phase, reinforcement was provided on a non-contingent basis in that the coupon booklets were provided after each breath test regardless of the blood/alcohol level. During the final 3-week phase, reinforcement was again made contingent upon a 0.00 blood/alcohol level.

Blood/alcohol levels for each phase of the study are presented in Fig. 5.1. Levels tended to be high during the baseline phase, ranging from 0.00% to 0.27%. During contingent reinforcement blood/alcohol levels were markedly decreased with only one being above 0.00. Non-contingent reinforcement resulted in increased drinking while reinstatement of contingent coupon booklets resulted in a steady decline in blood/alcohol levels.

Although this study was limited in time, the results illustrate that contingent reinforcement can markedly alter alcohol consumption in a chronic alcoholic. The most important aspect of this experiment is related to the methodology and assessment procedures used. Use of the single case experimental design in which treatment is instituted, withdrawn, and then reinstated allows the experimenter to rule out the role of extraneous therapeutic factors (e.g., therapeutic demand characteristics, attention-placebo factors) in explaining the results. Such a design

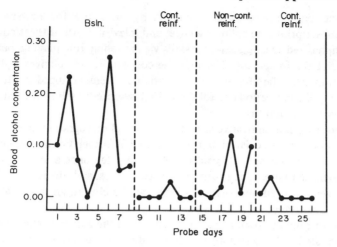

Fig. 5.1. Bi-weekly blood/alcohol concentrations for each phase (Miller, Hersen, Eisler, and Watts, 1974).

provides an excellent model for single case investigations. In addition, blood/alcohol concentrations as measured by random breath tests offer an objective and convenient method of scheduling consequences of drinking behavior and of assessing therapeutic results in the natural environment. This is especially relevant for operant treatment techniques since specific behaviors must be consequated, and drinking behavior *per se* seldom occurs in the presence of treatment personnel.

Such basic external reinforcements as canteen booklets or money are probably not potent enough to sustain long periods of sobriety. Hence, naturally occurring events could be rearranged to decrease the likelihood of excessive drinking. In this regard, activities that occur at a high frequency in the natural environmental (e.g., working, socializing) may be arranged so that they occur contingently upon decreased alcohol consumption. Bigelow, Liebson, and Lawrence (1973) have used the opportunity to work each day as a reinforcer for taking Antabuse. Clients are required to ingest Antabuse in the presence of clinic staff as a pre-condition to working each day.

Realistically, a more comprehensive approach utilizing both a wide selection of reinforcers for decreases in drinking and social punishment or loss of reinforcers for excessive drinking may be needed to achieve stable, long-term results. Close community contacts (e.g., home visits) are also necessary to maintain such a program. Hunt and Azrin (1973) instituted this notion in their community reinforcement approach to alcoholism. State hospital patients were provided with vocational counseling, marital and family counseling, social counseling, and reinforcer-access counseling. The latter included attempts to improve the patient's home environment by arranging for newspaper and magazine subscriptions, telephone service, and television. All of these counseling services emphasized teaching specific skills via modeling, role playing, behavioral rehearsal, and reinforcement. Through the cooperation of relatives and friends pleasurable marital, family, and social activities were arranged so that they occurred only during periods of sobriety. Follow-up counseling continued on a periodic basis for 6 months.

An interesting and innovative aspect of the social reprogramming consisted of the development of a social club for patients. A former tavern was converted into a social club and patients paid a membership fee once a month. The club provided social activities in the form of dances, parties, and movies. No alcoholic beverages were allowed and anyone arriving at the club in an intoxicated state was refused admittance.

This reinforcement program was compared with the existing hospital program which consisted of twenty-five 1-hour didactic sessions on alcoholism. Information, corroborated by a family member, was obtained regarding (1) days when drinking occurred, (2) days unemployed, and (3) days spent away from home. Percent of time since discharge (6 months) spent in each of these categories for the community-reinforcement group and the control group is presented in Figure 5.2.

The community-reinforcement group spent significantly less time drinking, unemployed, and away from home. In addition, reinstitutionalization time was only 2% for the reinforcement group while it was 27% for the control group.

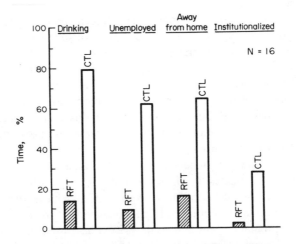

Fig. 5.2. A comparison of the key dependent measures for the reinforcement and control groups since discharge: mean percentages of time spent drinking, unemployed, away from home, and institutionalized (Hunt and Azrin, 1973).

Patients in the reinforcement group also earned more money and spent more time in structured social activities than the control group.

While this study is both interesting and innovative, the effects of contingent reinforcement *per se* on outcome are somewhat unclear due to methodological problems in the design. Nathan (in press) points out that the alcoholics in the reinforcement group received not just different but more treatment than the controls. In addition, successful outcome of the reinforcement group may have been related to their greater social and vocational stability. A study in which both groups received identical services with the exception of the contingent arrangement of reinforcement would clarify these points.

Comprehensive operant treatment approaches offer considerable promise and certainly deserve more extended analysis. Incorporation of more objective assessment procedures such as periodic blood/alcohol level determinators would enhance these applications. This is particularly relevant since success with some alcoholics may require a more gradual process of shaping successively lower blood/alcohol levels rather than expecting immediate cessation of chronic drinking patterns.

References

BARLOW, D. H. and HERSEN, M. Single case experimental designs. *Archives of General Psychiatry*, 1973, **29**, 319–25.

BIGELOW, G. and LIEBSON, I. Cost factors controlling alcoholic drinking. *Psychological Record*, 1972, **22**, 305–14.

BIGELOW, G., LIEBSON, I. and GRIFFITHS, R. Experiment analysis of alcoholic drinking. Paper presented at the American Psychological Association, Montreal, 1973.

BIGELOW, G., LIEBSON, I. and LAWRENCE, C. Prevention of alcohol abuse by reinforcement of incompatible behavior. Paper presented at the Association for Advancement of Behavior Therapy, December, 1973.

BOUDIN, H. M. Contingency contracting as a therapeutic tool in the deceleration of amphetamine use. *Behavior Therapy*, 1972, **3**, 604–8.

COHEN, M., LIEBSON, I. and FAILLACE, L. A. The modification of drinking in chronic alcoholics. In N. K. Mello and J. H. Mendelson (Eds.) *Recent advances in studies of alcoholism: An interdisciplinary symposium*. Washington, D.C.: U.S. Government Printing Office, 1971.

COHEN, M., LIEBSON, I. and FAILLACE, L. A. The role of reinforcement contingencies in chronic alcoholism: An experimental analysis of one case. *Behavior Research and Therapy*, 1971, **9**, 375–9.

COHEN, M., LIEBSON, I., FAILLACE, L. A. and SPEERS, W. Alcoholism: Controlled drinking and incentives for abstinence. *Psychological Reports*, 1971, **28**, 575–80.

HAUSERMAN, N., WHALEN, S. R. and BEHLING, M. Reinforced racial integration in the first grade: A study in generalization. *Journal of Applied Behavior Analysis*, 1973, **6**, 193–200.

HUNT, G. A. and AZRIN, N. H. A community reinforcement approach to alcoholism. *Behavior Research and Therapy*, 1973, **11**, 91–104.

JONES, R. J. and AZRIN, N. H. An experimental application of a social reinforcement approach to the problem of job finding. *Journal of Applied Behavior Analysis*, 1973, **6**, 345–54.

KAZDIN, A. E. and BOOTZIN, R. R. The token economy: An evaluative review. *Journal of Applied Behavior Analysis*, 1972, **5**, 343–72.

KRASNER, L. Behavior therapy. *Annual review of psychology*, 1971, **22**, 483.

LEWINSOHN, P. M. The behavioral study and treatment of depression. In M. Hersen, R. M. Eisler, and P. M. Miller (Eds.) *Progress in behavior modification*. New York: Academic Press, 1975.

LIEBSON, I., BIGELOW, G. and FLAMER, R. Alcoholism among methadone patients: A specific treatment method. *American Journal of Psychiatry*, 1973, **130**, 483–5.

MILLER, P. M. and BARLOW, D. H. Behavioral approaches to the treatment of alcoholism. *Journal of Nervous and Mental Disease*, 1973, **157**, 10–20.

MILLER, P. M., HERSEN, M. and EISLER, R. M. Relative effectiveness of instructions, agreements, and reinforcement in behavioral contracts with alcoholics. *Journal of Abnormal Psychology*, 1974, **83**, 548–53.

MILLER, P. M., HERSEN, M., EISLER, R. M., EPSTEIN, L. H. and WOOTEN, L. S. Relationship of alcohol cues to the drinking behavior of alcoholics and social drinkers: An analogue study. *Psychological Record*, 1974, **24**, 61–6.

MILLER, P. M., HERSEN, M., EISLER, R. M. and WATTS, J. G. Contingent reinforcement of lowered blood/alcohol levels in an outpatient chronic alcoholic. *Behavior Research and Therapy*, 1974, **12**, 261–3.

114

MILLER, P. M., STANFORD, A. G. and HEMPHILL, D. P. A social-learning approach to alcoholism treatment. *Social Casework*, 1974, **55**, 279–84.

NATHAN, P. E. Alcoholism. In H. Leitenberg (Ed.) *Handbook of behavior modification*. New York: Appleton-Century Crofts, in press.

NATHAN, P. E. and O'BRIEN, J. S. An experimental analysis of the behavior of alcoholics and non-alcoholics during prolonged experimental drinking. *Behavior Therapy*, 1971, **2**, 455–76.

NARROL, H. G. Experimental application of reinforcement principles to the analysis and treatment of hospitalized alcoholics. *Quarterly Journal of Studies on Alcohol*, 1967, **28**, 105–15.

OKULITCH, P. V. and MARLATT, G. A. Effects of varied extinction conditions with alcoholics and social drinkers. *Journal of Abnormal Psychology*, 1972, **72**, 205–11.

ROZYNKO, V. V., FLINT, G. A., HAMMER, C. E., SWIFT, K. D., KLINE, J. A. and KING, R. M. An operant behavior modification program for alcoholics. Paper presented at the Western Psychological Association, April, 1971.

SKINNER, B. F. *Science and human behavior*. New York: Macmillan, 1953.

SKINNER, B. F. *Contingencies of reinforcement: A theoretical analysis*. New York, Appleton, 1969.

SKINNER, B. F. *Beyond freedom and dignity*. New York: Knopf, 1971.

STUART, R. B. Behavioral contracting within families of delinquents. *Journal of Behavior Therapy and Experimental Psychiatry*, 1971, **2**, 1–11.

STUART, R. B. and LOTT, L. A. Behavioral contracting with delinquents: A cautionary note. *Journal of Behavior Therapy and Experimental Psychiatry*, 1972, **3**, 161–9.

SULZER, E. S. Behavior modification in adult psychiatric patients. In Ullman, L. P. and Krasner, L. (Eds.) *Case studies in behavior modification*. New York: Holt, Rinehart, & Winston, 1965, 196–9.

VOGEL-SPROTT, M. D. and BANKS, R. V. The effect of delayed punishment on an immediately rewarded response in alcoholics and nonalcoholics. *Behavior Research and Therapy*, 1965, **3**, 69–73.

CHAPTER 6

Marital Interaction

Intense marital conflict, marital separation, and divorce are frequent concomitants of alcoholism. In a study of seventy alcoholic outpatients, Woodruff, Guze, and Layton (1972) found that 49% were divorced. Similarly, Ullman (1952) reported that 57% of his sample of alcoholic women were divorced or separated. Among the more chronic abusive drinkers, divorce rates are even higher. Miller (1973) surveyed a group of thirty-four chronic alcoholics whose average length of problem drinking was 11 years. Of this group, 79% were divorced or separated, 15% were currently married, and 6% had never married. The majority of those who were divorced reported that their excessive drinking was a major cause of marital conflict.

Marital difficulties and excessive drinking appear to be so interrelated that it has not been possible to determine which event precipitates the other. It is most likely that while excessive drinking increases marital tension, marital conflict also increases the likelihood of alcohol abuse. In any event, most clinicians agree that alterations in the relationship between an alcoholic and his spouse provide an atmosphere that is more conducive to sobriety.

Unfortunately, few reports are available with respect to either behavioral analysis of these marriages or therapeutic attempts at marital intervention using behavior modification procedures. There is, however, a plethora of anecdotal and theoretical descriptions of the alcoholic's marriage based on psycho-dynamically oriented principles. In these analyses it is assumed that the disordered marriage helps to maintain abusive drinking. The major focus has been on the role of the non-alcoholic wife in the etiology of her husband's drinking. Descriptions of husbands of alcoholic wives are scarce.

Wives of Alcoholics

In a comprehensive review of the literature on the wives of alcoholics Edwards, Harvey, and Whitehead (1973) succinctly concluded that, "... at present, the only tenable hypothesis is that these wives are not unique." Early reports of these wives (Baker, 1941; Price, 1945; Whalen, 1953), based primarily on psychoanalytic theory, characterized them as neurotic "culprits" who drove their husbands to drink in order to satisfy their own pathological needs. They are often described as controlling, hostile women who keep their husbands dependent by mothering them. Futterman (1953) further assumed that the wife "needed" to be married to an alcoholic and that she would decompensate psychologically if her husband remained sober for any length of time.

Little supportive evidence exists for these propositions. For example, Mitchell (1959), Ballard (1959), and Kogan and Jackson (1964) found that wives of alcoholics were no more pathological (indeed, many were less so) than wives who were experiencing general marital difficulties. It appears that the alcoholic's marriage might be disturbed regardless of his drinking. In addition, Haberman (1964) and Bailey, Haberman, and Alksne (1962) found that instead of deteriorating when their husbands became abstinent, such wives functioned much better during these periods of sobriety.

A more plausible analysis of the alcoholic's marriage is that there is a reciprocal relationship between the wife's behavior and her husband's drinking. The stress induced by the condition of the husband leads to characteristic behavior patterns in the wife which at times may prove to be counter-therapeutic. Jackson (1954) presented supportive evidence for this position, assuming that the behavior of the alcoholic's spouse changes systematically as abusive drinking increases. Orford and Guthrie (1968) identified five specific behavior patterns exhibited by these wives: (1) safeguarding family interests, (2) withdrawing from the marriage, (3) attacking, (4) acting out, and (5) protecting the husband. James and Goldman (1971) found that the use of these coping behaviors varied systematically as a function of the severity of the husband's drinking pattern (i.e., social drinking, excessive drinking, alcoholismic drinking, abstinent stage). It is also interesting to note that these investigators found that in over 70% of eighty-five couples studied, the wives married their husbands prior to the onset of his excessive drinking. This finding lends credence to the view that the wife's behavior seems to be an attempt to cope with a deteriorating marital situation.

Husbands of Alcoholics

Clinical and experimental information on the husbands of alcoholic wives is practically non-existent. This deficit in the literature exists despite rather high estimates of the incidence of alcoholism in women ranging from 700,000 to 4.5 million (Lindbeck, 1972). As with male alcoholics, divorce is a frequent concomitant of the female's drinking. These women also tend to marry alcoholic men, especially in marriages subsequent to their first one. Ullman (1952) found that 80% of the second marriages of a group of alcoholic women involved an alcoholic husband. This situation, in which both partners abuse alcohol, decreases the likelihood that either will be able to modify their drinking patterns.

In a review of the literature on alcoholic women, Lindbeck (1973) found only scant information on marriages with most reports based on anecdotal data. These clinical data suggest that the husband of the female alcoholic responds to his wife's drinking in a variety of counterproductive ways (i.e., in a manner similar to that of the wives of alcoholic men). Denial of the problem seems to be a frequent characteristic of these husbands. Public denial is facilitated by the fact that female alcoholics have a greater tendency to drink secretly than do their male counterparts (Belfer, Shader, Carroll, and Harmatz, 1971).

Alcoholic Couples

Frequently, both partners in a marriage drink excessively. This situation presents a complex interactional pattern which is especially resistant to change. Physical separation of these couples often must precede introduction of procedures to modify either partner's drinking. This step is necessary for several reasons. First, the mere presence of the marital partner may serve as a strong cue for drinking behavior. Second, even if both partners are attempting to change, neither one can serve as a model of appropriate behaviors and adequate adjustment for the other. Also, if one partner were to revert to abusive drinking early in the treatment regime, the other partner would have much greater difficulty in controlling his/her drinking.

Although there have been no systematic analyses of these marriages, Steinglass, Weiner, and Mendelson (1971) and Steinglass and Weiner (1970) have studied pairs of close relatives (father—son, brother—brother) in which both individuals were alcoholics. Their theoretical and methodological approach to these pairs can be readily applied to the study of alcoholic couples. Their conceptualization is one of a *systems approach* in which alcoholic behavior can best be understood in terms of its relationship to the ongoing interpersonal and environmental "system" in which it occurs. Thus, experimental investigation of a husband's drinking in an isolated experimental setting may reveal conclusions which are erroneous if he does most of his drinking with his wife or drinking buddies.

This empirical systems analysis would seem to be an appropriate model for gathering much needed data on these marriages. Closed-circuit television monitoring of such interactions would allow for a more objective appraisal of both verbal and non-verbal behaviors. Extended observations of this type over a period of time would yield detailed analysis of the marriage together with objective formulations on the most efficacious methods of therapy.

Social-Learning Formulation

A behavior modification approach to the alcoholic's marriage is based on a social-learning formulation of social interaction. A basic tenet of this approach is that marital behavior is learned. Furthermore, this learning occurs by way of functional relationships between behaviors and their consequences. Thus, a husband engages in a particular set of verbalizations or motor actions which in turn elicit particular responses from his wife. Her responses to some types of behavior will be reinforcing and thus increase the likelihood that her husband will behave in that way again. On the other hand, she may either socially punish or ignore other kinds of behaviors which will then decrease in frequency. What determines her responses to her husband is in part determined by her past experiences in social contexts (i.e., her own family, other men she has known, etc.) and partly by the present situation in which the interaction occurs.

As with other theoretical approaches, the behavioral viewpoint assumes that certain interactional patterns present in the alcoholic's marriage actually maintain abusive drinking. Clinically, such marriages are characterized by each partner's general avoidance of the other, together with a high frequency of quarrels about drinking (James and Goldman, 1971). Stuart (1969) refers to this pattern as "negative scanning" and has found it to be typical of conflictual marriages in general. His term describes marital interactions in which one spouse systematically attends to (via looking, smiling, nagging) certain negative behaviors of his or her partner. Concomitantly, positive behaviors are generally ignored. Laws of operant conditioning would predict that alcoholic behaviors (alcohol related conversation, alcohol purchases, alcohol on breath, alcohol consumption) that are attended to and hence reinforced by the spouse will increase in frequency. On the other hand, positive behaviors (refusing an alcoholic drink, associating with non-drinking companions, spending time with the children) which are ignored will be extinguished and decrease in frequency of occurrence.

This phenomenon is well illustrated by Hersen, Miller, and Eisler (1972) in one of the few descriptive experimental analyses in this area. Rather than focusing exclusively on the alcoholic or his spouse, these investigators studied reciprocal interaction patterns between four chronic alcoholics and their wives. The couples had been married from 22 to 29 years with a mean of 26 years. Mean history of abusive drinking for the husbands was 9 years. Using a videotape assessment system as described in Chapter 2 (Eisler, Hersen, and Agras, 1973a, 1973b), each couple was monitored via closed-circuit television while they conversed in a laboratory studio designed to simulate a living-room situation. Couples were monitored for a total of 24 minutes with instructions to vary conversation content occurring at 6-minute intervals. After an initial warm-up phase, each couple was requested to converse for 6 minutes about any topic other than the husband's alcohol problem. At the conclusion of this interval the couple was asked to talk only about the husband's drinking problem for 6 minutes. Six minutes of non-alcohol related and 6 minutes of alcohol related conversation were repeated during the final two phases of videotaping.

Subsequent to the experiment, two observers independently rated each phase of the design on measures of looking and speech duration. Mean percentage of agreement for these raters was high, ranging from 95% to 100%. Videotaped segments of all phases were also rated for the occurrence of alcohol related words to ensure that the couples followed instructions. These ratings indicated that the couples did follow directions by maintaining conversation on the assigned topic.

Results are depicted in Figure 6.1 which presents mean data for the four couples. Mean duration of looking by wives during the first non-alcohol segment ranged from 26 to 43 seconds, and for husbands from 11 to 24 seconds. During the first alcohol segment wives drastically increased their looking to a range of 57 to 70 seconds. Reinstatement of non-alcohol related conversation resulted in a decrease in the wives' looking. In the last phase, looking again increased in relation to alcohol content. The looking of the husbands showed a slightly reversed trend. Speech data indicated equal speech duration for both husbands

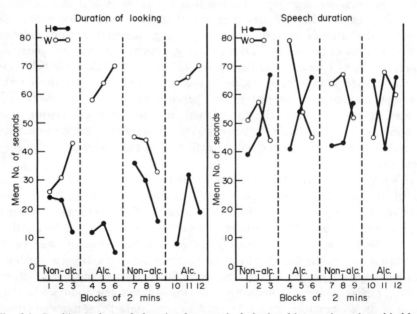

Fig. 6.1. Looking and speech duration for non-alcohol related interactions plotted in blocks of 2 minutes (Hersen, Miller, and Eisler, 1973). Reprinted by permission from *Quarterly Journal of Studies on Alcohol*, Vol. 34, pp. 516–520, 1973. Copyright by Quarterly Journal of Studies on Alcohol, Inc., New Brunswick, N.J. 08903.

and wives during all phases. Thus, these wives unwittingly attended more to alcohol related speech and ignored more appropriate conversation. In reality, an interactive pattern probably exists in which the husband's alcoholic behaviors serve as discriminative stimuli for increased attending by the wife. In turn, her attention reinforces alcoholic behavior and continues the cycle.

Stuart's (1969) comments regarding an operant-interpersonal approach to marital problems are also relevant to the alcoholic marriage. He observed that there are two characteristic patterns present in most conflictual marriages. The first is *control-coercion* in which one member seeks to gain positive reinforcement from the other in exchange for negative reinforcement. Negative reinforcement refers to an aversive event (e.g., nagging or excessive drinking) which, when removed, increases the probability of occurrence of the behavior which preceded its removal. In other words, the message from the spouse to the alcoholic is, "If you will stop drinking, I will stop nagging." As perceived by the alcoholic the situation is reversed, namely, "If you will stop nagging, I will stop drinking so much." Such patterns of interaction are quite unsuccessful in altering the marital partner's behavior and instead engender intense negative emotional feelings. Such emotional states may then serve as cues for either more drinking or more nagging. Often, however, these patterns do modify verbal behavior. That is, the alcoholic learns that if he says, "I promise never to take another drink," the spouse's nagging decreases. The decrease in her nagging, a positive event to the alcoholic, reinforces his verbal promises and increases the likelihood that he will continue to *promise* to discontinue his drinking. It is unlikely, however, that his actual drinking behavior will be affected by these control-coercive maneuvers.

The second pattern mentioned by Stuart (1969) is that of *withdrawal*, by which one partner simply avoids or escapes from the negative behaviors of the other. This avoidance of the problem behaviors only serves to further maintain marital dissatisfaction.

Stuart (1969) also proposes three assumptions regarding troubled marriages:

(1) Marital interactions at any point in time are the most rewarding of all available alternative behaviors. Thus, excessive alcohol consumption in the evening would be more rewarding to the alcoholic than conversing with his/her spouse or playing with the children. Treatment might focus on increasing the positive reinforcing value of the family members.

(2) Ideal marital interactions imply mutual reciprocity in the exchange of rewards, duties and responsibilities. Thus, in "happy marriages" it is implicit that when the wife cooks a good meal or has washed the car, the husband will reciprocate by washing the dishes or taking his wife out to a movie. In the alcoholic's marriage, the non-alcoholic spouse often is forced to take on a majority of the family responsibilities and is seldom

rewarded for doing this. On the other hand, the alcoholic's attempts to assume responsibility often result in criticism from the spouse (e.g., "I knew you couldn't handle that. I should have done it myself"), which only serves to further decrease the likelihood of such behavior.

(3) Couples must be able to use mutual reward to influence each other's behavior. When this fails, negative means of control are used almost exclusively. As already mentioned, these patterns are not conducive to successful relationships.

Altering Marital Interactions

There are two basic objectives in modifying the alcoholic's marriage. First, alcohol related interactional patterns which are assumed to maintain abusive drinking must be altered. This might involve teaching the spouse to attend more systematically to sober behaviors and socially punish alcoholic ones. Concomitantly, the alcoholic partner is taught to reinforce his spouse for positive reactions (e.g., commenting positively about his sobriety) and withhold reinforcement for negative reactions (e.g., nagging). The second goal involves altering general marital patterns to provide an atmosphere that is more conducive to sobriety. Couples might be taught how to reinforce one another, or how to interact in a more direct, positive manner. The characteristic alcoholic marriage with few positive interactional statements can hardly be satisfying to either partner. The major behavioral techniques used to accomplish these goals include social skills training for both partners and contingency management (e.g., via behavioral contracting).

Social Skills Training

As discussed above, the alcoholic and his spouse exhibit poor social interactional skills. Weiss, Hops, and Patterson (1972) consider that the three areas in most need of alteration in such marriages are affectional exchanges, problem solving, and mutual behavior change attempts. Similarly, Eisler and Hersen (1973) set three major goals for behavioral marital intervention:

(1) Develop new problem solving behaviors.
(2) Express positive and negative affect.
(3) Apply new skills to a variety of family situations.

Two phases of intervention appear to be necessary to accomplish these goals. *First*, couples must be taught the necessary social-interactional skills and then given practice at using them under controlled conditions. *Second*, these newly acquired interactions must be scheduled and programmed to occur in the natural environment. Thus, a combination of social skills or assertive training precedes the use of behavioral contracting.

In the initial therapeutic sessions with alcoholics and their spouses, an objective analysis of their interpersonal behaviors is required. The previously described videotape assessment system devised by Eisler, Hersen, and Agras (1973a, 1973b) is useful in this regard. A variety of specific behavioral goals of social skills training could be accumulated in this manner. Such goals might include:

(1) Increase positive statements to partner (e.g., "That dinner was great, Honey").
(2) Increase frequency of smiling at partner.
(3) Increase amount of looking at partner.
(4) Increase direct expression of feelings between partners (e.g., "When you nag me about my past drinking, I get irritated and feel like having a drink. Let's agree not to mention it again").
(5) Increase physical contact (e.g., hugging, kissing).
(6) Increase frequency of outings together (e.g., to movies, dinner).
(7) Increase shared responsibilities and solving family problems as a team.
(8) Decrease alcohol-related conversation.
(9) Decrease negative, critical, and sarcastic comments.
(10) Decrease conversation about past misdeeds of either partner.

These specific behaviors can be promoted through the use of instructions, prompts, modeling, videotaped feedback, behavioral rehearsal, and social reinforcement in marital counseling sessions. Such behavioral patterns must be taught one at a time for maximum therapeutic effects. Generally, the husband and wife are instructed to change one aspect of their behavior (e.g., "Try to smile more at your husband/wife, especially when he/she is making positive, goal-oriented statements") at a time. Through such devices as a small transistorized transmitter and earplug receiver, the wife can either be prompted to smile at appropriate times or be socially reinforced for complying with the instructions. Prompts and feedback for verbal content can also be provided. As the couple becomes more proficient in interacting, such prompts can gradually be faded out.

Once a number of new behavior patterns have been taught, "homework" assignments are given to allow the couple to practice more appropriate interactions in the natural environment. These assignments might be very simple in the initial stages of treatment. The couple might be instructed to spend 20 minutes each evening discussing a mutually pleasurable topic. Emphasis during this interaction might be placed on whichever behaviors (e.g., smiling, looking, mutually reinforcing) were being taught during that particular week.

Frequently, specific types of social skills must be stressed in the training process. For example, marital situations requiring assertiveness are particularly stressful for alcoholics since they frequently are deficient in this behavior. Assertive behavior refers to the direct expression of personal rights and feelings (both positive and negative). While this behavior pattern and its relationship to alcoholism was discussed in an earlier chapter, a brief example here will serve to demonstrate its importance in the marital relationship. A case reported by Eisler, Miller, Hersen, and Alford (1974) illustrates the effects of assertive training with an alcoholic both on his marital relationship and his drinking behavior.

The subject was a 52-year-old manager of a large automotive service station who had a 6-year history of excessive, sporadic drinking. Drinking episodes generally followed intense marital conflict. Issues involved in the marital discord were the disciplining of their retarded daughter, the amount of time the husband spent with his wife, and the husband's drinking even moderately. The subject reported an inability to cope with disagreements of this nature and usually allowed his wife to predominate.

The couple was videotaped while discussing their marital difficulties both before and after the husband received intensive assertive training. Additionally, blood/alcohol levels were determined from breath samples taken at weekly intervals on a random basis for 6 weeks prior and subsequent to assertive training.

During treatment the husband was trained on ten simulated marital encounters typical of his interactions with his wife. A surrogate wife (research assistant) role-played the marital encounters. For example, a typical scene structured for the husband's response was as follows:

> You've just come home from work about an hour later than usual. You had to stay late to finish a difficult job. As soon as you come in the door, your wife rushes up to you very upset. She says, "Don't tell me you've been working all this time. I know you've been drinking again."

Based on observations of the couple's initial interaction, four target behaviors were selected to be modified in the husband's training in assertion: (1) duration of looking; (2) duration of speech; (3) requests for the interpersonal partner to change her behavior; and (4) latency of response. The husband received direct instructions, behavioral rehearsal, and performance feedback in order to improve assertive responses.

Pre- and post-treatment marital videotapes were rated on (1) speech duration; (2) looking duration; (3) references to the husband's drinking; and (4) requests for the spouse to change his or her behavior. Figure 6.2 shows data from the first 20 minutes of marital interaction before and after training presented in blocks of

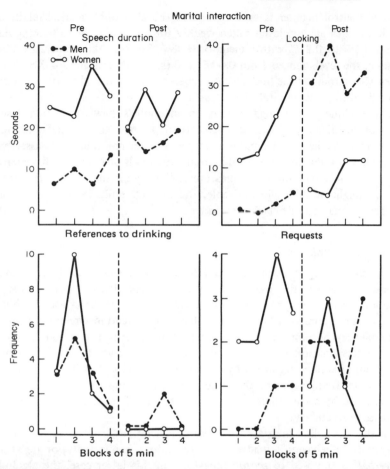

Fig. 6.2. Pre- and posttreatment measures of marital interaction for speech duration, looking duration, references to husband's drinking, and behavioral requests (Eisler, Miller, Hersen, and Alford, 1974). Reprinted by permission from *Archives of General Psychiatry*, 1974, **30**, 643–9.

5 minutes. Ratings indicated that the husband's duration of speech and duration of looking increased considerably following training, whereas the wife showed substantial decreases on both measures. Frequency of statements related to the husband's drinking showed a sharp decrease for both spouses following the husband's assertive training. Requests for changes in the spouse's behavior increased from a very low rate to a moderate rate in the husband, while the wife changed from a high rate of behavioral requests to a more moderate rate. It is interesting to note that the pre-test marital interaction in which the husband plays a rather passive-avoidant role and the wife behaves in a more active,

coercive-control manner is very typical of the alcoholic's marital relationship. Finally, breath alcohol levels taken weekly for 6 weeks prior to training ranged from 0.01% to 0.21% with a mean of 0.08%. For 6-weekly intervals following training, the levels ranged from 0.00% to 0.04% with a mean of 0.02%. Thus, it appears that training the husband to be assertive in simulated marital encounters generalized to actual marital interaction.

These clinical data suggest that an alcoholic's newly acquired assertive behavior significantly affects the behavior of his wife in interpersonal marital encounters. As he became more assertive, she became much less assertive on these measures. Possibly, the ideal marital situation is one in which both partners are more equivalent on these measures. While joint marital-assertive training sessions might be clinically advisable, the present results indicate that training one partner may be sufficient in some cases.

Behavioral Contracting

One method for facilitating new interactions between the alcoholic and his spouse is through the use of *behavioral* or *contingency contracting*. This technique places emphasis on the *consequences* of behavior. Within the social-learning approach to marital intervention, rearrangement of behavioral consequences becomes a primary focus of treatment. The rationale is that if appropriate behaviors of one marital partner are followed by rewards (increased attention, affection) furnished by the other partner, such behaviors will tend to increase in frequency. On the other hand, inappropriate behaviors that are consequated by social punishment or withdrawal of rewards by the spouse will decrease in frequency.

In the alcoholic's marriage, such contingencies either occur in reverse (thus, objectionable behavior is inadvertently rewarded), haphazardly, or are attached to *verbal* as opposed to *motor* behaviors. In this latter case, the alcoholic is praised for his promises to quit drinking rather than his positive actions in this regard. Such patterns also lead to the use of threats to invoke a contingency which are seldom carried through. The spouse often threatens, "I will divorce you if you take one more drink." Again, this leads to changes in the alcoholic's *verbal* behavior and at times, perhaps, a temporary decrease in his drinking behavior. The wife's behavior is rewarded and she is then more likely to use this threat in the future. The non-alcoholic spouse, however, seldom separates from the alcoholic contingent upon his drinking. She may, indeed, only leave after many years of frustration and despair. The use of separation as a consequence of excessive drinking can often be a powerful therapeutic tool when used systematically in a contingent manner. Indeed, many alcoholics suddenly become "motivated" to change and enter into treatment programs soon after their spouse has left them.

Behavioral contracting offers a systematic way of scheduling negative consequences for unacceptable behaviors (e.g., excessive drinking) and positive consequences for appropriate behaviors (e.g., moderate drinking or total abstinence). As described by Stuart (1969) and Weiss, Hops, and Patterson (1972), contracting has proven to be a very successful method of altering chronically disordered marriages. Essentially, the contract is a written document, often signed by both marital partners and the clinician, specifying behaviors which are to be increased or decreased. Contingencies are attached to each partner's compliance or non-compliance with the agreement.

During initial sessions the general social-learning approach to marital difficulties must be discussed with the couple. Couples traditionally perceive problem behaviors of their spouse as being internally determined (e.g., "If he weren't so stubborn, things would be okay") as opposed to functionally determined by reciprocal interactions between the two. Also, couples may perceive such a contractual bargaining approach as being too simplistic and mechanical to solve their complex marital problems. With assurance and encouragement from the clinician together with small improvements subsequent to early sessions, these apprehensions are usually allayed.

After these initial discussions the couple must be taught to pinpoint behaviors and their consequences. For example, rather than speaking in global terms such as, "My husband has a bad attitude," the wife is encouraged to specify her husband's verbal and motor behaviors that she would like to occur more often or less often. For example, she may want him to come home at a specified time, converse with her for at least a half hour each evening, limit his alcohol consumption to one drink per evening, and pay the monthly bills. The husband may want his wife to decrease her nagging about his drinking, increase frequency of sexual intercourse, and discuss with him a more systematic method of disciplining the children. Certain marital inventories such as the one devised by Knox (1971) may help in this process. Such books as Patterson's (1971) *Families* are easily read and can be recommended to the couple.

Training in "labelling functional relationships" (Weiss, Hops, and Patterson, 1972) must also occur. Couples must learn to identify social consequences of specific behaviors. That is, "When my husband arrived at home late for dinner, I started to cry, left his presence, and ran to my room." This observation provides more relevant data on the interaction than if the wife had reported, "He hurt my feelings last night by being so inconsiderate." An advantage of such labeling "... is that role expections of family members are clearly applied to *observable*, behavior" (Eisler and Hersen, 1973), thus reducing non-productive verbal exchanges focusing on vague perceptions of interactions. It is often useful to instruct couples to record relevant behavioral sequences soon after they occur. This tends to ensure more accurate, objective observations of both verbal and non-verbal behaviors and also provides a means of assessing alterations in interactional patterns as treatment continues. Records can then be kept in graphic form so that the couple can easily see the progress that they are achieving. Figures 6.3 and 6.4 provide examples of such graphing. Daily records on number of daily nagging episodes or number of affectional statements objectify assessment of success.

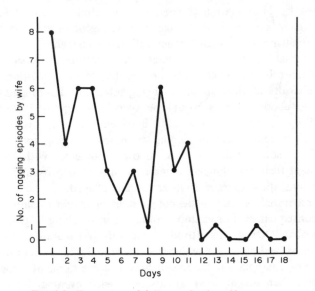

Fig. 6.3. Frequency of daily nagging by wife.

The contract is then negotiated and prepared in written form. Contents of the agreement are often expressed in "trade offs" or social bartering. That is, the husband agrees to limit his drinking to one alcoholic beverage per day if his wife limits her nagging to one reference to drinking per day. Or he might agree to spend one half hour talking with his wife in the evening and helping his son with his school work in return for more frequent sexual intercourse with his wife.* Thus, natural occurring behaviors are simply scheduled in a functional relationship to one another.

The contract should state the required behaviors and their contingencies very clearly. It must deal only with observable behaviors. Thus, a wife's drinking at home during the day could not be controlled in this type of contract since the husband would not be able to verify the occurrence of this behavior. Contracts

* It may be noted that sexual problems, notably impotence and orgasmic dysfunction, are a frequent concomitant of excessive drinking. If necessary, sexual retraining can be instituted concomitantly with contracting. Techniques such as those described by Masters and Johnson (1970) and Knox (1971) have proven to be quite effective in this regard.

should also stress positive social consequences for appropriate behaviors. Therapeutic success is often more rapid when initial contracts are kept simple, dealing only with a few behavior patterns. Contracts remain negotiable at all times with the clinician often acting as the arbitrator. As new functional social relationships become habitual the formal written contract can be gradually faded out.

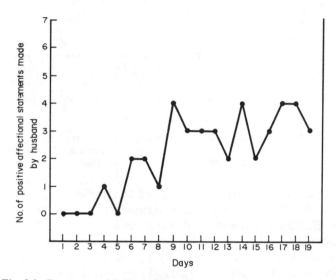

Fig. 6.4. Frequency of daily positive affectional statements by husband.

A case report by Miller (1973) provides a clinical example of the successful use of contracting with an excessive drinker and his wife. The subject was a 44-year-old male who consumed between 4 to 6 pints of bourbon per week. According to his reports, his wife's frequent critical comments and disapproving glances in reference to his drinking tended to increase his consumption. A baseline record of alcohol consumption charted by the husband (and corroborated by the wife) for 2 weeks prior to treatment indicated a mean consumption of seven to eight "drinks" (defined as 1½ oz. of alcohol either straight or mixed) a day. Under the terms of a behavioral contract the husband agreed to limit his consumption to between one and three drinks a day in the presence of his wife. Drinking in excess of this or in any other situation (as determined by actual observation, liquor on his breath, or intoxicated behavior) resulted in a monetary fine of $20.00 payable to his wife (to be spent as frivolously as possible on a non-essential item) and withdrawal of attention by the wife. The contract required the wife to pay a similar fine (both were working independently) if she engaged in negative verbal or nonverbal responses to her

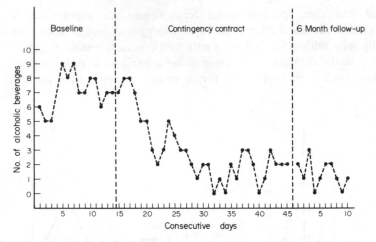

Fig. 6.5. Number of alcoholic beverages consumed (From Milton, P. M. The use of behavioral contracting in the treatment of alcoholism: A case study. *Behavior Therapy*, 1972, 3, 593–6. Reprinted with permission from Academic Press.)

husband's drinking. Also, each spouse agreed to provide increased attention and affection to the other for complying with the stipulations of the contract. Daily records of drinking behavior were recorded and are presented in Fig. 6.5. Soon after the contract was initiated the husband's drinking dropped within acceptable limits. Drinking stabilized by the thirtieth day of the study, with some abstinent days apparent. A 10-day probe period at a 6-month follow-up contact revealed maintenance of the moderate drinking pattern. The couple also reported improved marital relations in other areas.

Obstacles to Behavior Change

The specifics of husband–wife interactions are often easily taught via social skills training and subsequently scheduled via behavioral contracting. However, whether or not these new response styles are initiated in the natural environment is a more complex problem. The clinician, then, must ensure that the new interactional behaviors are initiated when they are scheduled to occur. For example, that the spouse will, indeed, praise her alcoholic partner when he remains sober or that the alcoholic takes his wife out to dinner contingent upon her decreased nagging. Once the new behaviors are initiated, the clinician must ensure that they will be maintained by the environment. Such maintenance cannot be left to chance, and application of reinforcement for these new interactions must be systematically scheduled.

The initiation of new interactional patterns is at times difficult due to a number of factors. The most prominent of these involves the past history of the couple. That is, they have been interacting so poorly for so long that their old response styles (e.g., coercion, avoidance) strongly compete with the new ones (e.g., direct confrontation, positive conversation). It is often helpful to give the couple extended practice (over-learning), in the therapy setting, for their new response styles. Conflictual situations, with the ensuing emotional involvement, can be recreated (with the therapist present) so that old patterns can be extinguished while new ones are being reinforced. In staged role playing sessions of typical marital encounters, couples often become as involved as they would in the real-life situation. Extensive practice in such simulated encounters helps to build in new responses so that they are more likely to occur *in vivo*.

It is always helpful to provide each partner with concrete alternatives to old response patterns. For example, a husband who is simply instructed to refrain from nagging when his alcoholic wife talks about having a drink may have great difficulty in complying since nagging in that situation would strongly compete with silence. In fact, saying nothing may be aversive to the husband who perceives such action (or lack of it) as not standing up for his rights in the marriage. He is more likely to alter his behavior if provided with a specific alternative to nagging. That is, whenever his wife discusses drinking he is to: (a) immediately leave her presence, or (b) change the subject. Both of these responses are incompatible with nagging since the spouse cannot change the subject and nag about drinking at the same time.

Another hindrance in initiation of behavior change in some cases is the extreme sensitivity of the non-alcoholic spouse to alcohol related stimuli. This is most often seen in alcoholic marriages of long duration in which the mere sight or mention of alcohol sets off a chain of coercive verbal behaviors. It is also prevalent in marriages in which the non-alcoholic partner is an abstainer with strong religious or moral judgments about drinking, even in moderation. This issue was prominent in a study by Cheek, Franks, Laucius, and Burtle (1971) in which wives of alcoholics were trained to use behavior modification techniques to change family interactions. A group of these wives attended ten weekly meetings during which they received instructions on pinpointing, recording, and consequating behaviors. They were to apply these techniques to the three most disruptive aspects of their alcoholic husbands' behavior: aggressiveness, social withdrawal, and failure to accept a responsible adult role in the family. Excessive drinking was not directly modified. Unfortunately, none of the wives were able to consistently apply the newly acquired responses. It seems that these wives were so sensitized to their alcoholic husbands' behavior that the tension and anger induced when dealing with them inhibited behavioral changes. The authors suggest a two-pronged behavioral program to combat this phenomenon. In this approach systematic desensitization (Wolpe, 1969) procedures would be applied to the wife so that scenes of alcohol related behaviors and general marital conflictual situations are paired with relaxation. This treatment should then allow the wife to take better advantage of the second phase of the program during which behavioral rehearsal and contingency contracting are used.

Along these same lines, Knox (1971) asserts that the wife's sensitivity to alcohol stimuli may be a particular problem when drinking in moderation rather than complete abstinence is the treatment goal. He also suggests the use of systematic desensitization to scenes of her husband's drinking. This should decrease the likelihood of her anxiety and/or negative verbal comments in such situations. Knox also suggests instructing the wife to drink her usual non-alcoholic beverages out of a cleaned, empty beer can in order to change the stimulus value of alcohol-related items.

A related obstacle to marital change involves the fact that, at times, providing a reward to the marital partner is actually aversive to the spouse (Tharpe and Wetzel, 1969). This is particularly true if the relationship has been characterized by passive-avoidance or coercive-control. Both partners have become highly aversive to one another and positive comments or mutual rewards seem incompatible with the current negative atmosphere in the marriage. In this instance rewards may be small at first and gradually faded in to the interaction. Stuart (1969), for example, has used a token system in which marital partners reward or punish the other by giving or taking tokens which are in turn traded in for reinforcements (e.g., fishing time, new dress, evening out to dinner). Initial dispensation of reward in this manner, although somewhat artificial, may facilitate positive interactions. Positive verbalizations, which have a low probability of occurrence in disturbed marriages, may then be gradually faded in as tokens are dispensed. After a while, the token system would be completely replaced with a more natural social reinforcement system.

References

BAILEY, M. B. Alcoholism and marriage: A review of research and professional literature. *Quarterly Journal of Studies on Alcohol*, 1961, 22, 81–97.

BAILEY, M. B., HABERMAN, P. and ALKSNE, H. Outcomes of alcoholic marriages: endurance, termination, or recovery. *Quarterly Journal of Studies on Alcohol*, 1962, 23, 610–23.

BAKER, H. M. Observations on prisoners. *Journal of Criminal Psychopathy*, 1941, 2, 367–75.

BALLARD, R. G. The interrelatedness of alcoholism and marital conflict. Symposium, 1958, 3. The interaction between marital conflict and alcoholism as seen through MMPI's of marriage partners. *American Journal of Orthopsychiatry*, 1959, 29, 528–46.

BELFER, M. L., SHADER, R. I., CARROL, M. and HARMATZ, J. S. Alcoholism in women. *Archives of General Psychiatry*, 1971, 25, 540–4.

CARTER, R. D. and THAMES, E. J. A case application of signaling system (SAM) to the assessment and modification of selected problems of marital communication. *Behavior Therapy*, 1973, 4, 629–45.

CHEEK, F. E., FRANKS, C. M., LAUCIUS, J. and BURTLE, V. Behavior modification training for wives of alcoholics. *Quarterly Journal of Studies on Alcohol*, 1971, 32, 456–61.

CLIFFORD, B. J. A study of the wives of rehabilitated and unrehabilitated alcoholics. *Social Casework*, 1960, 41, 457–60.

EDWARDS, P., HARVEY, C. and WHITEHEAD, P. C. Wives of alcoholics: A critical review and analysis. *Quarterly Journal of Studies on Alcohol*, 1973, 34, 112–32.

EISLER, R. M. and HERSEN, M. Behavioral techniques in family-oriented crisis intervention. *Archives of General Psychiatry*, 1973, 28, 111–16.

EISLER, R. M., HERSEN, M. and AGRAS, W. S. Videotape: A method for the controlled observation of nonverbal interpersonal behavior. *Behavior Therapy*, 1973, 4, 420–5.

EISLER, R. M., HERSEN, M. and AGRAS, W. S. Effects of videotape and instructional feedback on nonverbal marital interaction: An analog study. *Behavior Therapy*, 1973, 4, 551–8.

EISLER, R. M., MILLER, P. M., HERSEN, M. and ALFORD, H. Effects of assertive training on marital interaction. *Archives of General Psychiatry*, 1974, 30, 643–9.

FUTTERMAN, S. Personality trends in wives of alcoholics. *Journal of Psychiatric Social Work*, 1953, 23, 37–41.

HABERMAN, P. W. Psychological test score changes for wives of alcoholics during periods of drinking and sobriety. *Journal of Clinical Psychology*, 1964, 20, 230–2.

HEDBERG, A. G. and CAMPBELL, L. M. A comparison of four behavioral treatment approaches to alcoholism. *Journal of Behavior Therapy and Experimental Psychiatry*, in press.

HERSEN, M., MILLER, P. M. and EISLER, R. M. Interactions between alcoholics and their wives: A descriptive analysis of verbal and nonverbal behavior. *Quarterly Journal of Studies on Alcohol*, 1973, 34, 516–20.

JACKSON, J. K. The adjustment of the family to the crisis of alcoholism. *Quarterly Journal of Studies on Alcoholism*, 1954, 15, 562–86.

JAMES, J. E. and GOLDMAN, M. Behavior trends of wives of alcoholics. *Quarterly Journal of Studies on Alcohol*, 1971, 32, 373–81.

133

KNOX, D. *Marriage happiness: a behavioral approach to counseling*. Champaign, Illinois: Research Press Company, 1971.

KOGEN, K. L. and JACKSON, J. K. Patterns of atypical perceptions of self and spouse in wives of alcoholics. *Quarterly Journal of Studies on Alcohol*, 1964, **25**, 555–7.

LINDBECK, V. L. The woman alcoholic: a review of the literature. *International Journal of the Addictions*, 1972, 7, 567–80.

MASTERS, W. H. and JOHNSON, V. E. *Human sexual inadequacy*. Boston: Little, Brown, 1970.

MILLER, P. M. An analysis of chronic public drunkenness offenders with implications for behavioral intervention. *International Journal of the Addictions*, in press.

MILLER, P. M. The use of behavioral contracting in the treatment of alcoholism: A case report. *Behavior Therapy*, 1972, 3, 593–6.

MITCHELL, H. E. The interrelatedness of alcoholism and marital conflict. Symposium, 1958, 4. Interpersonal perception theory applied to conflicted marriages in which alcoholism is and is not a problem. *American Journal of Orthopsychiatry*, 1959, 29, 547–59.

ORFORD, J. and GUTHRIE, S. Coping behavior used by wives of alcoholics: A preliminary investigation. *International Congress on Alcohol and Alcoholism*, 1968, 1, 97.

PATTERSON, G. R. *Families*. Champaign, Illinois: Research Press Company, 1971.

PRICE, G. M. A study of the wives of twenty alcoholics. *Quarterly Journal of Studies on Alcohol*, 1945, 5, 620–7.

STEINGLASS, P. and WEINER, S. Familial interaction and determinents of drinking behavior. In N. K. Mello and J. H. Mendelson (Eds.) *Recent advances in studies of alcoholism: An interdisciplinary symposium.* Washington, D.C.: U.S. Government Printing Office, 1970, 687–705.

STEINGLASS, P., WEINER, S. and MENDELSON, J. A systems approach to alcoholism: A model and its clinical application. *Archives of General Psychiatry*, 1971, 24, 401–8.

STUART, R. B. Operant – interpersonal treatment for marital discord. *Journal of Consulting and Clinical Psychology*, 1969, 33, 675–82.

THARPE, R. G. and WETZEL, R. J. *Behavior modification in the natural environment*. New York: Academic Press, 1969.

ULLMAN, A. The psychological mechanism of alcohol addiction. *Quarterly Journal of Studies on Alcohol*, 1952, 13, 600–9.

WEINER, S., TAMERIN, J. S., STEINGLASS, P. and MENDELSON, J. H. Familial patterns in chronic alcoholism; A study of a father and son during experimental intoxication. *American Journal of Psychiatry*, 1971, **127**, 1646–51.

WEISS, R. L., HOPS, H. and PATTERSON, G. R. A framework for conceptualizing marital conflict, a technology for altering it, some data for evaluating it. Paper presented at the Fourth Annual International Conference on Behavior Modification, Banff, Alberta, Canada, March 1972.

WHALEN, T. Wives of alcoholics: Four types observed in a family service agency. *Quarterly Journal of Studies on Alcohol*, 1953, 14, 632–41.

WOLPE, J. *The practice of behavior therapy*. New York: Pergamon Press, 1969.

WOODRUFF, R. A., GUZE, S. B. and CLAYTON, P. J. Divorce among psychiatric out-patients. *British Journal of Psychiatry*, 1972, 121, 289–92.

CHAPTER 7

Controlled Social Drinking

Introduction

Traditionally, the singular goal of alcoholism treatment has been complete and total abstinence for the client. The widely held belief that this is the only realistic aim of treatment has gone unchallenged for decades. Recently, however, clinical and experimental evidence has demonstrated that some alcoholics, even chronic ones, have been able to achieve moderate, controlled drinking patterns and maintain them over extended periods of time. Such evidence, although highly controversial, has provided an impetus for three major research trends that have added significantly to the field. *First*, intensive investigations of the disease model of alcoholism upon which the notion of total abstinence is based have flourished. These studies (refer to Chapter 1) have failed to support one of the basic concepts of the disease model, namely, the "loss of control" hypothesis. Thus, it is apparent that under certain circumstances alcoholics do evidence control over their drinking and are not inevitably driven (by "irresistible cravings") to continued, excessive drinking after consuming small to moderate amounts of alcohol. *Second*, closer analysis, via direct systematic observations, of the individual components of social versus alcoholic drinking patterns is apparent. With the exception of nationwide sociological surveys of drinking practices (Cahalan, Cisin, and Crossley, 1969), relatively little data have been available on the specific nature of moderate drinking as it differs from excessive drinking patterns. *Third*, the accumulation of descriptive data paved the way for clinical investigations of treatment procedures geared toward inculcating controlled, social drinking patterns in alcoholics.

Clinical Evidence

A number of clinical reports of sustained social drinking by former alcoholics appeared during the 1950s (Lemere, 1953; Shea, 1954; Selzer and Holloway, 1957). Although the percentage of clients undergoing treatment who were able to drink in moderation after treatment was small (ranging from 3% to 16% of the population reported), these findings were noteworthy in that they

135

challenged a traditionally held belief. Little attention was given to these reports until a paper by D. L. Davies, Dean of the Institute of Psychiatry at the Maudsley Hospital in London, appeared in 1962. In this report Davies describes seven former chronic abusive drinkers who were all drinking in a moderate, controlled manner for continuous periods ranging from 7 to 11 years after treatment. None had been intoxicated during the follow-up period. What is perhaps the most noteworthy factor is that none of these patients received extensive psychotherapy or continuous follow-up assistance. Each was hospitalized from 2 to 5 months with treatment consisting of Antabuse, discussions, and social-vocational assistance. Each of these patients, however, made significant changes in occupation and/or social relationships in which heavy drinking was typical. Although this report was presented in a very careful, objective manner with rather conservative conclusions, the reactions to it were profound. Nevertheless, critiques questioning the legitimacy of complete abstinence criteria in alcoholism treatment continue to flourish (Pattison, 1968; Sobell and Sobell, 1973).

Social Drinkers Versus Alcoholics

Prior to attempts at inculcating controlled social drinking patterns in alcoholics, some very basic questions had to be answered. These questions related to the nature of the social drinking process. While researchers had been studying alcoholic drinking patterns for years, very little information was available on the drinking of non-alcoholic individuals.

Sociological and clinical data indicated that social drinkers appear to drink in more socially circumscribed situations than alcoholics. That is, their drinking is more likely to occur at social gatherings, during special holidays or celebrations, prior to a meal or with a meal in the case of wine. While it may be used to alleviate stress on an occasional basis, this is not a habitual state of affairs. While the questions of why, when, and where social drinkers consume alcohol still remain somewhat unclear, the "how" of social drinking has been delineated in experimental investigations. In a study preliminary to actually teaching alcoholics the skills of social drinking, Schaefer, Sobell, and Mills (1971) and Sobell, Schaefer, and Mills (1972) obtained baseline drinking information on both alcoholics and social drinkers. In the initial study subjects included sixteen male chronic alcoholics in an alcoholism treatment program at Patton State Hospital and fifteen males from the local community who described themselves as social drinkers. The groups were matched on age but unfortunately not on education. The social drinkers were significantly better educated (Mean = 16.53 years) than the alcoholics (Mean = 11.42 years). The subjects were allowed to drink in a simulated bar within the hospital. Subjects were observed in small groups and allowed to consume a total of 6 ounces of liquor or its equivalent in beer. Staff members located in the bar recorded specific componets of drinking behavior.

Interestingly, both groups ordered approximately the same number of drinks (5.3 and 5.2 respectively). Alcoholics tended to order straight drinks while social drinkers consumed mixed drinks. In addition, alcoholics took larger gulps of drinks than did social drinkers. Figure 7.1 illustrates the magnitude of sips, in ounces, for both the alcoholics and social drinkers.

This figure is noteworthy in that it sets norms to be followed when teaching social drinking skills. That is, sips for mixed drinks for social drinkers ranged from 0.2 ounce to approximately 0.4 ounce. Fewer differences were obtained when beer was the beverage consumed.

In a more extensive analysis Sobell, Schaefer, and Mills (1972) replicated this study using twenty-six alcoholics and twenty-three social drinkers. Unfortunately not only were educational levels of these groups significantly different, with social drinkers being better educated, but also the social drinkers were

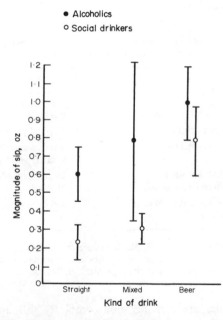

Fig. 7.1. Magnitude of sips (in liquid ounces) averaged and showing 95% confidence interval for sixteen male alcoholics and fifteen male social drinkers during experimental drinking session in a bar as a function of kind of drink consumed.

From Schaefer, H. H., Sobell, M. B., and Mills, K. C. Baseline drinking behaviors in alcoholics and social drinkers: Kinds of drinks and sip magnitude. *Behav. Res. & Therapy*, 1971, 9, 23–7. Reprinted by permission of H. H. Schaefer.

significantly younger than the alcoholics (29 years as compared to 38 years). Cahalan, Cisin, and Crossley (1969) have shown on the basis of self-report survey data that age and education are significant variables in regard to differences in drinking patterns.

Procedures of this study were identical to those of the previous one with the exception that the drinkers were allowed to order as much as 16 ounces of 86 proof whiskey as opposed to being limited to 6 ounces. With this increased limit, differences in the total amount consumed by the alcoholics and social drinkers were observed. Alcoholics ordered a mean of 15.27 drinks as compared to a mean of 6.65 drinks for the social drinkers. The difference between ordering straight versus mixed drinks and sip magnitude were similar to the results obtained in the first study. In addition, social drinkers took two to three times longer to consume a drink than alcoholics (1550 sec. as opposed to 590 sec. for mixed drinks). An unexpected result related to the time between sips. Alcoholics took significantly longer time in between sips than social drinkers for beer and straight drinks. No such differences were apparent, however, when mixed drinks were being consumed. Table 7.1 summarizes these data and presents behavioral profiles of alcoholics and social drinkers.

TABLE 7.1   Behavioral Profiles of Alcoholics and Normal Drinkers
(Sobell, Schaefer, and Mills, 1972)

Alcoholic	Normal drinker
1. Will almost always drink more than twelve drinks within a 4-hour period	1. Very seldom drinks more than twelve drinks within a 4-hour period
2. Generally orders straight drinks	2. Typically orders mixed drinks
3. Takes a larger size sip, no matter what type of drink	3. Takes a smaller size sip, no matter what type of drink
4. Drinks much faster than a normal drinker; sometimes three times as fast	4. Drinks considerably slower than an alcoholic
5. Sips more slowly than normal drinkers, but larger mouthful per sip	5. Takes many rapid and small sips

From Table 1 (p. 264) from: Sobell, M. B., Schaefer, H. H. and Mills, K. C. Differences in baseline drinking behavior between alcoholics and normal drinkers. *Behav. Res. & Therapy*, 1972, **10**, 257–67. Permission given by Mark B. Sobell.

While these profiles are certainly not complete, this analysis provides an objective starting point from which to build drinking profiles. A more naturalistic analysis in the community environment, while more limited in experimental control, would seem to provide more realistic data on day-to-day drinking patterns. Matching subjects on age and educational variables is essential and a replication of the above studies with this in mind would seem warranted.

Differences in drinking patterns may represent an artifact of socioeconomic status and/or age. Drinking norms may then have to be developed for these groupings separately. It seems doubtful that, in a society with no formal training on how to drink, a single pattern of normal versus alcoholic drinking will be found.

Treatment Approaches

After the initial interest in descriptively gathering baseline information on drinking patterns, the next step was to construct, implement and evaluate treatment programs to inculcate controlled, social drinking patterns in alcoholics. The several methods that have been reported include the use of aversive procedures, bio-feedback, operant approaches, instructions-feedback-modeling and comprehensive treatments. Social drinking as a treatment goal is still a relatively new area and the studies evaluating treatments in each of these areas are relatively few.

Aversive Procedures

In one of the first studies with the goal of social drinking for alcoholics, Mills, Sobell, and Schaefer (1971) treated thirteen hospitalized male alcoholics using aversive procedures. Treatment was conducted in a hospital dayroom that had been converted into a bar. Subjects were seated at the bar, two at a time, and electrodes attached to a shock generator were taped to their fingers. They were instructed to freely order drinks but to do so in a socially acceptable manner. This included ordering mixed drinks, sipping drinks, and consuming a maximum of 3 ounces of 86-proof liquor. The subject received a strong electric shock to his fingers if he either ordered a straight drink and gulped it (defined as any more than one-seventh of the total volume of the drink) or if he ordered more than three drinks. Mild shock was administered if the subject either ordered a straight drink and sipped or ordered a mixed drink and gulped. No shocks were administered if the subject drank in the manner in which he was instructed.

Results were presented in terms of drinking in the experimental bar and drinking during follow-up contracts in the natural environment. Of the nine subjects who completed at least fourteen training sessions, all demonstrated significant changes toward more appropriate social drinking skills as the sessions progressed. Follow-up data at 6-week and 6-month intervals were not promising. At 6 weeks after hospital discharge, only two subjects in the experimental group were able to drink socially with three subjects remaining abstinent. In a control group that did not undergo the behavioral treatment none were drinking socially but two remained abstinent. While specifics of the 6-month follow-up were not available the authors reported that there was "... a decrease in subjects reporting less alcoholic behavior and an increase in the drunk category while 'improved' frequency remained the same." (p. 26) The authors suggest the use of social reinforcement of social drinking habits together with periodic booster follow-up treatments in order to enhance generalization to the community environment.

Roitzsch and Kilpatrick (1973) utilized a variation of this method to induce social drinking patterns in four male alcoholics. During initial sessions each subject was placed in a simulated bar setting and allowed to fix himself a drink in his usual manner. Records were obtained on the amount of alcohol poured, amount of ice and/or mixer, and the amount of time required to consume the drink. During a separate session measures of heart rate, respiration, and exosomatic electrodermal activity (EDR) were obtained while the subject mixed and consumed a drink. Treatment consisted of sequentially presenting electric shock to the hand contingent upon pouring more than 45 cc of alcohol in the glass, adding less than 155 cc of ice and mixer to the alcohol, and consuming the drink in less than 30 minutes. Sessions were scheduled until the criterion of three no-shock sessions were attained. Subsequent to this training, each subject was once again assessed physiologically, while he consumed a drink in his original fashion. All subjects attained the required drinking habits from between eleven to twenty-three sessions. Each subject also increased autonomic emotionality to drinking, as measured physiologically by EDR frequency, from the pre- to post-conditioning assessment session. Thus the procedures led to a conditioned emotional response in reaction to inappropriate drinking habits. The authors are currently planning subsequent studies using control groups to evaluate long-term clinical effects of this procedure.

These studies demonstrate that alcoholics can readily learn the skills of social drinking through conditioning procedures. It is unlikely, however, that such conditioning, *per se*, has any long-term influence over the maintenance of social drinking in the natural environment. While these techniques may help to initiate these patterns, more comprehensive treatment strategies are necessary to sustain success.

Blood/Alcohol Discrimination Training

A second method used to generate controlled drinking patterns involves teaching the client to discriminate his own blood/alcohol levels and then to use this information to maintain moderate concentration of alcohol in his system during drinking episodes. During discrimination training the client is requested to judge his blood/alcohol level at periodic intervals while he is consuming alcoholic beverages. Feedback is then provided on the accuracy of his judgements via breathalyzer assessments. The client is instructed to focus on his own idiosyncratic emotional and/or physiological states (e.g., numbness, facial "tingling") associated with various blood/alcohol concentrations.

Once the client can accurately discriminate these levels he must be taught to use them. This second phase, or control training, has been administered in different ways. Some investigators use an aversive conditioning (avoidance learning) paradigm in which the client is instructed to drink freely. Electric shock is then made contingent upon levels of blood/alcohol above a specified point (e.g., above 0.05%). Usually the level is set at a point corresponding to the consumption of two to three 1½ ounce alcoholic beverages within 1 hour. Shock can be avoided by drinking moderately. Less aversive methods have also been used in this regard. The client can be reinforced either socially or monetarily for maintaining a blood/alcohol concentration (BAC) below a certain level with corresponding loss of reinforcers for high blood/alcohol levels.

Lovibond and Caddy (1970) used a BAC discrimination training procedure to train outpatient alcoholics to become moderate drinkers. Treatment consisted of a 2-hour discrimination training session followed by a series of conditioning trials. During discrimination training subjects were asked to drink pure alcohol mixed in fruit juice with breathalyzer analyses being taken every 15 to 20 minutes. At each analysis the subject was required to estimate his current blood/alcohol concentration on the basis of his subjective feelings. He then received feedback as to his actual blood/alcohol level. During conditioning sessions shock electrodes were attached to the patient's chin and face. The patient was instructed to drink alcohol freely and was told to expect shocks at blood/alcohol levels of 0.065% or higher (reported to be equivalent to two to three double martinis consumed within 1 hour). Shocks were then delivered on this basis over six to twelve sessions. Approximately thirty to seventy shocks were administered.

The results indicated that alcoholics can quite easily learn to discriminate their blood/alcohol levels within ±0.01%. Follow-up data (16 to 60 weeks) on twenty-eight subjects completing treatment indicated that twenty-one were drinking in a controlled fashion (0.07% blood/alcohol concentration or less), three drank only in excess of this level once or twice per week, and only four drank above that level frequently. Unfortunately, these data are based on self-report of alcohol intake together with reports from relatives. Periodic breathalyzer analyses could have corroborated these findings. A group of thirteen control subjects receiving random as opposed to contingent shocks during treatment did not significantly alter their drinking behavior.

In a similar but more extensive analysis, Silverstein, Nathan, and Taylor (1974) examined the effects of feedback, social reinforcement, and token reinforcement in training alcoholics to estimate their blood/alcohol levels (BAL).

Four male chronic alcoholics were exposed to a two-phased treatment regime. Phase I began with a baseline period during which subjects were instructed to consume alcohol and then, at intervals throughout the day, judge their level of intoxication on a 40-point scale. BAL measures were obtained via breathalyzer analysis at least ten times per day per subject. Subsequent to baseline, estimation training began. This training consisted of three cycles with each cycle lasting 2 days. They included (a) feedback as to actual BAL after each judgement together with discussion of the emotional and physiological cues associated with varying levels, (b) random feedback averaging 50% of the trials, and (c) random feedback together with reinforcement (points exchangeable for money or alcohol) for accurate estimations. Estimation training was followed by a 2-day baseline period during which feedback and reinforcement were withheld.

During Phase II subjects were required to maintain a moderate BAL (80 mg/100 cc) over a period of time. A shaping procedure was used to train this ability. Initially BALs within the range of 30 to 130 mg/100 cc were reinforced with points. This range was gradually narrowed until subjects were finally reinforced only for BALs between 70 to 90 mg/100 cc.

A follow-up assessment was also conducted by requiring subjects to record daily drinking behavior and send this information to the investigators. Family members and friends were used to corroborate this information. Results indicated that the subjects were able to estimate their blood/alcohol levels most accurately when feedback was provided. Reinforcement did not appear to add significantly to this ability. Unlike Lovibond and Caddy's (1970) subjects, however, these subjects took many hours to learn to discriminate accurately and never reached the accuracy of Lovibond and Caddy's subjects. Also, Silverstein et al.'s subjects lost their ability to discriminate when external feedback was no longer provided. Thus, these subjects were able to maintain specified BALs as long as external feedback was provided to them. Follow-up results indicated that only one of the four subjects drank in a controlled manner during the follow-up period. However, at an 80-day follow-up session this subject was not able to estimate his BALs accurately.

While this study presents a very promising system by which discrimination training can be provided, the results are open to alternative interpretation. For example, it may be that the subjects were relying on external cues of the drinking behavior to maintain certain BALs. That is, they learned to count their drinks, pace themselves, etc. It would have been interesting to evaluate changes in these behaviors concurrently. It would be possible to inject alcohol so that these cues were not apparent and thus rule out their influence.

In a more recent investigation, Bois and Vogel-Sprott (1974) attempted to control for the influence of these external factors in a discrimination training procedure. Nine male social drinkers were provided with discrimination training with breathalyzer feedback during the experimental sessions. Procedures of training were similar to those described in the above mentioned studies. These social drinkers not only learned to accurately estimate low BAL levels during training but also, unlike Silverstein *et al.*'s (1974) alcoholic subjects, were able to maintain accurate judgements subsequent to training without the aid of feedback. Perhaps this ability of social drinkers acts as a deterrent to abusive drinking. Alcoholics may be deficient in these skills and more dependent, even after discrimination training, on external feedback as to the accuracy of their judgements. In a similar manner, obese individuals are less able to discriminate "hunger" on the basis of internal cues and thus must rely on the external environment (Schachter, 1971). This reliance, however, contributes to their abusive eating patterns.

A related issue with which Bois and Vogel-Sprott's study dealt illustrated the importance of the point in the drinking sequence at which judgements are made concerning BALs. It was found that the social drinkers could estimate BAL very accurately (±0.005%) when this level was rising or at its peak but not when it was falling. The authors suggest that this may be related to adaptation to sensations over time making it more difficult to detect cues associated with falling BALs. It would be interesting to compare these results with equivalent data on alcoholics. Alcoholics may actually be superior at judgements during falling BALs. Nathan and O'Brien (1971) have indicated that an alcoholic's drinking appears related to the maintenance of a high BAL level. It appears that he may discriminate decreases in these levels (via tremulousness, agitation, etc.) and drink to reestablish his previous baseline level.

Finally, Bois and Vogel-Sprott's data on the influence of external versus internal cues in making BAL judgements is not completely clear-cut. During some sessions the salience of external cues in relation to BAL judgements was lessened. The subject received a brandy glass containing 100 ml. of 7-Up, a drop of peppermint, and a cherry. Each subject was instructed to drink freely and to decide when he had reached a low BAL within the 0.04 to 0.06%. The "mint julep cocktail", as it was called, sufficiently distinguished the taste and amount of alcohol being consumed. During the next two sessions external cues were made more salient by instructing the subjects to mix and drink their customary beverages (e.g., martini, beer).

When these cues were absent, the difference between their judgements and those made with the assistance of external cues was not statistically significant. It appears, however, that these cues do play some role in judgements although the exact interaction is unclear. At the present time it seems that, clinically, a combination approach in which both internal and external cues are available to the alcoholic would lead to the most accurate discrimination training. More investigations are definitely needed to further delineate the capacities of alcoholics to maintain BAL discrimination over time.

Contingency Management

Operant conditioning strategies have also been used extensively in training controlled drinking skills. Essentially, consequences in the environment are arranged so that drinking above a certain level (e.g., 4 ounces of whiskey) results in punishment and drinking below that level produces reinforcement. Since the studies investigating this area have been discussed in Chapter 5, they will not be repeated here.

Instructions-Feedback-Modeling

If social drinking is viewed as a behavioral skill that one can acquire through learning, then techniques that have been successful in teaching other behavioral skills could be used in this regard. Thus far, most of the techniques used to induce appropriate drinking skills involve some form of aversive control. However, a number of studies have indicated that new behaviors can be easily taught via simple instructions, feedback, and/or modeling. In fact, such positive techniques would be preferred over the aversive ones since they often produce more stable behavior patterns and provide a treatment that is much less unpleasant for the client.

Occasionally, simple instructions to the client serve to change his behavior. While instructions alone serve to initiate changes in behavior, the effects are often short-lived and reinforcers for "instruction following" must be provided to maintain behavior. Instructions, however, are useful in teaching a new set of behaviors in which the client is deficient.

In a preliminary investigation, Miller and Becker (1975) examined the influence of instructions on the acquisition of the components of moderate drinking in two alcoholics. In addition, the study was designed to analyze the effects of modifying one component (e.g., sip size) on other components of drinking. Both subjects were chronic alcoholics voluntarily admitted to an inpatient alcoholism treatment program. The study was conducted in a laboratory room renovated to simulate a living room setting complete with couch, chairs and lamps, and a television set. On a side table adjacent to the couch on which the subject was sitting were placed the following: glasses, 100 cc of bourbon, 300 cc of mix (either water or Coke), and a shot glass. Subjects were seen individually once a day for 20 days with each session being videotaped. During each session the subject was instructed to fix himself a "drink" as he normally would if he were out of the hospital. Number of sips, intersip interval, percent of alcohol to mix, and mean sip amount (total amount consumed divided by the number of sips) were recorded. The study was divided into four phases with 5 days in each phase. Phase 1 constituted a baseline condition during which the subject was allowed to drink freely. Prior to each session in phase 2, he was instructed to take smaller sips. Prior to each session in phase 3 he was instructed to take smaller sips *and* to lengthen the time in between his sips. In phase 4 the instructions of diluting drinks by adding more mix and/or less alcohol was added. Thus, a multiple baseline across behaviors design (Barlow and Hersen, 1973) was used.

Results for Subject 1 are presented in Figure 7.2. During baseline, mean sip amount averaged between 21 and 23 cc per sip (30 cc = 1 ounce). Following instructions to take smaller sips, mean sip amount decreased markedly to a range of 8 to 12 cc. Incidentally, number of sips increased. It is interesting to note that

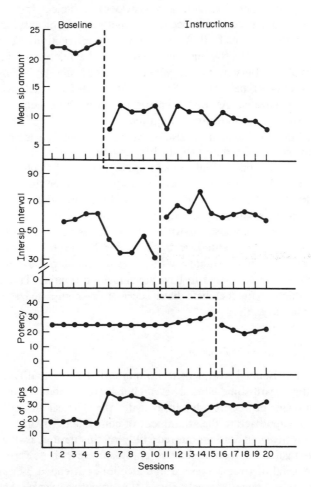

Fig. 7.2. Sequential effects of instructions on mean sip amount, intersip interval, potency, and number of sips for each drinking session (Miller and Becker, 1975).

as the subject took smaller sips, he began to sip at a faster rate as indicated by decreases in intersip interval. Instructions to lengthen intersip interval resulted in increases in this measure. Concomitantly, however, percent of alcohol to mix increased, indicating the subject was mixing "stronger" drinks. The subject complied with the final instructions by mixing more diluted alcoholic beverages. In a sense, the subject appeared to be attempting to compensate for changes in one component by making changes in another geared toward either faster drinking or more alcohol consumption. He was, however, able to acquire components of social drinking skills as a function of instructions. While Subject 2 also acquired these skills, he did not show the reactive inter-relationship in component behaviors as was evident in Subject 1.

Some clients may need more specific instructions and/or extensive feedback as to the extent to which they are following instructions. The fact that instructions were so effective may be related to the relative simplicity of the behaviors involved. Hersen, Eisler, Miller, Johnson, and Pinkston (1973), in studies of social skills, have also indicated that focused instructions can modify simple social behaviors. As the behavior becomes more complex, however, specific feedback and/or modeling is required.

Feedback and modeling may also serve to enhance the learning of social drinking skills. While Marlatt (1974) has demonstrated that observations of models of excessive drinking lead to increases in amount of alcohol consumed by college students, these procedures have not as yet been used in a systematic way in social drinking treatments. Patients could be provided with immediate feedback on their sip amount, intersip interval, or percent of alcohol to mix in their drinks. This may also assist them in assessing this information for themselves so that in natural settings feedback can be provided through self-monitoring. Providing patients with a live or videotaped example of social drinking skills would also seem to have advantages in training. Training in group settings in which some members have successfully completed social drinking training may be advisable.

Comprehensive Treatment Programs

Seldom is one isolated treatment technique sufficient to modify any behavior pattern. In this regard some clinical researchers have combined a number of the above mentioned procedures to investigate the clinical effectiveness of a broad-spectrum approach to the attainment of controlled drinking.

In an innovative but seldom quoted study of this nature, Ewing and Rouse (1972) investigated a comprehensive program geared toward outpatient alcoholics. A total of twenty-one chronic alcoholics attended 3-hour treatment sessions scheduled once a week for 12 consecutive weeks. Sessions con-sisted of group meetings scheduled in a setting resembling a living room and complete with various alcoholic beverages, ice, and mixers. Subjects were instructed to fix themselves drinks during the meetings. They received explicit instructions on social drinking skills such as mixing drinks, sipping rather than gulping, drinking slowly, and spacing drinks. During some sessions the therapists modeled these appropriate drinking skills by mixing and consuming drinks during the session. Breathalyzer readings were obtained at the beginning of the session (to ensure that patients had not been drinking before they arrived) and every 20 minutes during the session. Patients who were found to have a high (80 mg%) blood/alcohol content upon arrival were asked to leave and return sober the following week. As part of blood/alcohol discrimination training, patients were asked to judge these levels on the basis of their subjective experiences and appropriate feedback was then provided on their accuracy. In addition, random electric shock to the face was applied contingent upon drinking subsequent to a blood/alcohol concentration reading of 60 mg%. The therapists also used these drinking sessions to discuss negative consequences of excessive drinking and alternative modes of behavior. Spouses were encouraged to accompany patients to these sessions. The purpose of this attendance was to (a) desensitize the spouse to the patient's moderate drinking and (b) teach her ways of reinforcing successful attempts at controlled, social drinking at home. Patients were also requested to keep diaries of their drinking in between sessions.

Patients were evaluated on a rating scale designed to assess drinking, relations with spouse, family, and friends, work history, and health history. A maximum of 3 points was provided in each of these categories based on reports from the patient, family members, local physicians, or social workers. Since no control group was used, results are reported in terms of comparing patients on the basis of number of sessions attended. Follow-up periods ranged from 4 to 20 months and were unfortunately limited due to the rather high drop-out rate. Of six patients who had completed twelve sessions, three were maintaining a pattern of controlled social drinking. Out of a maximum improvement score of 12 on the categories maintained above, this group's mean overall rating was 5.5. Of patients who had completed from four to eleven sessions none were maintaining controlled drinking patterns (although one who had completed eleven sessions had gained much more control over his drinking than he had in the past). The mean overall improvement score for this group was only 0.90. None of the patients who completed less than four treatment sessions was maintaining sobriety and all were rated low on overall improvement (mean = 0.55). Unfortunately, the number of patients actually completing treatment was small (N = 6) and those not completing treatment do not actually comprise an adequately matched control group. Certainly, inclusion of continuous outpatient treatment sessions gradually spaced out over longer periods of time may have helped many of the patients sustain improvement.

In a more controlled and far more extensive analysis, Sobell and Sobell

(1973a, 1973b, 1973c) present probably the best total evaluation of a comprehensive treatment aimed toward social drinking skills available. Expanding on their original research using exclusively aversive procedures (Mills, Sobell, and Schaefer, 1971), the Sobells assigned (on the basis of the judgement of the therapist and the desires of the patient) a total of seventy chronic alcoholics to either a treatment goal of total abstinence or one of controlled, social drinking. Subjects in each group were then randomly assigned to either a behavioral treatment program or one in which conventional methods were used. The behavioral treatment included behavioral self-analysis, self-management training, social skills training, videotape feedback of both drunken and sober behavior, a programmed failure experience, and aversive conditioning. During aversive conditioning "abstainers" received electric shocks contingent upon any drinks while "controlled drinkers" were shocked only if they (a) ordered a straight drink, (b) took a sip larger than one-sixth of the glass' total volume, (c) ordered a drink within 20 minutes of a previously ordered drink, (d) ordered a total of more than three drinks.

A major part of this program which is lacking in most others of this nature included teaching alternative behavioral responses to situations leading to excessive drinking. The importance of such an approach has been greatly under-estimated in alcoholism treatment programs aimed either at controlled drinking or abstinence. In the Sobells' study, ten sessions were devoted to stimulus control training which consisted of the following:

1. Elucidating stimulus controls for heavy drinking.
2. Generating a universe of possibly effective alternative responses to those situations.
3. Evaluating the probable consequences of exercising each response.
4. Practising the most beneficial alternative responses under simulated conditions (Sobell and Sobell, 1973, p. 57).*

In order to evaluate the success of this inpatient program, a variety of assessment data were obtained at 6 weeks, 6 months, 1 year, and 2 years after discharge. This information included the number of days that the subject was intoxicated (more than 10 ounces of alcohol), number of days of controlled drinking (6 ounces or less), number of abstinent days, number of abstinent days resulting from hospital or jail incarceration, vocational status, use of therapeutic supports (AAs, counseling services), and an evaluation of general adjustment by a friend or relative.

* From Sobell, M. B. and Sobell, L. C. Individualized behavior therapy for alcoholics. *Behavior Therapy*, 1973, 4, 49—72.

TABLE 7.2   2-Year Follow-Up Results for Subjects in the Patton Experiment
(Sobell and Sobell, 1973)*

Group[a]	Measure	Year 1	Year 2
CD-E, N=20	n located for complete follow-up	20	19[b]
	Daily drinking disposition—		
	Mean % of days abstinent	45.29	65.85
	Mean % of days controlled drinking	25.19	23.76
	(Total mean % of days functioning well)	(70.48)	(89.61)
	Mean % of days drunk	14.02	7.87
	Mean % of days incarcerated in hospital	11.34	1.61
	Mean % of days incarcerated in jail	4.16	0.92
	Percentage of subjects found to be functioning well >80% of all days	55.00	78.90
CD-C, N=20	n located for complete follow-up	19	18[c]
	Daily drinking disposition—		
	Mean % of days abstinent	25.66	37.34
	Mean % of days controlled drinking	9.56	6.13
	(Total mean % of days functioning well)	(35.22)	(43.47)
	Mean % of days drunk	49.88	43.36
	Mean % of days incarcerated in hospital	5.55	2.14
	Mean % of days incarcerated in jail	9.35	6.03
	Percentage of subjects found to be functioning well ⩾80% of all days	10.50	22.22
ND-E, N=15	n located for complete follow-up	15	13[d]
	Daily drinking disposition—		
	Mean % of days abstinent	65.06	61.29
	Mean % of days controlled drinking	3.33	3.32
	(Total mean % of days functioning well)	(68.39)	(64.61)
	Mean % of days drunk	13.99	18.85
	Mean % of days incarcerated in hospital	11.77	6.49
	Mean % of days incarcerated in jail	5.85	10.05
	Percentage of subjects found to be functioning well ⩾80% of all days	33.33	53.87
ND-C, N=15	n located for complete follow-up	14[e]	14[e]
	Daily drinking disposition—		
	Mean % of days abstinent	32.35	43.62
	Mean % of days controlled drinking	6.13	1.56
	(Total mean % of days functioning well)	(38.48)	(45.18)
	Mean % of days drunk	39.85	35.91
	Mean % of days incarcerated in hospital	6.29	8.43
	Mean % of days incarcerated in jail	15.38	10.48
	Percentage of subjects found to be functioning well >80% of all days	7.14	21.43

* Reprinted by permission from Sobell, M. B., and Sobell, L. C. The need for realism, relevance, and operational assumptions in the study of substance dependence. Paper presented at the International Symposium on Alcohol and Drug Research, Toronto, October, 1973.

(Notes to references a—e appear on page 150.)

Notes to Table 7.2 appearing on page 149:

[a] Groups were controlled drinker, experimental (CD-E): controlled drinker, control (CD-C); non-drinker, experimental (ND-E); and non-drinker, control (ND-C).

[b] If complete data are obtained on the one missing CD-E subject, the total mean percentage of days functioning well for subjects in this group should decrease very slightly.

[c] If complete data are obtained for one of the two missing CD-C subjects (one CD-C subject has never been located), the total mean percentage of days functioning well for subjects in this group should decrease somewhat.

[d] One ND-E subject died shortly after the completion of his first year of follow-up because of non-alcohol-related causes. If complete data are obtained for the one missing ND-E subject, the total mean percentage of days functioning well for subjects in this group should remain about stable or increase slightly.

[e] One ND-C subject died about 8 weeks after discharge of barbiturate related causes (automobile accident, see Sobell and Sobell, 1972).

Follow-up data at all intervals indicated that the experimental subjects, both controlled drinkers and abstainers, were functioning better than the control group. Table 7.2 presents the follow-up information on subjects 2 years subsequent to treatment (Sobell and Sobell, 1973). The composite number reflects the percentage of subjects in each group found to be functioning well > 80% of all days. Of the controlled drinkers, 78.90% of the subjects receiving behavioral treatment were functioning well as compared to 23.50% in the control group. For subjects with the goal of abstinence, 53.87% of the experimental subjects were functioning well as compared to 21.43% of the control subjects. While these data appear very promising they are difficult to evaluate in comparison with other studies due to the different manner in which the results were analyzed. Most other evaluative studies of alcoholism treatment assess results in terms of total number of patients who are completely abstinent for 1 year after the completion of treatment. The Sobells' manner of assessing success, however, seems to be more clinically relevant than other studies. That is, merely because an individual becomes intoxicated once or twice within a year after treatment, he should definitely not be labeled as a therapeutic failure. It is hoped that more investigators will utilize this new evaluation system in the future.

Social Drinking Versus Abstinence

Now that controlled social drinking appears to be a possibility how does the clinician decide who is an appropriate candidate for this goal? Unfortunately, there are as yet few experimental data on which such judgements can be based. While most of the studies above randomly chose alcoholics for such treatment, others used specific criteria for inclusion. In the Sobell and Sobell (1973) study controlled drinking subjects were initially chosen on the basis of the following criteria: (1) could not identify with abstinence groups (e.g., AA), (2) requested social drinking as a goal, (3) had successfully practiced social drinking at some time in the past, and (4) had significant social supports for such behavior in their community environment. While such criteria are based more on clinical judgements than on empirical data, they offer a starting point from which such predictors can be evaluated.

Recently, Orford (1973) compared characteristics of patients whose drinking was "totally uncontrolled" versus those exhibiting "controlled drinking". None of these subjects had undergone treatment geared toward social drinking but were all selected from a group of seventy-seven patients who received traditional treatment of varying intensity ranging from one counseling session of frequent contact (up to a year's time) with a psychiatrist. The study was not designed to evaluate traditional psychiatric care but rather to follow up the drinking patterns of these patients over a 2-year period to differentiate controlled versus uncontrolled drinkers. On the basis of periodic reports of drinking from both the patient and his wife the proportion of drinking weeks during which drinking did not exceed 5 pints of beer or its equivalent in one day was calculated. On the basis of a dichotomy between the extensive upper and extreme lower portion of patients on this measure, twenty-two uncontrolled drinkers were compared with fourteen individuals whose drinking was mainly controlled. While no significant differences were found on the basis of age, the controlled drinkers were less chronic in terms of their alcohol dependence than the uncontrolled drinkers. While severity of family problems as a function of drinking were similar for both groups, the uncontrolled drinkers evidenced a history of significantly more morning drinking, tremors, hallucinations, and time lost from work. Uncontrolled drinkers tended to be arrested more frequently. There was a non-significant trend for controlled drinkers to express more negative attitudes and few positive attitudes regarding drinking than the uncontrolled drinkers. Uncontrolled drinkers more often thought of themselves as alcoholics. In addition uncontrolled drinkers were more likely to choose complete abstinence as their therapeutic goal. As far as stability is concerned, both controlled and uncontrolled drinking patterns remained highly stable over the 2-year period under study.

Conclusions and Future Trends

Current research has seriously questioned the validity of the disease model of alcoholism together with the "loss of control" hypothesis. Such research has provided a basis upon which alternative treatment goals can now be evaluated. The major alternative appears to be the possibility that some alcoholics, through specialized treatment procedures, can learn to drink in moderation, in a controlled, social manner. The emphasis here is certainly on *controlled* drinking and not just social drinking. Since the alcoholic has abused alcohol in the past he must constantly monitor both his drinking behavior *per se* and those events which have in the past been antecedents to excessive consumption.

This alternative treatment goal may have distinct clinical advantages. Our society is certainly a drinking-oriented one in which moderate social use of alcohol is encouraged and reinforced. An individual who must totally abstain from alcoholic beverages must also be willing to identify with certain religious and/or social groups or be subject to frequent temptations and pressures from others to drink. In this regard, younger problem drinkers may refrain from treatment due to a resistance to a life of abstinence. The controlled drinking goal offers these individuals an alternative which may be much more acceptable to them.

Concomitantly, there are a number of precautions which must be raised with regard to this relatively new approach. Some may see this as a panacea for the treatment of alcoholism and attempt to prematurely and indiscriminately apply this goal. Faddism is a notorious phenomenon in the behavior change area with new treatment approaches readily being applied on a widescale basis with only little evidence for their effectiveness. Two recent examples of this are the sensitivity group craze and the current popularity of transactional analysis. Surely by the time this book appears in print some other forms of therapeutic change will be "sweeping the country". Research into controlled drinking as a goal must continue in an open-minded scientific atmosphere.

Along these lines, research reports in this area also do not imply that all currently abstinent former alcoholics should be able to drink in moderation. Such drinking would definitely require specialized treatment strategies. In addition, the types of alcoholics who can accomplish this goal have yet to be identified.

Much more information is needed on the specific treatment techniques that might be most effective in inculcating social drinking patterns. Certainly, blood/alcohol level discrimination training, aversion procedures, modeling, performance feedback, social skills training, and self-management training appear promising. Once social drinking skills are taught, however, they must be reinforced and maintained by the environment. That is, one can be taught the mechanics of a new skill quite easily but whether he will use that skill is a more complex matter. As with the goal of abstinence, a total program of behavior change and environmental modifications must be adopted. Use of procedures simply to change the components of drinking behaviors are not likely to alter lifelong drinking habits. For example, the author is aware of a recent case of a young, 28-year-old black college student who was using alcohol to excess on a periodic basis. Upon examination it was determined that his drinking behavior was similar to that characteristic of alcoholics. That is, he gulped drinks, drank rapidly, and drank straight drinks. He was therefore taught, through videotape feedback and specific instructions, the components of social drinking. In addition, his girlfriend was advised to reinforce, with extra attention and recognition, appropriate social drinking as it occurred in the natural environment. The client easily learned social drinking behavior and successfully drank in moderation for approximately 5 months. At the end of that time, however, a highly emotional argument with his girlfriend precipitated his going to a local bar and becoming intoxicated. He continued this excessive drinking behavior two to three times a week for 2 to 3 months thereafter. While this client knew *how* to drink in a controlled fashion, he also knew *how* to drink to attain a rapid state of intoxication. Under periods of stress, he simply chose to drink in an alcoholic manner. Treatment, then, was incomplete since he did not learn ways to appropriately handle certain stressful interpersonal situations which were likely to induce poor drinking habits.

References

BARLOW, D. H. and HERSEN, M. Single-case experimental design. *Archives of General Psychiatry*, 1973, **29**, 319–25.
BOIS, C. and VOGEL-SPROTT, M. Discrimination of low blood alcohol levels and self-titration skills in social drinkers. *Quarterly Journal of Studies on Alcohol*, 1974, **35**, 86–97.
CAHALAN, D., CISIN, I. H. and CROSSLEY, H. M. American drinking practices: A national study of drinking behavior and attitudes. Monograph No. 6. New Brunswick, N.J.: Rutgers Center of Alcohol Studies, 1969.
DAVIES, D. L. Normal drinking in recovered alcohol addicts. *Quarterly Journal of Studies on Alcohol*, 1962, **23**, 94–104.
EWING, J. A. and ROUSE, B. A. Outpatient group treatment to inculcate controlled drinking behavior in alcoholics. Paper presented at International Congress on Alcoholism and Drug Dependence, Amsterdam, Sept. 1972.
HERSEN, M., EISLER, R. M., MILLER, P. M., JOHNSON, M. B. and PINKSTON, S. G. Effects of practice, instructions, and modeling on components of assertive behavior. *Behavior Research and Therapy*, 1973, **11**, 443–51.
LEMERE, F. What happens to alcoholics. *American Journal of Psychiatry*, 1953, **109**, 674–6.
LOVIBOND, S. H. and CADDY, G. Discriminated aversive control in the moderation of alcoholics' drinking behavior. *Behavior Therapy*, 1970, **1**, 437–44.
MARLATT, G. A. Modeling effects in alcohol consumption: A laboratory analogue. Presented at Association for Advancement of Behavior Therapy, Chicago, 1974.
MILLER, P. M. and BECKER, J. The effects of instructions on alcoholic drinking behavior. Paper presented at the meeting of the Southeastern Psychological Association, Atlanta, 1975.
MILLS, K. C., SOBELL, M. B. and SCHAEFER, H. H. Training social drinking as an alternative to abstinence for alcoholics. *Behavior Therapy*, 1971, **2**, 18–27.
NATHAN, P. E. and O'BRIEN, J. S. An experimental analysis of the behavior of alcoholics and nonalcoholics during prolonged experimental drinking: A necessary precursor of behavior therapy? *Behavior Therapy*, 1971, **2**, 455–76.
ORFORD, J. A comparison of alcoholics whose drinking is totally uncontrolled and those whose drinking is mainly controlled. *Behavior Research and Therapy*, 1973, **11**, 565–76.
PATTISON, E. M. A critique of alcoholism treatment with special reference to abstinence. *Quarterly Journal of Studies on Alcohol*, 1966, **27**, 49–71.
ROITZSCH, J. C. and KILPATRICK, D. G. Conditioning temperate drinking behavior: Can the alcoholic learn to drink less and enjoy it more? Presented at the Association for Advancement of Behavior Therapy, Miami, 1973.
SCHACHTER, S. Some extraordinary facts about obese humans and rats. *American Psychologist*, 1971, **26**, 129–44.
SCHAEFER, H. H., SOBELL, M. B. and MILLS, K. C. Baseline drinking behaviors in alcoholics and social drinkers: Kinds of sips and sip magnitude. *Behavior Research and Therapy*, 1971, **9**, 23–7.
SELZER, M. L. and HOLLOWAY, W. H. A follow-up of alcoholics committed to a state hospital. *Quarterly Journal of Studies on Alcohol*, 1957, **18**, 98–120.

SHEA, J. E. Psychoanalytic therapy and alcoholism. *Quarterly Journal of Studies on Alcohol*, 1954, **15**, 595–605.

SILVERSTEIN, S. J., NATHAN, P. E. and TAYLOR, H. A. Blood alcohol level estimation and controlled drinking by chronic alcoholics. *Behavior Therapy*, 1974, **5**, 1–15.

SOBELL, M. B., SCHAEFER, H. H. and MILLS, K. C. Differences in baseline drinking behavior between alcoholics and normal drinkers. *Behavior Research and Therapy*, 1972, **10**, 257–67.

SOBELL, M. B. and SOBELL, L. C. Individualized behavior therapy for alcoholics. *Behavior Therapy*, 1973a, **4**, 49–72.

SOBELL, M. B. and SOBELL, L. C. Alcoholics treated by individualized behavior therapy: One year treatment outcome. *Behavior Research and Therapy*, 1973b, **11**, 599–618.

SOBELL, M. B. and SOBELL, L. C. Evidence of controlled drinking by former alcoholics: A second year evaluation of individualized behavior therapy. Presented at American Psychological Association, Aug., 1973c.

SOBELL, M. B. and SOBELL, L. C. The need for realism, relevance and operational assumptions in the study of substance dependence. Paper presented at International Symposium on Alcohol and Drug Research, Toronto, Oct. 1973.

CHAPTER 8

Comprehensive Behavioral Approaches

Introduction

Although most behavioral treatment programs emphasize the utilization and evaluation of one or two major treatment procedures, the ultimate clinical treatment for alcoholism would involve a comprehensive package. This package, however, must be empirically based so that only those procedures which have been demonstrated to be effective are used. The objective is to bring together an efficient treatment which requires minimal amounts of time and effort to administer. In addition to effectiveness, cooperation of participants must also be taken into account. Thus, *positive* therapeutic strategies are to be preferred over *punitive* or *aversive* ones.

On the basis of present knowledge in the field a satisfactory comprehensive program would include procedures to accomplish the following objectives:

1. *Decrease the positive value of abusive drinking*
   Procedures that currently appear to have promise in this endeavor are self-management training, covert conditioning, and Antabuse maintenance.
2. *Increase alternative behaviors*
   This involves social skills training, relaxation training, and perhaps recreational retraining.
3. *Rearrange environment to increase likelihood of sobriety*
   Two major components of this element of the program are marital counseling and social counseling. Marital counseling involves interpersonal skills training, contingency contracting, and training in parenting skills. Social counseling may involve altering social consequences of excessive drinking, providing a social environment that is conducive to abstinence or moderate drinking, and job counseling, placement, and/or retraining.
4. *Individualize therapeutic goals*
   The goals must be individualized to fit the needs of the individual. That is, with very chronic, Skid Row alcoholics the goal may be simply to extend the length of time in between drinking episodes rather than demanding complete abstinence. Also, with the recent evidence questioning the validity of the disease concept of alcoholism, the program must be flexible

156

enough to allow for either complete abstinence or controlled social drinking.

5. *Maintain and support changes*

   One of the most important aspects of treatment success is often related to the intensity of the follow-up program. Too often, alcoholism treatment programs administer various behavior change strategies, discharge the client, and then evaluate his success at various intervals. No ongoing therapeutic assistance is provided. In this sense, treatment is mistakenly based upon a medical model in which an individual enters a hospital with an "illness" and through appropriate treatment is "cured".

6. *Build in an ongoing evaluation system*

   In addition to continuing treatment, follow-up sessions must include assessment data on the client's progress. Such data would include self-reports, reports from relatives, friends, employers, breathalyzer analyses obtained at random intervals, and reports from hospitals, courts and jails. Evaluation of the client's social, emotional, marital, and vocational functioning is also essential. In this sense there is no fundamental difference between treatment and research.

Thus far, few truly comprehensive behavioral alcoholism programs have been reported. Lazarus (1965) was one of the first clinicians to describe a combined approach in the context of a case study. His "broad spectrum" orientation places major emphasis on anxiety reduction as the main therapeutic goal. Aversion therapy was combined with systematic desensitization, assertive training, hypnosis, and marital counseling in order to suppress drinking responses and teach new ways of coping with antecedent stressful events.

Since that time several multimodal behavioral programs have been implemented. Notable among these are those by Sobell and Sobell (1973) and Hunt and Azrin (1973) which have already been described. Three additional programs will be described in some detail to provide more explicit examples of the clinical applications of this approach.

Examples

Program 1

McBrearty, Dichter, Garfield, and Heath (1968) of Temple University established a comprehensive alcoholism program at Eagleville Hospital and Rehabilitation Center in Pennsylvania. Initiation of this project was fostered by the lack of success of more traditional treatment programs together with the rather narrowed focus of single technique-oriented behavioral programs. The treatment package was divided into six elements:

1. *Didactic Training for Behavioral Change*
   During this phase of treatment patients were taught, in a group setting, basic principles of behavior modification. They learned to evaluate and modify their drinking behavior on a functional basis by delineating specific antecedents and consequences of excessive alcohol consumption.

2. *Aversive Conditioning Procedures*
   Electrical aversion therapy was used in association with the thought, smell, and taste of alcohol. In one aversion therapy sequence, words (e.g., beer, gin, alcohol) were projected onto a screen. Shock was delivered to the fingers after each word was presented. Following nine alcohol related words a word such as "relax" was presented. At that point no shock was delivered and the patient was instructed to drink a glass of juice or soda. During other sessions, electric shocks were delivered contingent upon smelling and sipping alcoholic beverages.

3. *Covert Sensitization*
   A combination of covert sensitization and covert reinforcement were used in the manner described in Chapter 4. Thoughts and feelings of nausea were associated with drinking while feelings of calm and relaxation were associated with thoughts of avoiding or rejecting alcohol.

4. *Relaxation Training and Systematic Desensitization*
   Patients were provided with relaxation training both individually and in groups of three to four. Systematic desensitization was then administered using imagined scenes of anxiety-producing situations that precede alcohol abuse. These authors noted that heterosexual anxiety was frequently reported by patients to be most bothersome to them.

5. *Training of Behavioral Deficits*
   This phase of treatment consisted of social skills training in which the patient learned new ways of responding to difficult interpersonal situations by means of behavioral rehearsal in "behaviordrama" or role playing. Self-control responses were also incorporated into this phase so that the patient was provided with experience in making new responses to situations which have elicited drinking behavior in the past. For example, on "therapeutic passes" the patient was instructed to go to several bars and practice walking by them without entering. These passes also provided a method of periodically assessing the effects of treatment in the actual environment.

6. *Application of Contingency Management Procedures*
   Generally, this procedure included the use of an inpatient token economy system in which points were earned for appropriate behaviors.

Program 2

The second program is that described by Rozynko, Flint, Hammer, Swift, Kline, and King (1971) at Mendocino State Hospital in California. Among the assumptions upon which this program was based were two that deserve special mention. First, the authors assumed that most problem drinkers have disordered interpersonal relationships which require special therapeutic intervention. This emphasis on the important influence of other people in abusive drinking patterns was often ignored in earlier behavioral approaches. Secondly, it was noted that since there are such a massive number of alcoholics with relatively few professionals or paraprofessionals to treat them, treatment programs must be applicable to large numbers of people at relatively small cost and little professional time.

Treatment was administered over a period of approximately 6 months in an inpatient setting. Consistent with a learning as opposed to a disease model of alcoholism, participants in the program were referred to as "students" rather than patients. The program was divided into phases as outlined in Table 8.1. The first adaptation week consisted mainly of orientating students to the ward routine and the rationale of the program. The next 17-week phase was divided into three components: cognitive-perceptual instruction, desensitization, and assertive training.

Cognitive-perceptual instructions taught the student basic principles of behavior from a social-learning framework. Emphasis was placed on the functional analysis of drinking behavior particularly in terms of modifying

TABLE 8.1   Program Stages of the Operant Behavior Modification Program
(Rozynko, Flint, Hammer, Swift, Kline, and King, 1971)*

1 week Adaptation week	17 weeks Student status	4 weeks Graduate student status	4 weeks Discharge status
1. Orientation to ward 2. First relaxation training 3. Psychological testing 4. Introductory lectures and discussions	*Cognitive-Perceptual* 1. Operant theory 2. Application to life situations *Desensitization* 1. Standard hierarchies 2. Individualized hierarchies *Assertive Training* 1. Scripts 2. "Talk and hear"	1. Class moderators 2. Interviewer of TBMs 3. Individualized classes 4. Individualized hierarchies	1. Vocational rehabilitation 2. Job hunting 3. Preparation for community return

* Reprinted by permission.

cognitive antecedents such as "I'm no good. I might as well get drunk, nobody cares about me." Periodically a Terminal Behavioral Measure was administered to assess progress. This procedure consisted of a 5- to 10-minute interview regarding one of the topics of behavior analysis and/or modification under study. The student was reinforced verbally and monetarily for correct answers to questions and general spontaneous remarks about alcohol abuse which were consistent with therapeutic goals.

Relaxation training and systematic desensitization were used to reduce tension levels especially those associated with interpersonal relationships. Students were encouraged to initiate desensitization procedures on their own in response to idiosyncratic anxiety-producing persons, places, or situations.

Finally, students were trained, via role-played scripts, assertive ways to handle situations in which they must express personal rights or feelings. Students were encouraged to practice these new responses with each other by directly expressing both positive and negative feelings on the ward.

Along with these specific treatments, motivation to participate in and advance through the program is provided through a token economy system. Students were free to participate in as few or as many therapeutic activities as they wished. However, participation and accomplishments in these activities earned "credit slips" which could be exchanged for money at the end of each week.

After the 17-week treatment phase, the participant became a "graduate student". During this time he assumed more responsibility and assisted in the administration of treatment to "undergraduates". He also could devote more individual time to aspects of the program in which he needed more improvement. During the final month, students spent their time finding housing, employment, and generally preparing themselves for life outside of the hospital.

At the time of the report of this program, evaluation of its efficacy had not been complete. The description here, however, serves to illustrate the way in which a number of behavioral strategies can be used in an integrated manner.

Program 3

Miller, Stanford, and Hemphill (1974) described a behavioral program for alcoholics at the Veterans Administration Center in Jackson, Mississippi. This multimodel treatment project is administered through an 8-week inpatient program followed by a year of outpatient follow-up treatment. A token economy ward system was used to foster sustained cooperation and to initiate and reward more adaptive behavior patterns. Behaviors that are deemed to be conducive to sobriety outside of the hospital were emphasized. Patients earned points, recorded on index cards, for a variety of activities, such as reporting on time to treatment sessions, actively participating during a treatment session, appropriately handling day-to-day conflicts with staff or other patients, and carrying out hospital work assignments. Points could be traded in for time off the ward, extended bed time, and day or weekend passes away from the hospital. Patients' rooms were locked during the day to encourage off-ward activity. Intoxication during the week or upon return from a pass resulted in a loss of points together with a 3-day suspension of all ward privileges.

To encourage responsibility patients were required to plan their entire day each morning. At this time they planned their own schedule of work, treatment, and recreational activities. Thus, they scheduled the ways they would both earn and spend points. Patients were encouraged to continue this method of planning their days after discharge from the hospital so that free time and drinking would be less likely to occur.

Major therapeutic activities included a self-modification group, a group to develop more adaptive coping behaviors, marital counseling, and job counseling. The self-modification group sessions included a variety of procedures to assist the patients to control their behavior. Table 8.2 outlines the procedures used and assignments required of the participants.

Didactic sessions on functional analysis of behavior along the lines of social-learning principles were combined with sessions teaching relaxation training, covert sensitization, self-management skills, and social and recreational skills. Between sessions patients were provided with assignments to complete. These included such activities as reading relevant materials on alcohol abuse, recording specific antecedents and consequences of their past two drinking episodes, and practicing covert sensitization scenes.

In other group sessions patients were confronted with inadequate or inappropriate ways in which they handle interpersonal and/or emotional situations. Role-playing, modeling, feedback, and verbal reinforcement were used to initiate new behavior patterns such as expressing feelings more directly and assertively or engaging in less self-related conversation.

Family members were required to involve themselves in the treatment process by attending counseling sessions. These sessions were geared toward teaching more positive interactional patterns and more direct ways of handling conflict. Use of videotape feedback and behavioral rehearsal helped to teach these new behavioral patterns. Contracts were frequently negotiated between the couple in terms of reciprocal agreements to engage in specified behaviors at home. For example, the husband may agree in writing to faithfully take his Antabuse daily in the presence of his wife if she agrees to refrain from nagging about his past drinking episodes.

One of the most important aspects of the program involved job counseling. Twice weekly patients attended "job school" during which they learned methods of preparing a job résumé, interviewing for jobs, and handling a

TABLE 8.2   Outline for Self-Management Skills Training Course
12 sessions, 3 × per week
Short written test prior to sessions 2 through 12

Session	Topics	Assignments
1	Social-learning approach to alcohol abuse – introduction and rationale	Read handouts
2	Analysis of drinking behavior – antecedents and consequences	Functional analysis of last three drinking episodes
3	Analysis of drinking behavior – alternative responses	Read handouts
4	Social-skills training – introduction and rationale	Read "Your Perfect Right"
5	Role playing of general scenes – modeling, videotape feedback, rehearsal	Detailed description of three specific scenes relevant to individual's drinking (e.g., unexpressed anger toward spouse)
6	Role playing of relevant scenes – alcohol related (i.e., refusing a drink) and non-alcohol related	Try out new behavior in at least two real situations
7	Covert sensitization and reinforcement	Practice scenes
8	Covert sensitization and reinforcement	Practice scenes
9	Relaxation training	Practice relaxation and use when appropriate
10	Self-control techniques self-monitoring, ultimate aversive consequences	Devise a self-control contract
11	Self-control techniques – rearranging contingencies, incompatible behavior	Devise a total self-modification system – goals and procedures
12	Conclusion – self-modification – how to implement and maintain changes	

difficult interaction with supervisors or coworkers. Interviews were role-played, with patients alternately assuming the role of either an employer or a prospective employee. Feedback was provided with modeling used to enhance progress. At times agreements were negotiated between the patient and his prospective employer regarding Antabuse intake. Frequently patients agreed to take Antabuse in the presence of the boss or his designate each morning upon arrival at work.

After discharge, patients were scheduled for monthly treatment sessions during which they attended either "job school", a social skills–self-management oriented group, or both. Treatment success was evaluated via a number of self-report measures, reports from relatives, employers, or friends, videotaped segments of interactions with peers or spouses, analogue drinking tasks, and, occasionally, breathalyzer analyses administered on a random basis. Although the program evaluation is not as yet complete, results thus far appear promising. Preliminary results indicate that 62% of a sample of 100 patients completing the program were either abstinent or drinking in a more controlled manner at follow-up evaluations ranging from 8 to 24 months.

Specialized Populations

In addition to the use of behavioral strategies within programs that are geared toward general alcoholic populations, these procedures may also provide a viable means of meeting the treatment needs of specialized alcoholic groups. The problems of women, American Indians, youth, and aged alcoholics are often exacerbated by certain confining social, economic, vocational, or cultural restrictions placed on them by the nature of their role in society. In addition, alcoholics seen through the criminal justice system, either the chronic public inebriate or the drunken driver, provide particular treatment difficulties due to their chronicity and/or lack of motivation to enter treatment. Traditional counseling oriented alcoholism programs are often not beneficial to the Skid Row alcoholic since they fail to deal with his most immediate problems of social and economic deprivation. Finally, industries lose millions of dollars each year because of alcoholic employees. The difficulty here is related to the fact that the alcoholic employee must first be identified and he, himself, must at least recognize that he has a problem that needs treatment. Also industries must have a program that can be administered in such a way that the employee's work activities are not severely interrupted. This involves a rapid program of behavior change that can be administered on an outpatient basis, preferably through the industry itself.

Specific behavioral strategies that might be useful with some of these populations are described below. In some instances, such as with female alcoholics, few specialized ongoing behavioral treatment programs exist. With other groups, such as Skid Row alcoholics, a great deal of both descriptive and treatment evaluation studies are available to provide a precedent for the use of specific behavioral procedures.

Skid Row Programs

The debilitated social and economic conditions of the Skid Row alcoholic have been documented in numerous sociological and psychological surveys and reports (Alford, 1965; Blumberg, Shipley, and Moore, 1971; Jackson and Conner, 1953; Miller, in press; Pittman and Gordon, 1958). The Skid Row label typically refers to alcoholics who live in the deteriorated areas of the inner city (usually in cheap hotels or boarding houses), have few stable environmental supports, work sporadically at unskilled jobs on a day-to-day basis, have limited social or vocational skills, and are repeatedly arrested for public intoxication. Actually, the name Skid Row derives from Yessler Street in Seattle, Washington (Pitman, 1965). In the late 1800s this sloped street was used to "skid" logs into Puget Sound. In order to accommodate the loggers working in this area, a number of cheap bars and hotels opened up along this street. Hence the name Skid Road or Skid Row.

Thus far, traditional treatment strategies have been least effective with the Skid Row group. Failures are partly due to the closely knit drinking groups characteristic of this population in which excessive drinking is potently reinforced and encouraged. A "drink" is always available even to the financially destitute since drinking buddies will readily share a bottle with another Skid Row resident. The reasoning behind this cooperative behavior appears to be related to the fact that in the future the roles may be reversed with the provider in need of a drink from the recipient. This reciprocal sharing ritual applies only to alcohol, however, since food, even to the hungry, is a non-transferable commodity.

In a recent survey of the Skid Row Community, Miller (in press) found that while the Skid Row alcoholic often wants to change his way of living, his environment is geared toward maintaining his chronic alcohol abuse. While excessive use of alcohol is expected, there are few opportunities to engage in alternative behaviors that might provide satisfactions. Society outside of the Skid Row area quickly labels and frequently rejects the chronic inebriate due to his obvious deteriorated physical condition. Attempts to initiate interactions with relatives, non-Skid Row friends, or employers are often met with criticism, even when he or she is completely sober.

Research evidence (Heilbrun and Norbert, 1972; Nathan and O'Brien, 1971) indicates that the excessive drinking of the Skid Row group is maintained by *external* factors, such as availability of alcohol or presence of drinking buddies, as opposed to *internal* factors (depression, anxiety). Cessation of drinking after an extended binge is also externally determined by arrest or lack of availability of alcohol.

Thus, it appears that a successful treatment program must deal with two issues. First, it must bring meaningful *external* factors to bear on the alcoholic to maintain his cooperation and modify his drinking. Contingency management programs based on the principles of operant conditioning would accomplish this goal. Secondly, in addition to the alcohol problem *per se*, treatment must alter the basic social, economic, vocational, and medical deficiencies of the individual. In this regard, behavioral programs geared toward teaching job finding skills (Jones and Azrin, 1973) and general interpersonal skills (Hersen and Miller, 1973) have been developed.

Most Skid Row treatment programs are administered through the police or municipal courts. This is due to the fact that the Skid Row individual becomes most visible to society in relation to his public drunkenness arrests. In most communities public intoxication is still considered to be a criminal offense and accounts for approximately two million arrests annually in the United States (Nimmer, 1972). This rather high incidence actually represents a "revolving door" phenomenon (Pittman and Gordon, 1958) in which a few chronic alcoholics are repeatedly arrested, released and rearrested. In addition to the waste of human resources, the financial costs of these arrests are staggering. Even a moderate sized city (pop. 250,000) may spend as much as $250,000 annually (in terms of police officers' salaries, court costs, meals to inmates) to arrest and process public inebriates. In a larger metropolitan area this figure might run into the millions. Sobell and Sobell (in press) calculated the incarceration costs (both jail and hospital) for one chronic alcoholic to be $11,543.17 over a 2-year period of time.

In connection with the criminal justice system, court-imposed threats of incarceration have been used to initiate participation and sustain cooperation in Antabuse maintenance (Bourne, Alford, and Borocok, 1972; Haynes, 1973) or halfway house rehabilitation (Baker, 1973; Coffler and Hadley, 1973) programs. Haynes (1973), for example, reported the use of contingency management within an Antabuse program administered through the Municipal Court of Colorado Springs, Colorado. Within this special program, chronic Skid Row alcoholics were allowed to take Antabuse daily for a year in lieu of a 90-day jail sentence. As described in an earlier chapter, Antabuse taken daily deters alcohol intake since it results in extremely unpleasant physiological reactions if alcohol is ingested following its use. Participants were required to take Antabuse tablets in the presence of their probation officer at least twice per week. Failing to take Antabuse resulted in immediate arrest and reinstatement of the 90-day jail sentence. Results at the end of one year indicated that 66 of 138 participants had consistently maintained Antabuse intake. In addition this program resulted in a marked decrease in arrests for public drunkenness for the entire group involved in the project, even those breaking probation early in treatment. While such results are promising, the all-or-nothing punishment contingency of the program certainly has limitations. Participants were not given an opportunity to learn by experience so that those who failed to take Antabuse even once received little benefit from the treatment. A shaping procedure would have allowed for successively more potent punishment to be applied to each instance of failure to ingest Antabuse. For example, the first instance might have resulted in a 3-day jail sentence, the next a 10-day sentence, and so on.

While these court programs have been effective on a limited level they often are not comprehensive enough to meet the needs of the Skid Row alcoholic. In addition, threats of punishment do not produce lasting "motivation" for behavior change since abusive drinking patterns reoccur as soon as the negative contingencies are no longer in operation. Under the new Uniform Alcoholism and Intoxication Treatment Act, decriminalizing public drunkenness, such coercive methods are no longer available in many states.

An alternative which offers the promise of more sustained improvements is the use of positive contingency management. While reinforcing contingencies have been demonstrated to be effective in reducing alcohol consumption in controlled laboratory settings (Cohen, Liebson, and Faillace, 1971; Cohen, Liebson, Faillace, and Speers, 1971; Bigelow, Liebson, and Griffiths, 1973; Miller, Hersen, and Eisler, 1974) and with individual outpatient chronic alcoholics (Miller, Hersen, Eisler, and Watts, 1974; Sulzer, 1965), they have not been utilized on a large scale *in vivo* basis.

An exception is a recent project by Miller (1975) in which positive contingencies were used to provide assistance to a sample of chronic Skid Row alcoholics who had a history of frequent arrests (at least eight in a 12-month period of time) for public intoxication. The specific goals of the project were to increase work behavior, decrease alcohol consumption, and decrease the number of public drunkenness arrests. All participants in the study were chronic alcoholics who resided in a rooming house, hotel, or mission within the central downtown area of the city. All worked sporadically on a day-to-day basis. Out of twenty subjects, ten received a behavioral intervention treatment while ten served as the control group.

The program was administered through various community agencies in the inner city area which regularly dealt with the Skid Row population. Subjects in the control group received services from these agencies on a non-contingent basis regardless of their behavior. The behavioral intervention group, however, received goods and services only as long as they remained sober. This agreement established a reciprocal relationship between the agencies and the client which required responsibility on his part in the form of a commitment to alter his drinking patterns. Under special cooperative agreements with various community agencies, clients were provided with housing, employment, medical care, clothing, meals, cigarettes, and counseling in exchange for attempts to control their drinking. Drinking was assessed via direct observations of intoxication and periodic breathalyzer analyses gathered on a random basis approximately every 5 days. Evidence of intoxication reported by any agency or determined by the breath test resulted in an immediate 5-day suspension of eligibility for all goods and services. Clients could even be terminated from their employment and dismissed from their living quarters during this time. Thus, until the 5-day suspension had passed, they met their needs without the aid of community resources. An obvious necessity for this program was a very close working relationship among all agencies so that the client could not obtain needed goods and services regardless of his drinking.

TABLE 8.3   Mean Number of Public Drunkenness Arrests for 2 Months Prior to and
2 Months During Intervention
(Miller, 1975)*

	Pretreatment M	During intervention M	Difference
Intervention group	1.70	0.30	−1.40
Control group	1.40	1.30	−0.10

* Reprinted by permission. From Miller, P. M. A behavioral intervention program for chronic public drunkenness offenders. *Archives of General Psychiatry*, 1975, **32**, 915–18.

Data on number of public drunkenness arrests, number of hours worked per week, and blood/alcohol levels obtained were accumulated 2 months before and 2 months after the initiation of the program. Table 8.3 illustrates the mean number of arrests for public drunkenness for the behavioral intervention group and the control group prior to and subsequent to the program.

While mean number of arrests significantly decreased from 1.70 to 0.30 for the behavioral group, it remained approximately the same for the control group. In fact only three behavioral clients were arrested during the project while nine of the ten control subjects were arrested at least once during this time (see Fig. 8.1).

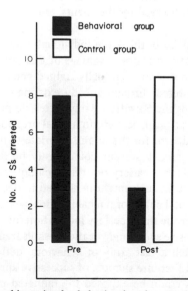

Fig. 8.1. Number of subjects in the behavioral and control groups who were arrested for public drunkenness at least once prior to and during treatment (figure constructed from data presented in Miller, 1975).

TABLE 8.4   Mean Number of Hours Worked Per Week for 2 Months Prior to and
2 Months During Intervention
(Miller, 1975)*

	Pretreatment M	During intervention M	Difference
Intervention group	3.2	12.0	+8.8
Control group	4.4	3.2	−1.2

* Reprinted by permission. From Miller, P. M. A behavioral intervention program for chronic public drunkenness offenders. *Archives of General Psychiatry*, 1975, **32**, 915–18.

As indicated in Table 8.4, mean number of hours worked per week by the behavioral group increased significantly from 3.2 to 12. Control subjects evidenced a slight decrease from 4.4 to 3.2 hours. It may be noted that those participants in the behavioral group who did not increase their work behavior were all receiving some type of monthly disability payments. This pay was essentially not contingent upon the performance of any productive behaviors and served as a counter-therapeutic factor with these individuals.

Breathalyzer analyses of five individuals tested periodically before and after the behavioral intervention program indicated marked decreases in mean blood/alcohol levels from 0.05% to 0.002%. Since these were random probe measures excessive drinking at other times could not be ruled out. However, intoxication was also being observed by the clients' employer and by the staff of each community agency.

Such a program is beneficial both to the individual himself and to the police and court systems of the city. A major advantage of this rather simple approach lies in the fact that it does not require specially trained personnel or even special funding but can be administered through already existing community agencies. While some agencies, such as the Salvation Army, often do provide their services contingent upon sobriety, all agencies within a local area must be consistently working together in this endeavor for the public inebriate to benefit.

This contingency management system could easily be incorporated into a halfway house setting in which a variety of other techniques could also be used. While the goals with some individuals might be limited to decreasing arrest rates, others may benefit from a total behavioral rehabilitation system. The contingency management system can provide the necessary motivation for behavior change and be supplemented with extensive social and vocational skills training. Since the Skid Row alcoholic evidences such a vast array of behavioral deficits progress would probably be slow and would require shaping of successive approximations of the required end result. Clients could be exposed to graduated phases of increasing responsibility similar to the "student-learning" paradigm of Rozynko *et al.* (1971) and also that used by Synanon with drug abusers (Dreissler, 1972).

Female Alcoholics

For the most part, females in our society who abuse alcohol have been consistently overlooked in terms of research and treatment. Most information concerning female alcoholism is anecdotal in nature. Recently, however, more specific descriptive data are being accumulated.

While males are both more likely to drink and more likely to abuse alcohol the number of women who drink is increasing (DHEW, 1971). According to a recent governmental survey (DHEW, 1974), approximately 47% of adult women drink alcohol at least once a month or more. This survey also found that those women who drink the most are in the younger (21 to 29 years) age group.

Compared to their male counterparts, a greater proportion of alcoholic women are secretive drinkers. Publicly, the female alcoholic presents herself as a socially well-adjusted individual and is rarely seen intoxicated in public. She is more likely to be a problem to herself and her immediate family than to her community or to the legal authorities (Blane, 1968; Kinsey, 1966). The immediate precipitants of excessive drinking in the female are often related to her sex and include premenstrual tension, the demands of small children, boredom, dissatisfaction with her marital role, insecurity in her feminine role, poor self-image, and fears of social incompetence (Belfer, Shader, Carroll and Hatmetz, 1971; Lindbeck, 1972). In addition women usually begin excessive drinking at a later age than men but reach chronic abusive drinking patterns in a shorter period of time (Schuckit, 1972).

Behavioral approaches can provide a framework of empiricism within which more objective studies on the nature of alcoholic female drinking patterns can be evaluated. An excellent example is provided in a recent study by Tracey, Karlin and Nathan (1974) at the Rutgers Alcohol Behavior Research Laboratory. Four alcoholic females were observed on this inpatient experimental unit for a period of 22 days. The subjects could earn points via an operant reinforcement system which they could spend on either alcohol or time out of social isolation. Results indicated that while subjects drank substantial amounts of alcohol, their drinking was mainly controlled in that they never became grossly intoxicated. In addition, they spent more points for socialization time than for alcohol. Surprisingly, they preferred to drink with others rather than alone. This finding appears to contradict the often cited notion that women tend to be solitary, secretive drinkers. It may be noted, however, that none of the women drank to the point of intoxication in the social condition. Perhaps these women do drink to intoxication more frequently when they are alone but this behavior was not observed due to the fact that their drinking was being monitored by others (i.e., the experimenters). Thus, while social drinking in females may occur in interpersonal settings, excessive drinking may be more likely to occur in a solitary environment.

Other objective analyses of female alcoholism could be conducted in more naturalistic settings. Miller and Becker (1975) are currently evaluating *in vivo* drinking patterns of ten chronic alcoholic women. All subjects are married to provide corroboration by family members of self-report information. Each subject is required to keep written daily records of her activities for a 2-week period of time. Emphasis will be placed on stressful social interactions with her husband, children, neighbors, or employer. She will also be asked to record all drinking episodes, time of their occurrence, amount consumed, and precipitating factors. Husbands or other family members are also asked to record these episodes noting all social-environmental antecedents and consequences.

Clinically, certain behavioral treatment modalities, such as social skills training, may meet the special needs of female alcoholics. This is particularly the case where the lack of skills to function out of the traditional female role is evident. It is apparent that more detailed descriptive information is needed in this area before specific treatment programs for women can be initiated.

Employees

Since many alcoholics are working regularly, they often pose a considerable problem on the job. The National Institute on Alcohol Abuse and Alcoholism (Dept. HEW, 1974) estimates that over 9.35 billion dollars are lost to industry each year because of absenteeism, loss of efficiency, poor decision making, or accidents related to excessive drinking. Industrial programs to combat this problem frequently focus on the identification and referral of the "troubled employee". Emphasis is placed on confronting the individual with his poor performance or absenteeism (usually on Monday), rather than with his alcohol problem *per se*. He or she is given the opportunity of obtaining help for the problem or facing punitive action. Many firms utilize Alcoholics Anonymous meetings within the company itself.

Behavior modification programs aimed at the troubled employee are few. Bigelow, Liebson, and Lawrence (1973) used an operant approach in which the opportunity to work each day served as a reinforcer for Antabuse taking. Since all of the subjects in these studies ingested Antabuse each day without fail, the role of the contingencies *per se* in bringing about improvements is not clear. Perhaps the results were related to simply identifying the alcoholic and threatening him with job loss. A longer term program of this type would probably clarify this issue.

Another behavioral approach might involve the use of positive contingencies rather than a response cost as in the case of pay loss for one day. Tondo and Miller (1974) are currently evaluating the efficacy of such a program. Emphasis is placed on assisting the alcoholic and his employer to negotiate a written contract regarding Antabuse taking. The patient agrees to take Antabuse on Monday, Wednesday, and Friday in the presence of his employer or a designated supervisor. In some cases the employer may be willing to provide a small monetary bonus contingent upon each episode of Antabuse ingestion. In other cases the alcoholic may agree to provide a weekly deposit from his paycheck, 20% of which will be refunded subsequent to his ingesting Antabuse on the designated days. It seems as though this positive approach may have some advantages over a response cost system. Alcoholic clients often react very negatively to aversive contingencies so that punishment of their behavior often leads to binge drinking.

Certainly more information is needed on various employee oriented approaches. Within a behavioral system the work situation can serve as a potent "motivator" for continued sobriety. With many alcoholics the reinforcement value of the work setting is prepotent over all other reinforcers in his environment including the family. This may be due to a realization that once employment is terminated, funds to purchase alcohol will no longer be available.

Conclusion

Comprehensive behavioral programs have shown promise in alcoholism treatment and certainly deserve further evaluation and refinement. These programs illustrate the ways in which the focus of behavior therapy in the field of alcoholism has changed from emphasizing one rather simple conditioning procedure (i.e., aversion therapy) to dealing with the entire repertoire of an individual's behavior.

It appears that treatment must be moved more into the environment of the client and must involve not only changes in his responses to difficult situations, but also alterations in the way the environment responds to him. The technology to accomplish this goal is slowly being accumulated. Future work in this area should focus on the development of behavioral treatment packages individually tailored to meet the needs of the varied alcoholic populations discussed above.

References

ALFORD, J. A. Medical and psychiatric aspects. In *The court and the chronic inebriate*. Washington, D.C.: U.S. Government Printing Office, 1965, pp. 16–20.

BAKER, T. B. Halfway houses for alcoholics: Shelters or shackles. *International Journal of Social Psychiatry*, 1973, **18**.

BELFER, M. L., SHADER, R. I., CARROLL, M. C. and HARMATZ, J. S. Alcoholism in women. *Archives of General Psychiatry*, 1971, **25**, 540–4.

BIGELOW, G., LIEBSON, I. and GRIFFITHS, R. R. Experimental analysis of alcoholic drinking. Paper presented at American Psychological Association, Aug. 1973.

BIGELOW, G., LIEBSON, I. and LAWRENCE, C. Prevention of alcohol abuse by reinforcement of incompatible behavior. Presented at Association for Advancement of Behavior Therapy, Dec., 1973.

BLANE, H. T. *The personality of the alcoholic*. New York: Harper & Row, 1968, pp. 107–19.

BLUMBERG, L. U., SHIPLEY, T. E. and MOORE, J. O. The skid row man and the skid row status community. *Quarterly Journal of Studies on Alcohol*, 1971, **32**, 909–41.

BOURNE, P. G., ALFORD, J. A. and BOROCOCK, J. Z. Treatment of skid row alcoholics. *Quarterly Journal of Studies on Alcohol*, 1972, **33**, 990–8.

COFFLER, D. B. and HEDLEY, R. G. The residential rehabilitation center as an alternative to jail for chronic drunkenness offenders. *Quarterly Journal of Studies on Alcohol*, 1973, **34**, 1180–6.

COHEN, M., LIEBSON, I. and FAILLACE, L. The role of reinforcement contingencies in chronic alcoholism: An experimental analysis of one case. *Behavior Research and Therapy*, 1971, **9**, 375–9.

COHEN, M., LIEBSON, I., FAILLACE, L. and SPEERS, W. Alcoholism: Controlled drinking and incentives for abstinence. *Psychological Reports*, 1971, **28**, 575–80.

DEISSLER, K. J. Synonan, how it works, why it works. In P. H. Lackley (Ed.) *Progress in drug abuse*. Springfield, Illinois: Charles C. Thomas, Publisher, 1972, pp. 49–61.

Department of Health, Education, and Welfare. *Alcohol and health*. Washington, D.C.: U.S. Government Printing Office, 1971.

Department of Health, Education, and Welfare. *Alcohol and health: New knowledge*. Washington, D.C.: U.S. Government Printing Office, 1974, p. 12.

HAMMER, C. E. A behavioral control and data collection system in a comprehensive program for alcoholics. Paper presented at American Psychological Association, 1971.

HAYNES, S. N. Contingency management on a municipally administered antabuse program for alcoholics. *Journal of Behavior Therapy and Experimental Psychiatry*, 1973, **4**, 31–2.

HEILBRUN, A. B. and NORBERT, N. Self-regulatory behavior in skid row alcoholics. *Quarterly Journal of Studies on Alcohol*, 1972, **33**, 990–8.

HERSEN, M., EISLER, R. M. and MILLER, P. M. Development of assertive responses: Clinical, measurement, and research considerations. *Behavior Research and Therapy*, 1973, **11**, 505–21.

HUNT, G. M. and AZRIN, N. H. The community-reinforcement approach to alcoholism. *Behavior Research and Therapy*, 1973, **11**, 91–104.

JACKSON, J. R. and CONNER, R. The skid row alcoholic. *Quarterly Journal of Studies on Alcohol*, 1953, **14**, 468–86.

JONES, R. J. and AZRIN, N. H. An experimental application of a social reinforcement approach to the problem of job finding. *Journal of Applied Behavior Analysis*, 1973, **6**, 345–54.

KINSEY, B. A. *The female alcoholic*. Springfield, Ill.: Charles C. Thomas, Publisher, 1966.

LINDBECK, V. L. The woman alcoholic. *International Journal of the Addictions*, 1971, **7**, 567–80.

McBREARTY, J. T., DICHTER, M., GARFIELD, Z. and HEATH, G. A behaviorally oriented treatment program for alcoholism. *Psychological Reports*, 1968, **22**, 287–98.

MILLER, P. M. A behavioral intervention program for chronic public drunkenness offenders. *Archives of General Psychiatry*, 1975, **32**, 915–18.

MILLER, P. M. An analysis of chronic drunkenness offenders with implications for behavioral intervention. *International Journal of the Addictions*, in press.

MILLER, P. M. and BECKER, J. A behavioral analysis of alcoholism in women. Unpublished manuscript. University of Mississippi Medical Center, 1975.

MILLER, P. M., HERSEN, M. and EISLER, R. M. Relative effectiveness of instructions, agreements, and reinforcement in behavioral contracts with alcoholics. *Journal of Abnormal Psychology*, 1974, **83**, 548–53.

MILLER, P. M., HERSEN, M., EISLER, R. M. and WATTS, J. G. Contingent reinforcement of lowered blood/alcohol levels in an outpatient chronic alcoholic. *Behavior Research and Therapy*, 1974, **12**, 261–3.

MILLER, P. M., STANFORD, A. G. and HEMPHILL, D. P. A comprehensive social-learning approach to alcoholism treatment. *Social Casework*, 1974, May, pp. 279–84.

NATHAN, P. E. and O'BRIEN, J. S. An experimental analysis of the behavior of alcoholics and non-alcoholics during prolonged experimental drinking: A necessary precursor of behavior therapy? *Behavior Therapy*, 1971, **2**, 455–76.

NIMMER, R. 2,000,000 unnecessary arrests. In *Proceedings of the joint conference on alcohol abuse and alcoholism*. Washington, D.C.: U.S. Government Printing Office, 1972, pp. 86–97.

PITTMAN, D. J. The chronic drunkenness offender: An overview. In *The court and the chronic inebriate*. Washington, D.C.: U.S. Government Printing Office, 1965, pp. 6–24.

PITTMAN, D. J. and GORDON, E. W. Revolving door: A study of the chronic police case inebriate. Nonograph 2. New Brunswick, N.J.: Rutgers Center of Alcohol Studies, 1958.

ROZYNKO, V. V., FLINT, G. A., HAMMER, C. E., SWIFT, K. D., KLINE, J. A. and KING, R. M. An operant behavior modification program for alcoholics. Paper presented at the American Psychological Association, 1971.

SCHUCKIT, M. The alcoholic woman: A literature review. *Psychiatry in Medicine*, 1972, **3**, 37–43.

SOBELL, L. C. and SOBELL, M. B. The erudite transit. *International Journal of Social Psychiatry*, in press.

SOBELL, M. B. and SOBELL, L. C. Individualized behavior therapy for alcoholics. *Behavior Therapy*, 1973, **4**, 49–72.

SULZER, E. S. Behavior modification in adult psychiatric patients. In L. P. Ullman and L. Krasner (Eds.) *Case studies in behavior modification*. New York: Holt, Rinehart, & Winston, 1965, pp. 196–9.

TONDO, T. and MILLER, P. M. An experimental investigation of maintenance of Antabuse ingestion in alcoholics via employers. Unpublished data, University of Mississippi Medical Center, 1975.

TRACEY, D. A., KARLIN, R. and NATHAN, P. E. An experimental analysis of the behavior of female alcoholics. Presented at Association for Advancement of Behavior Therapy, Chicago, 1974.

CHAPTER 9

Conclusions and Future Trends

Clinical

Probably the most important contribution of behavior modification to the field of alcohol abuse lies in its emphasis on the merger between treatment and research. Within this scientific–evaluative context, treatment methods are evaluated and scrutinized simultaneously with their clinical application. In this sense there is essentially no distinction between clinical practice and research. Behavioral methodologies have provided ways to objectively assess treatment effects not only in regard to drinking behavior *per se* but also social, marital, emotional, and vocational functioning. Direct observations of behavior change are preferred over self-reports or inferences of therapeutic success based on clinical judgements. While self-reports are often necessary in clinical follow-up studies, their reliability must be established through random corroboration by friends, relatives, employers, legal authorities or hospitals. A recent study (Sobell and Sobell, in press) on self-reports by alcoholics, however, indicates that the validity of self-reported life history information (e.g., number of alcohol related arrests, number of alcohol related hospitalizations) was surprisingly high. One might expect, however, that data on actual day-to-day drinking may be subject to more inaccuracies.

In regard to clinical evaluation, criteria for success in treatment are becoming more individualized based upon each alcoholic's particular drinking and psycho-social behavior patterns. Thus, for some individuals moderate, controlled drinking may be a realistic goal which is more acceptable to the client than total abstinence. In other cases complete abstinence may be the only achievable goal. Within this model, one or even a few brief episodes of excessive drinking during treatment or follow-up does not necessarily indicate therapeutic failure. Instead of being compared with some artificially established success criterion (e.g., total abstinence for 1 year), the patient's progress is compared to his own baseline level of drinking and functioning prior to the initiation of treatment. In addition neither complete abstinence for a lengthy period of time nor maintenance of controlled drinking guarantees adequate functioning in other areas of life. Thus the general goal with all clients is not only to decrease alcohol intake but also to

174

increase their ability to function more effectively in numerous personal-social areas of life.

On the basis of these evaluation procedures, a variety of behavioral treatment procedures have been assessed with respect to their efficacy. The first procedures to be evaluated were also the oldest and most widely used. Thus, the aversion therapies, which historically had been the primary behavioral treatment for alcoholics, have been only recently assessed. Unfortunately, aversion therapies did not fare well under such close scrutiny. Currently, these procedures are steadily losing popularity and most probably will be used minimally if at all in future behavioral alcoholism programs. Essentially, there is a striking lack of evidence to substantiate the clinical efficacy of aversion therapy (especially electrical) with alcoholics. Verbal aversion possibly supplemented with chemical aversion sessions, and used in a self-control manner by patients, may prove useful. Lack of evaluative studies lends caution to the espousal of this combination of procedures.

Operant strategies have received careful assessment of late and may contribute meaningfully to successful outcome. Basically, by rearranging social-environmental contingencies, alcoholics are either reinforced for sobriety or punished for excessive alcohol consumption. Although most studies investigating these procedures have been of a laboratory analogue type in which relatively simple behavioral consequences were altered, recent analyses have documented their efficacy under more complex conditions in the natural environment. Clinical applications of these strategies are often complicated by the necessity of using significant others in the environment to implement contingency management. The problems involved in training these individuals are often oversimplified in the clinical literature. Procedures must be developed to ensure that relatives, friends, and/or employers fulfill their parts of the therapeutic plan. Written contracts through which the behavioral expectations for these individuals are specified and subsequently reinforced have been successful in this regard. Certainly non-behavioral treatment programs often strive to involve community based significant others in this capacity. Behaviorists are attempting to delineate the process by which this can be most efficiently accomplished via explicit strategies of intervention and continuous assessment of interactions between these individuals and the alcoholic patient.

Two other behavioral strategies that offer promise but have not as yet been extensively utilized include social skills training and self-management training. Through these procedures alcoholics are taught alternative responses to antecedent situations which consistently lead to excessve use of alcohol. Emphasis is placed on providing the client with techniques to modify his or her own behavior and in turn deal more effectively with problem situations. The control of the individual's behavior is placed in his own hands as opposed to, in the case of operant contingency management systems, in the control of those around him. This approach is frequently more acceptable to the alcoholic since punitive—coercive methods often lead to his avoidance of contingencies through an extended drinking binge. Also, self-management and social skills training have the additional advantage of enhancing reported feeling of self-esteem and personal worth.

Eventually, empirically based comprehensive treatment systems expending minimal time and effort must be developed. This is not to say that a conglomeration of behavioral techniques should be applied to all alcoholic individuals but rather that specific *treatment packages* should be developed for different types of alcoholic patients. While the major framework of the treatment program would remain consistent, the *focus* of treatment would necessarily vary depending on the characteristics of the patients involved. Treatment of the Skid Row alcoholic might place more emphasis on rearranging environmental consequences of alcohol abuse together with stabilization of living and vocational situations. The middle-class female alcoholic with marital problems may be more likely to benefit from assertive training.

The means by which these treatment packages are developed are complicated by the diverse sources of variance that influence therapeutic outcome. McLean and Miles (1974) have categorized these variables as follows: client/patient (sex, age, etc.), psychological (expectancies, motivation), problem (e.g., chronicity), treatment (type and intensity), therapist (skills and sex), environmental (family, status, work, friends, etc.). In such a scheme, the optimum combination of treatment and therapist variables must be paired with particular psychosocial and environmental characteristics of the patients. Thus, over time, in a broad spectrum behavioral program, relationships among these variables could be established. Then, on the basis of an initial assessment of relevant patient variables (e.g., age, sex, chronicity of abusive drinking), patients can be matched with a focused treatment regime that is most likely to be successful for them. Unfortunately, most alcoholism programs provide exactly the same treatment for all participants. This treatment rationale appears to be based on an outdated notion that alcoholism constitutes an entity in and of itself much like other psychiatric diagnostic categories. In reality a variety of different individuals with different problems are likely to abuse alcohol. More importantly, however, variables maintaining excessive drinking in a group of alcoholic individuals vary widely. In one case, social and economic deprivation combined with social—environmental reinforcement contingencies may be involved while in another, individualistic problems in coping with interpersonal and marital stress may precipitate drinking episodes.

In essence, the solution to the development of successful alcoholism treatment strategies lies in an open-minded, empirical approach in which therapeutic techniques are utilized not for theoretical reasons but because they have been demonstrated to be effective. In addition to efficacy, treatments must be chosen on the basis of those requiring the least amounts of time and therapeutic involvement. Also, those treatments which are most likely to engender maximum cooperation from participants would be preferred.

Experimental

Historically, the quality of research in the alcoholism field has been highly variable with respect to objectivity of measurement procedures and the quality of experimental design. The constant proliferation of published reports on complex theoretical systems, etiological explanations based upon minimal research data, and detailed descriptions of case material has not significantly increased applicable knowledge regarding the development and/or treatment of alcoholism.

Using recently developed analogue drinking measures, however, a number of investigators are systematically gathering data on relationships between drinking patterns and a variety of antecedent and consequent events. The development of analogue drinking tasks under controlled conditions together with data indicating that the consumption of alcohol by alcoholics under such conditions is *not* clinically harmful has provided a methodology for more meaningful experimental studies. This type of research, although still considered controversial by some, will undoubtedly continue and provide a model for scientifically relevant alcoholism research studies.

Behavioral approaches also bring a broader range of research options to the study of alcoholism. In addition to the traditional group experimental design, the single case experimental design, used extensively in clinical behavioral analyses, has particular applicability to the alcoholism field. In this design the influence of a particular variable on the drinking behavior of a single individual is assessed. Typically, the variable under investigation is introduced, removed, and then reintroduced with concomitant changes in alcohol consumption noted. While there are numerous variations of this research strategy (Barlow and Hersen, 1974), a particularly useful one is the ABAB design.

Figure 9.1 presents a hypothetical example of this design as it might be used to examine the effects of alcohol cues on alcohol consumption. The subject might be provided access to alcohol during a 20-minute drinking session for each of 12 days. During the first 3 days, constituting the baseline phase, no cues are presented. During the next 3 days the room in which drinking occurs might be saturated with alcohol cues such as an extensive array of alcoholic beverages, pictures of social drinking scenes, audio tapes of bar noises, etc. These first two phases would then be repeated over the last two 3-day intervals. The exact relationship between cues and drinking behavior can then be graphically illustrated.

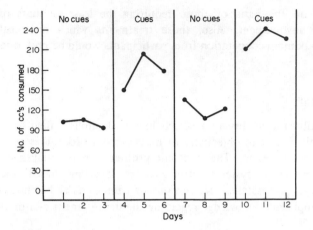

Fig. 9.1. Hypothetical example of a single case experimental design illustrating the effects of visual alcohol cues on alcohol consumption.

Experimental designs of this type are also useful in treatment evaluation studies. Using repeated single subject analyses the most efficacious components of individual treatment techniques can be determined. Such analyses enable a refinement of treatment strategies which then allow a more comprehensive group evaluative study. Variations of this basic design as they relate to treatment evaluation are presented at length in a recent book by Hersen and Barlow (in press).

Societal

Behavioral research data may eventually have marked relevance to prevention of alcoholism. On a societal level, behavioral techniques designed to teach controlled, social drinking patterns have particular applicability. Mass education campaigns aimed at fostering responsible social drinking may prove to be quite effective. Both the National Institute on Alcohol Abuse and Alcoholism and agencies of the Licensed Beverage Industry have already disseminated information through the mass media stressing the importance of not pressuring others, particularly at social gatherings, to "have one more for the road". More specifically, if individuals can be taught not only *how* to drink but also *when, where,* and *why* to drink early in their lives, they may be less likely to become abusive drinkers. Currently our society allows youngsters to learn the use of alcohol on their own or through their peer group. This often leads to drinking "to be a man" or to see who can consume the most alcohol without showing the effects. An open minded attitude in which drinking is accepted as a reality would seem to be more appropriate. Within this framework structured educational experiences regarding alcohol and alcoholism could be provided for high school and college aged students. Courses could even include guided practical experience in learning the components (e.g., small sips, diluted alcohol mixture) of moderate social drinking.

In addition, more emphasis could be placed on early intervention with children in populations which are most likely to abuse alcohol. Intervention geared toward teaching adaptive social skills in addition to responsible drinking may significantly lessen the probability of alcoholism in these individuals.

References

BARLOW, D. H. and HERSEN, M. Single case experimental designs. *Archives of General Psychiatry*, 1974, **29**, 319–25.

HERSEN, M. and BARLOW, D. H. *Strategies for studying behavior change: Single case experimental designs*. New York: Pergamon Press, in press.

McLEAN, P. D. and MILES, J. E. Evaluation and the problem-oriented record in psychiatry. *Archives of General Psychiatry*, 1974, **31**, 622–5.

SOBELL, L. C. and SOBELL, M. B. Self-reports by alcoholics. *Journal of Nervous and Mental Disease*, in press.

Author Index

Abramson, H.   3, 19
Agras, W. S.   39, 41, 43, 45, 64, 70, 73, 119, 123, 133
Alberti, R. E.   81, 83, 96
Alford, H.   124, 133
Alford, J. A.   163, 165, 172
Al-Issa, I.   87, 97
Alksne, H.   117, 133
Allman, L. R.   13, 19, 85, 96
Anant, S. S.   64, 73
Ashem, B.   64, 73
Azrin, N. H.   57, 73, 99, 111, 114, 157, 164, 172, 173

Baekeland, F.   3, 20
Baer, P. E.   29, 44, 58, 75
Bailey, M. B.   117, 133
Baker, H. M.   116, 133, 165, 172
Baker, T. B.   165, 172
Ballard, R. G.   117, 133
Bandura, A.   7, 8, 19, 64, 67, 71, 73
Banks, R. V.   101, 115
Barlow, D. H.   23, 41, 45, 48, 64, 65, 70, 73, 99, 110, 114, 145, 154, 177, 180
Barry, J. R.   36, 43
Becker, J.   144, 154, 170, 173
Bchling, M.   99, 114
Belfer, M. L.   118, 133, 169, 172
Bersh, P.   71, 75
Bigelow, G.   14, 19, 20, 107, 109, 111, 114, 166, 170, 172
Blake, B. G.   57, 60, 73, 86, 87, 96
Blanchard, E. B.   81, 82, 96
Blane, H. T.   23, 43, 169, 172
Blumberg, L. U.   163, 172
Bois, C.   142, 154
Bootzin, R. R.   105, 114
Borocock, J. Z.   165, 172
Boudin, H. M.   99, 107, 114
Bourne, P. G.   165, 172
Briddell, D. W.   14, 19
Bridges, W.   71, 73
Broz, W. R.   35, 50, 51, 67, 68, 74, 75
Brunner-Orne, M.   3, 19
Burt, D. W.   30, 43, 58, 59, 73
Burtle, V.   131, 133

Caddy, G.   141, 142, 154
Cahalan, D.   1, 7, 19, 135, 138, 154
Callahan, E. J.   70, 73
Campbell, D.   54, 55, 74
Campbell, P.   49, 54, 55, 73, 75
Cappell, H.   12, 19
Carroll, M. C.   118, 133, 169, 172
Carruth, M.   15, 20
Cautela, J. R.   46, 62, 63, 64, 73, 92, 96
Chapman, R. F.   30, 43, 58, 59, 73
Charnoff, S. M.   3, 20
Chatterjee, B.   71, 73
Cheek, F. E.   131, 133
Christelman, W. C.   4, 21, 26, 45
Cisin, I. W.   1, 7, 19, 135, 138, 154
Clancy, J.   49, 54, 55, 73
Clayton, P. J.   116, 134
Coffler, D. B.   165, 172
Cohen, M.   28, 29, 43, 106, 107, 114, 166, 172
Conger, J. J.   9, 19
Conner, R.   163, 172
Coopersmith, S.   80, 96
Corbett, L. O.   6, 20, 26, 29, 43
Cornelison, F. S.   6, 20, 29, 43
Cox, L. E.   89, 96
Crossley, H. M.   1, 7, 19, 135, 138, 154
Cutter, H. S.   6, 19

Davidson, R. S.   27, 43, 56, 73
Davies, D. L.   154
Davison, R. S.   67, 76
Deissler, K. J.   168, 172
Demming, B.   6, 21, 31, 44, 81, 97
Dent, J. Y.   46, 52, 73
Dichter, M.   157, 173
Donner, L.   64, 73
Dvorak, B. A.   53, 75

Edlin, J. V.   51, 74
Edwards, P.   116, 133
Eisler, R. M.   7, 13, 16, 19, 20, 21, 27, 30, 33, 37, 39, 40, 43, 44, 45, 61, 67, 75, 78, 80, 81, 82, 83, 84, 85, 90, 95, 96, 97, 107, 110, 114, 119, 122, 123, 124, 127, 133, 146, 166, 173

181

Emmons, M. L.   81, 83, 96
Emrick, C. D.   2, 9, 19
Epstein, L.   16, 21, 27, 44, 90, 94, 96, 97
Erickson, C.   71, 73
Ewing, J. A.   8, 19, 146, 154

Faillace, L. A.   26, 28, 29, 43, 106, 107, 166, 172
Falkowski, W.   61, 62, 67, 74
Farrar, C. H.   55, 74
Feldman, M. P.   58, 74
Ferster, C. B.   90, 96
Flamer, R. N.   26, 43, 107, 114
Fletcher, D. A.   32, 44
Flint, G. A.   105, 115, 159, 168, 173
Fort, T.   12, 19
Franks, C. M.   9, 19, 47, 50, 74, 131, 133
Friedman, P. H.   40, 43
Friken   46, 75
Fulkerson, S. E.   36, 43
Fuller, G. B.   91, 97
Futterman, S.   117, 133

Garfield, Z.   157, 173
Gary, V.   95, 96
Gerrein, J. R.   3, 20
Goldfried, M. R.   87, 96
Goldman, M.   15, 20, 117, 119, 133
Goodwin, D. W.   8, 20
Gordon, E. W.   163, 165, 173
Götestam, K. G.   92, 96
Gottheil, E.   6, 20, 26, 29, 43
Grasberger, J. C.   6, 20, 29, 43
Greenberg, L.   8, 20
Griener, J. M.   89, 96
Griffiths, R. R.   14, 20, 107, 114, 166, 172
Gringer, W.   71, 74
Guthrie, S.   95, 96, 117, 134
Guze, S. B.   8, 20, 25, 43, 116, 134

Haberman, P. W.   117, 133
Hallam, R.   61, 62, 67, 74
Hammer, C. E.   105, 115, 159, 168, 173
Harmatz, J. S.   118, 133, 169, 172
Harvey, C.   116, 133
Hauserman, N.   99, 114
Haynes, S. N.   165, 172
Heath, G. A.   157, 173
Hedley, R. G.   165, 172
Heilbrun, A. B.   164, 172
Heilbruun, G.   51, 74
Hemphill, D. P.   30, 44, 61, 67, 75, 106, 115, 160, 173
Henbest, R.   31, 44, 69, 75
Herman, C. P.   12, 19

Hermanson, L.   8, 20
Hersen, M.   13, 16, 20, 21, 27, 30, 33, 36, 37, 39, 40, 41, 43, 44, 45, 60, 61, 64, 65, 67, 75, 78, 80, 81, 82, 83, 84, 85, 90, 95, 96, 97, 107, 110, 114, 119, 122, 123, 124, 127, 133, 145, 146, 154, 166, 173, 177, 180
Higgins, R. L.   13, 20, 85, 96
Hill, M. J.   23, 43
Hilsman, G.   13, 21, 37, 44, 80, 85, 97
Hletko, P.   51, 74
Holloway, W. H.   135, 154
Holz, W. C.   57, 73
Hops, H.   122, 127, 134
Hornick, E. J.   51, 75
Hsu, J. J.   59, 74
Hunt, G. A.   111, 114
Hunt, G. M.   157, 172

Ichok, G.   46, 74
Imber, S. D.   26, 43

Jackson, J. K.   117, 134
Jackson, J. R.   163, 172
Jacobsen, E.   86, 96
James, J. E.   117, 119, 133
Jellinek, E. M.   2, 4
Johnson, G. R.   56, 60, 67, 75
Johnson, M. B.   83, 96, 146, 154
Johnson, R. H.   51, 74
Jones, R. J.   99, 114, 164, 173

Kanfer, F. H.   37, 43, 89, 94, 96, 97
Kant, F.   50, 51, 74
Kantorovich, N. V.   46, 60, 74
Karlin, R.   169, 173
Karoly, P.   89, 94, 96, 97
Kasterbaum, R.   92, 96
Kazdin, A. E.   105, 114
Keller, M.   6, 20
Kendall, L.   3, 20
Kepner, E.   9, 20
Kilpatrick, D. G.   140, 154
King, R. M.   105, 115, 159, 168, 173
Kingham, R. J.   9, 20
Kinsey, B. A.   169, 173
Kissin, B.   3, 20
Kline, J. A.   105, 115, 159, 168, 173
Knox, D.   127, 132, 134
Ko, S.   46, 74
Kogen, K. L.   117, 134
Korn, S. J.   13, 20
Kosturn, C. F.   80, 97
Kraft, T.   87, 97
Krasner, L.   99, 114

Lanyon, R. I.   87, 97
Laucius, J.   131, 133
Laverty, S. G.   54, 55, 74, 75
Lawrence, C.   111, 114, 170, 172
Lawson, D.   27, 43
Lazarus, A.   82, 86, 97, 98, 157, 173
Leaf, R.   93, 98
Leitenberg, H.   64, 70, 73
Lemere, F.   50, 51, 55, 67, 68, 74, 75, 135, 154
Lester, D.   8, 20
Levitt, C. B.   90, 96
Lewinsohn, P. M.   99, 114
Liebson, I. A.   14, 20, 28, 29, 43, 106, 107, 109, 111, 114, 166, 170, 172
Lindbeck, V. L.   117, 118, 133, 134, 169, 173
Lindsley, O. R.   37, 43
Lockhart, R.   71, 74
Lott, L. A.   107, 115
Lovibond, S. H.   48, 56, 57, 74, 141, 142, 154
Lunde, S. E.   36, 44, 56, 60, 75
Lundwall, L.   3, 20

MacCulloch, M. J.   58, 74
MacCulloch, M. L.   58, 74
Madill, M. F.   55, 74
Mahoney, M. J.   77, 87, 88, 91, 93, 94, 97
Mandel, I.   71, 73
Manokar, V.   3, 20
Mardones, J.   8, 20
Marlatt, G. A.   6, 13, 15, 20, 21, 31, 44, 80, 81, 85, 96, 97, 101, 115, 146, 154
Marston, A. R.   40, 44
Martimor, E.   47, 74
Martin, L. K.   55, 74
Martin, P. L.   56, 60, 67, 75
Martorano, R. D.   84, 97
Masters, J. C.   78, 97
Mavisakalian, M.   67, 74
Mayfield, D.   12, 21
McBrearty, J. T.   157, 173
McCance, C.   36, 44
McCance, P. F.   36, 44
McCord, J.   9, 21
McCord, W.   9, 21
McFall, R. M.   40, 44
McGuire, R. J.   93, 97
McLean, P. D.   176, 180
McNamee, H. B.   12, 21
Melin, L.   92, 96
Mello, N. K.   6, 12, 14, 21, 26, 27, 28, 29, 44
Mendelson, J. H.   12, 14, 21, 22, 26, 27, 28, 29, 44, 118, 134

Merbaum, M.   87, 96
Merry, J.   6, 21
Mertens, G. C.   89, 91, 97
Miles, J. E.   176, 180
Miller, E. C.   53
Miller, M. M.   64, 70, 75
Miller, P. M.   7, 13, 16, 19, 20, 21, 23, 24, 26, 27, 30, 37, 40, 43, 44, 60, 61, 64, 65, 67, 74, 75, 78, 80, 81, 82, 83, 84, 85, 90, 94, 96, 97, 99, 106, 107, 110, 114, 115, 116, 119, 124, 129, 133, 134, 144, 146, 154, 160, 163, 164, 166, 170, 173
Mills, K. C.   32, 35, 44, 136, 137, 139, 148, 154, 155
Mitchell, H. E.   117, 134
Moller, N.   8, 20
Monohar, V.   3
Moore, J. O.   163, 172
Moore, R. C.   70, 73
Morosko, T. E.   29, 44, 58, 75
Murphy, B. F.   26, 43

Narrol, H. G.   105, 115
Nathan, P. E.   6, 12, 13, 14, 15, 17, 19, 20, 21, 28, 37, 39, 44, 85, 86, 93, 96, 97, 102, 113, 115, 141, 143, 154, 164, 169, 173
Nimmer, R.   165, 173
Norbert, N.   164, 172
Notterman, J.   71, 75
Nurnberger, J. I.   90, 96

O'Brien, J. S.   6, 12, 14, 17, 21, 28, 37, 39, 44, 102, 115, 143, 154, 164, 173
O'Hollaren, P.   50, 51, 67, 68, 74, 75
Okulitch, P. V.   101, 115
Orford, J. F.   58, 74, 117, 134, 151, 154
Osgood, C. E.   31, 44

Patterson, G. R.   122, 127, 134
Pattison, E. M.   136, 154
Pellizzari, E. D.   8, 20
Picken, B.   25, 43
Pinkston, S. G.   83, 96, 146, 154
Pittman, D. J.   163, 164, 165, 173
Porterfield, A. L.   12, 19
Powell, B. J.   55, 74
Price, G. M.   116, 134
Primo, R. V.   87, 97

Quinn, J. T.   31, 44, 69, 75

Rachman, S.   46, 47, 49, 61, 62, 64, 66, 67, 75
Rathus, S. A.   82, 97

Raymond, M. J.   29, 44, 49, 51, 75
Reid, J. B.   6, 21, 31, 44, 81, 97
Rimm, D. C.   78, 97
Roberts, D. L.   32, 44
Robinson, D.   5, 21
Roitzsch, J. C.   140, 154
Room, R.   7, 19
Rosenberg, C. M.   3, 20
Rossi, A. M.   28
Rouse, B. A.   8, 20, 146, 154
Rozynko, V. V.   105, 115, 159, 168, 173

Sanderson, R. E.   54, 55, 74, 75
Saslow, G.   37, 43
Schachter, S.   30, 44, 143, 154
Schaefer, H. H.   31, 32, 35, 44, 136, 137
    139, 148, 154, 155
Schoenfeld, W.   71, 75
Schroeder, H. G.   9, 21
Schuckit, M.   169, 173
Schulsinger, F.   8, 20
Schwab, E. L.   6, 19
Selzer, M. L.   135, 154
Shader, R. I.   118, 133, 169, 172
Shanahan, W. M.   51, 75
Shea, J. E.   135, 155
Shipley, T. E.   163, 172
Sibler, A.   3, 21
Silverstein, S. J.   141, 142, 143, 155
Simkins, L.   23, 45
Skinner, B. F.   7, 19, 37, 45, 99, 115
Skolda, T. E.   26, 43
Sluchevsky, I. F.   46, 75
Smith, B. S.   33, 45
Smith, J. W.   30, 43, 58, 59, 73
Sobell, L. C.   4, 5, 10, 21, 24, 25, 26, 32,
    45, 136, 147, 148, 149, 150, 155, 157,
    165, 174, 180
Sobell, M. B.   4, 5, 10, 21, 24, 25, 26, 32,
    35, 44, 45, 136, 137, 139, 147, 148,
    149, 150, 154, 155, 157, 165, 174, 180
Solomon, P.   14, 28
Speers, W.   107, 114, 166, 172
Stanford, A. G.   106, 115, 160, 173
Steffen, J. J.   86, 97
Steiner, C. M.   3, 21
Steinglass, P.   14, 21, 22, 118, 134
Stewart, M. A.   25, 43
Strel'Chuk, I. V.   46, 64, 75
Stuart, R. B.   107, 115, 119, 121, 127,
    132, 134
Stunkard, A.   89, 97
Suci, G. J.   31, 44
Sulzer, E. S.   109, 115, 166, 173
Summers, T.   24, 45
Sutherland, E. H.   9, 21

Swift, K. D.   105, 115, 159, 168, 173
Syme, L.   9, 22

Tamerin, J. S.   14, 22
Tannenbaum, P. H.   31, 44
Taylor, H. A.   13, 15, 19, 20, 85, 96, 141,
    155
Teasdale, J.   46, 47, 49, 64, 66, 75
Terrell, F.   87, 97
Thames, E. J.   133
Tharpe, R. G.   92, 97, 132, 134
Thimann, J.   51, 75
Thoresen, C. E.   77, 87, 88, 91, 93, 97
Thorne, F. C.   23, 45
Tondo, T.   170, 173
Tordella, C. L.   9, 21
Tracey, D. A.   169, 173
Traxel, W.   13
Tuason, V. B.   25, 43
Tupper, W. E.   50, 74, 75
Turner, D. W.   53

Ullman, A.   117, 134
Upper, D.   92, 96

Vallance, M.   93, 97
Vanderhoff, E.   49, 54, 55, 73
Vanderpool, J. A.   16, 22
Vanderwater, S. L.   55, 74
Voegtlin, W. L.   35, 49, 50, 51, 55, 67,
    68, 74, 75
Vogel-Sprott, M. D.   101, 102, 115, 142,
    154
Vogler, R. E.   36, 44, 56, 60, 67, 75

Wallach, E. S.   27, 43, 56, 73
Wallerstein, R. S.   53, 75
Ward, R. F.   26, 43
Watson, D. L.   92, 97
Watts, J. G.   32, 44, 110, 114, 166, 173
Webster, J. H.   94, 96
Weiner, H. B.   3, 22
Weiner, S.   14, 21, 22, 118, 134
Weiss, R. L.   122, 127, 134
Wener, A.   87, 97
Wetzel, R. J.   132, 134
Whalen, S. R.   99, 114
Whalen, T.   116, 135
Whitehead, P. C.   116, 133
Williams, A. F.   12, 22
Williams, J. G.   41, 45
Williams, R. J.   8, 22
Williams, T. K.   6, 21
Wilson, G. T.   62, 67, 75, 76, 93, 98
Winokur, G.   8, 20

Wisocki, P. A.   86, 98
Wolpe, J.   63, 82, 86, 98, 131, 134
Woodrow, K.   80, 96
Woodruff, R. A.   116, 134

Wooten, L. S.   16, 21, 27, 44, 90, 97
Yates, A. J.   47, 76
Zvonikov, M. Z.   54, 76

Subject Index

Alcoholics Anonymous   4–6
Antabuse maintenance
  behavioral contracts and   161–162
  efficacy of   53
  reinforcement of   107, 111, 170–171
  Skid Row   165
  treatment evaluation and   33
Anxiety   *see* Stress
Assertiveness   40, 78–85
Assertive training   78–85, 124–126,
  159–162
Aversion therapy
  chemical   29, 46, 49–55, 69, 175
  electrical   30, 46, 55–62, 139–140,
    141–142, 147, 148, 175
  verbal   46, 62–66, 69, 158, 161–162,
    175
Avoidance learning   48, 58–59, 100–101

Behavioral contracting
  Antabuse maintenance and   161–162
  components of   107–109
  marital counseling   126–130
Blood/alcohol concentration
  assessment and   25, 28, 32–33
  discrimination training   140–143
Booster conditioning sessions   67–68

"Choice situations"   29–31
  see also Taste rating test
Classical conditioning   48
Cognitive cues   11, 16
College students   34, 179
Comprehensive behavioral treatment
  case example of   157
  program examples of   157–163
Conditioned reflex therapy   *see* Aversion
  therapy
Controlled drinking
  abstinence versus   135, 150–151
  aversive procedures   139–140
  blood/alcohol discrimination training
    140–143
  clinical evidence of   135–136
  comprehensive treatment   146–150
  contingency management   144

instructions and   144–146
  self-management techniques   89–90
Covert contingency management   92
Covert sensitization   *see* Aversion therapy
Craving   6

Depression   40–42
Diagnosis
  American Psychiatric Association   2
  Jellinek   2
  National Council on Alcoholism   2–3
Disease model   4–6, 135
Disulfiram   *see* Antabuse maintenance
Divorce   116
Drug abuse   1, 107

Emotions   10–13
  see also Stress
Employees   *see* Vocational behaviors
Escape learning   48, 57–58, 100–101
Etiological explanations
  behavioral-empirical   9–17
  physiological   4–6, 8
  psychological   8–9
  sociological   7
Expectancy effects   70
Experimental bars   31, 136–138,
  147–148
Extinction   102–103

Family history   7
Female alcoholics
  marriages of   117–118
  stress and   12
  treatment of   64, 169–170
Follow-up   25–26, 148–150, 174–177

Group treatment
  aversion therapy   53–54
  contingency management   106

Homework assignments
  assertive training   83–84
  marital counseling   123–124

Indians   7, 163
Instructional control   70, 144–146
Interpersonal relationships   37–40

Loss of control   4–6, 135

Marriage
    alcoholic couples   118
    assessment of   37, 118, 119
    behavioral contracting in   126–130
    husbands of alcoholics   117–118
    social-learning formulation   119–122
    social skills training in   122–126
    wives of alcoholics   116–117
Military   34–35
Motivation   38–39, 77–78

Natural environment assessment   32–35
Negative reinforcers   100–101

Occupation   see Vocational behaviors
Operant assessment   17, 27–29, 169–170
Operant conditioning   99–115

Pain   17
Physicians   5
Physiological model   see Etiological
    explanations
Positive reinforcers   99–100
Prevention   178–179
Psychodynamic treatment   3, 8–9
Psychological model   see Etiological
    explanations
Punishment   48, 101–102

Relaxation training   85–87, 158–162

Schedules of reinforcement   103, 109
Self-control   see Self-management
Self-management   59, 87–94, 161–162

Self-monitoring   24–25
Self-reports   23–26
Sexual problems   128
Skid Row
    assessment and   26, 32–33
    prevalence of   1
    studies of   12–14, 39
    treatment of   163–168
Social drinking   7, 12, 136–139
    see also Controlled drinking
Social factors
    assessment of   37–40
    relationship to alcohol abuse   14–16
Sociological model   see Etiological
    explanations
Stress
    assertive deficits and   78, 80–81
    assessment of   41
    relationship to alcohol abuse   10–13,
        80–81
    relaxation training and   85–87
Systematic desensitization   85–87,
        131–132, 158–163
Systems approach   118

Taste rating test   6, 13, 15, 30–31,
        60–61, 65–66
Tension reduction hypothesis   12
Token economy   105–106, 160–162

Ultimate aversive consequences   90–91

Videotape   39
Vocational behaviors
    assessment of   42
    employee alcoholism programs
        170–171
    relationship to treatment success   36
    training of   161–162

TITLES IN THE PERGAMON GENERAL PSYCHOLOGY SERIES (continued)

Vol. 34.   R. M. LIEBERT, J. M. NEALE & E. S. DAVIDSON – *The Early Window: Effects of Television on Children and Youth*

Vol. 35.   R. COHEN *et al.* – *Psych City: A Simulated Community*

Vol. 36.   A. M. GRAZIANO – *Child Without Tomorrow*

Vol. 37.   R. J. MORRIS – *Perspectives in Abnormal Behavior*

Vol. 38.   W. R. BALLER – *Bed Wetting: Origins and Treatment*

Vol. 40.   T. C. KAHN, J. T. CAMERON & M. B. GIFFEN – *Psychological Methods in Evaluation and Counseling*

Vol. 41.   M. H. SEGALL – *Human Behavior and Public Policy: A Political Psychology*

Vol. 42.   G. W. FAIRWEATHER *et al.* – *Creating Change in Mental Health Organizations*

Vol. 43.   R. C. KATZ & S. ZLUTNICK – *Behavior Therapy and Health Care: Principles and Applications*

Vol. 44.   D. A. EVANS & W. L. CLAIBORN – *Mental Health Issues and the Urban Poor*

Vol. 45.   K. P. HILLNER – *Learning: A Conceptual Approach*

Vol. 46.   T. X. BARBER, N. P. SPANOS & J. F. CHAVES – *Hypnosis, Imagination and Human Potentialities*

Vol. 47.   B. POPE – *Interviewing*

Vol. 48.   L. PELTON – *The Psychology of Nonviolence*

Vol. 49.   K. M. COLBY – *Artificial Paranoia – A Computer Simulation of Paranoid Processes*

Vol. 50.   D. M. GELFAND & D. P. HARTMANN – *Child Behavior Analysis and Therapy*

Vol. 51.   J. WOLPE – *Theme and Variations: A Behavior Therapy Casebook*

Vol. 52.   F. H. KANFER & A. P. GOLDSTEIN – *Helping People Change: A Textbook of Methods*

Vol. 53.   K. DANZIGER – *Interpersonal Communication*

Vol. 54.   P. A. KATZ – *Towards the Elimination of Racism*

Vol. 55.   A. P. GOLDSTEIN & N. STEIN – *Prescriptive Psychotherapies*

Vol. 56.   M. HERSEN & D. H. BARLOW – *Single Case Experimental Designs: Strategies for Studying Behavior Change*

Vol. 57.   J. MONAHAN – *Community Mental Health and the Criminal Justice System*

Vol. 58.   R. G. WAHLER, A. E. HOUSE & E. E. STAMBAUGH II – *Ecological Assessment of Child Problem Behavior: A Clinical Package for Home, School, and Institutional Settings*

Vol. 59.   P. A. MAGARO – *The Construction of Madness – Emerging Conceptions and Interventions into the Psychotic Process*

Vol. 60.   P. M. MILLER – *The Behavioral Treatment of Alcoholism*

Vol. 61.   J. P. FOREYT – *Behavioral Treatments of Obesity*

Vol. 62.   A. WANDERSMAN, P. POPPEN & D. F. RICKS – *Humanism and Behaviorism: Dialogue and Growth*

Vol. 63.   M. NIETZEL, R. WINETT, M. MACDONALD & W. DAVIDSON – *Behavioral Applications to Community Problems*

Vol. 64.   J. FISCHER & H. GOCHROS – *Behavior Therapy with Special Problems*

Vol. 65.   M. HERSEN & A. BELLACK – *Behavioral Assessment: A Practical Handbook*